## More Praise for *Never Give in to Fear*

"Marti MacGibbon shows readers just how rou
gritty memoir of addiction...Her raw, honest, c
page. The road to recovery begins with her daugh
of tough crowds as her stand-up career restarts
her composure. In the end, readers will likely feel the restorative power that's symbolized in the memoir's striking closing image of a rare albino redwood, a symbol of healing...A dark yet inspiring look at conquering addiction and regaining hope."

—*Kirkus Reviews*

"*Never Give in to Fear* is a great title because Marti didn't give in and reading her story I probably would have. It's an incredible, inspiring, sometimes funny, often unbelievable journey to recovery. No matter what your personal journey is, this book will help you along the way."

—Alonzo Bodden, comedian, winner of NBC's Last Comic Standing: Tonight Show, and star of the Showtime special, "Who's Paying Attention."

"...Her narration is funny—she can laugh at her old self, even as she shows the reader the terror and loss she felt in the past...MacGibbon is self-aware, and is able to show the humor of the moment without losing the tense pacing of her story. The memoir whips along, hardly taking a breath. Comparable to Mary Karr's *Lit*...an excellent story, both inspiring and entertaining...Honest to a fault, in ruthless pursuit of the story, MacGibbon's memoir is captivating from the very first sentence...A memoir that offers hope, even in the worst of times, *Never Give in to Fear* is a terrific read. It's the perfect book for a reader in recovery, though MacGibbon's real-life adventures will be equally appealing to anyone who needs a little more adrenaline in their reading list."

—Foreword Clarion Reviews (Five Stars out of five)

"I absolutely love this book. I haven't read a drug infused adventure this good since Hunter Thompson's *Fear and Loathing in Las Vegas*. MacGibbon's book is funny, inspirational and always entertaining."

—Ritch Shydner, comedian, Tonight Show, Late Night with David Letterman, co-author, *I Killed: True Stories of the Road by America's Top Comics*

"It's amazing that Marti MacGibbon survived her harrowing life and had the guts to recount it...not too preachy, the author's candor and sense of humor keep the pages turning."

—bohemian.com

"Rarely do you find such inspiration in so riveting a story. Moment to moment, he story twists and turns in a white-knuckle fashion—I held my breath in suspense, yet at the same time got the perfect amount of comic relief...Her narration is so funny and real that I found myself laughing out loud while my heart was breaking...While there are plenty of books about people's real life experiences, only *Never Give in to Fear* delivers this much style and substance...It's not only the intensity of the story and the challenges that Marti overcame, it was how she did it and still remained funny as hell on the way."

—Karen Rontowski, comedienne,
of Late Night with David Letterman and Comedy Central

"Marti's natural humor and storytelling help balance out the book into a symmetrical tale of both hurt and healing...The book is successful as a motivating tool and touching story. In the end, her saving grace comes in an unlikely form, and it almost brought a tear to my eye. *Never Give In To Fear* is a book everyone needs to read. This is not only a story about the danger of drugs, but about the power of the human spirit."

—San Francisco Book Review

"Marti MacGibbon has written a terrific memoir...Marti, through her humor and great sense of story, takes us on a journey few, if any of us, could survive. And she survives it intact and with great style and humor."

—Mark Schiff, comedian, Tonight Show,
Late Night with David Letterman: co-author,
*I Killed: True Stories of the Road from America's Top Comics*

"Marti MacGibbon takes you on a journey of amazing pitfalls, dizzying heights, and the depths of deepest alcoholism and drug addiction. Her recovery and redemption lift the spirit, and bring joy to the heart. *Never Give in to Fear* is a book you will return to time and time again. Most important book I have read in the past five years."

—Paul Jacek, comedian, co-host of the internet sensation
"OH, MARY!" radio show on LA Talk Radio.

"Ms. MacGibbon's memoir is a raw, honest and powerful account of her journey into addiction and her extraordinary courage, humor, and sensitivity as she travels the path to recovery. *Never Give in to Fear* provides readers with remarkable insight into the human condition."

—Richard Nass, Ph.D, Associate Professor of Pharmacology and Toxicology,
Indiana University School of Medicine

# NEVER
## GIVE IN TO
# FEAR

## LAUGHING ALL THE WAY UP
## FROM ROCK BOTTOM

*ENHANCED EDITION*

# MARTI MACGIBBON

NOTE TO READERS: This book is a memoir, describing the author's present recollections of her experiences over a number of years. Characters' names have been changed, and some characters are composites. Dialogue and events have been retrieved from memory and have been condensed in some cases to impart the essence of what was said or took place.

Printed in the United States of America.

# CONTENTS

# ACKNOWLEDGMENTS

Infinite thanks to my husband, Christopher Fitzhugh: you are the love of my life and my hero; without you I wouldn't have lived to tell my story. Boundless thanks to my daughter Anne. And thank you, Yvonne Dauphin, for your careful and insightful editing.

Photos of me before I left Texas for California—so clean-cut!

# CHAPTER 1

# SLIPPERY SLOPE

MY LIFE AT HYPERSPEED. THAT'S WHAT I SEE NOW, LOOKING BACK. When I first arrived in California, I was living fast, as fast as I could—yet still haunted by a sense of inertia, as in nightmares when you're trying to run and your legs won't move, or trying to scream and no sound comes out. I never felt like I had enough time to accomplish what I needed to survive in life. I always rushed onward, blind to opportunity, self-realization, and love, toward self-destruction.

I loved California—every square inch of it. I loved L.A. with its cool desert nights and brilliant, pollution-enhanced sunsets, and San Francisco with its cold fog rolling in over the Golden Gate Bridge, and all points in between. I loved the dope and the sex and the rock n' roll.

I especially loved the redwood country north of San Francisco. In December 1984, when I discovered the Russian River, or rather it discovered me, I thought I was fleeing the city for a quieter, more peaceful existence, free from the frenetic energy of my crack addict housemates.

At that point in my life I was a recreational user, and my friends tended to be what clinicians call "high-functioning" addicts. In all fairness to my housemates I feel like I've gotta take a moment here to tell you that although they were strung out on smoking crack, they'd all graduated from excellent schools—U.C. Berkeley and Columbia—and they somehow managed to hold down yuppie jobs despite a ferocious preoccupation with crack.

I thought my three housemates were dope-hungry, but then, I hadn't experienced the River People yet. And I never dreamed I'd eventually become one of the River People. Nothing could've prepared me for that eventuality when, only a few months previously in September, I'd loaded up my Datsun Sentra, turned my back on Texas, and relocated to California with my head full of dreams—dreams of making it big as a standup comic.

I'd been honing my craft in the local comedy club in Austin and had progressed to the point of assessing myself ready for California. Instead of moving to Los Angeles, I'd chosen to try San Francisco first. In spite of being in the wrong city, I still landed an audition for the Tonight Show with Johnny Carson a few months after I arrived in California. They liked me and scheduled me for an appearance in December 1985. I was pretty, blonde, tall, statuesque, and funny. In those days the comedy scene was exploding, and a comic's appearance on Carson's show practically guaranteed a magnificent career would follow. So I felt lucky—and also certain that I could achieve anything I set my mind to. The problem was, back then my mind tended to be bent by drugs and alcohol, and my judgment was generally skewed at best.

I told myself that now I only needed to hunker down, work on my act, and save enough money to relocate to L.A. Once in Los Angeles, I'd perform as a regular at the Comedy Store. The Tonight Show people could keep an eye on me and groom me for my scheduled set. That's why I was now headed to the River. I'd arranged to rent a room for rock-bottom prices. Looking back now, I wonder why I didn't head straight for Los Angeles. Better to have lived in my car on Sunset near the Comedy Store! Instead I chose to sojourn in the redwoods for a spell. Insane in the brain!

I'd arrived in Monte Rio at Dennis Mooney's rustic bungalow on a chilly afternoon in early December. Dennis, a San Francisco native and triumphantly gay man, held a position in middle management at some corporation. I'd made his acquaintance over the phone through a very close friend of mine named Michael. After talking with me for a minute or two, Dennis agreed to let me rent his spare bedroom, dirt cheap, while I saved for my move to L.A. The way I figured it, I'd only need two months to get the money together. This spare room was furnished with a four-poster bed and an oak dresser. It reminded me of one of the rooms that Goldilocks snoozed in while the Three Bears were still out hiking.

Mooney and I hit it off right away. "Call me Moon," he laughed. "All my close friends do." He worked long hours, and spent almost every weekend in San Francisco, so I virtually had the place to myself. With my scheduled Tonight Show, I felt like the sky had opened up and everything was possible for me. I rode a winning streak that I thought would never end. I felt magnanimous, expansive. I loved everybody and everybody loved me.

During those days, I even entertained fantasies of winning back custody of my daughter—Annie, my bright and shining star. Annie's birthday was coming up. She'd be nine years old.

My dark secret, the center of all my pain, was that I'd been duped into signing over custody of my child when I got my divorce. I'd done it in desperation after suffering from a long depression; after being convinced I was mentally ill and unable to be a good mom. I'd never been able to forgive myself for what I saw as my terrible deed, regardless of mitigating circumstances.

At first, I'd only been able to see Annie for very brief stints. In most recent years I'd managed to win summer visitation rights. Between the summers with my sweet, beautiful little girl, I dedicated myself to working long hours at whatever job I could get until I was simply too tired to remember that I had a child. When I wasn't working, I drank or got high in a witless attempt to distract myself from the constant pain and guilt of separation.

I figured I could get a really cool apartment in West Hollywood by summer, where we'd have our visitation and I'd take her to see Madonna. Annie, like so many little girls in the '80s, was a big Madonna fan.

I sometimes imagined that I'd actually be hanging out with Madonna and all the big stars by the time summer rolled around. I'd be the coolest mom and I'd be able to make up for all my sins and shortcomings. Annie would love me, I'd be able to give her anything her heart desired, and we'd live happily ever after.

I missed my daughter constantly, yet I now lived in a delusional state of celebration, which set me up perfectly for what happened at the River, specifically at the Pink Elephant a couple of nights later. That was the night I met Evan.

———

THE RIVER, OR "RUSSIAN RIVIERA," AS IT'S KNOWN TO SOME OF US, is a resort area around eighty miles north of San Francisco, and it's known for its redwood groves and gorgeous scenery. The Russian river winds its way down through Mendocino County and into Sonoma County, flowing westward till it meets the Pacific Ocean. A number of small villages nestle among the redwoods along the banks of the river, drawing their sustenance from tourist dollars.

These tiny burgs have names like Forestville, Rio Nido, Guerneville, Monte Rio, Duncans Mills, and on the coast, Jenner. Back then, the people who lived in these towns were merchants and small business owners, regular working people, dedicated environmentalists, peace activists, gentle vegetarian hippies. The Shire, home of the hobbits; that's what it reminded me of the first time I rolled through.

Right. Frodo and Gandalf. Elves. That's what I thought. But see, I never met any of those nice little hippie-hobbit types, because when I hit town I was looking to score some coke. So I hooked up with the less savory element—the dope fiends, the winos, the crystal meth chefs. My kind of people. People I could trust.

The Pink Elephant was a bar in downtown Monte Rio. In fact, the Pink was the only bar in downtown Monte Rio, the only business, in fact, besides a grocery store and the Monte Rio Post Office. Towering redwood trees stand stately, all over the village of Monte Rio, and the Russian River flows through the center of town.

Atop the mountain behind the Pink Elephant is the Bohemian Grove, the secret society originally founded by right wing industrialists as a drinking club. The Grove in summer is a destination for bigwigs and neocons. When the limos glide down River Road toward the Grove's heavily guarded entrance gates, peace activists still gather to picket and protest, but they are much fewer in number today than in earlier decades.

I didn't join the protests. However, my addiction brought me into contact with small time criminals whose highest aspirations involved stealing stereos out of the black stretch limos.

I'd been in the Pink one time, the first night I arrived, for a cocktail with Moon, and when I crossed the threshold I was already tripping. When I exited Texas, I'd brought along an ample bag of psilocybin mushrooms, and we did the last of the stash that evening. Moon wanted to treat me to a hearty slice of Monte Rio nightlife. Bikers in leather jackets and chaps straddled the barstools—of course, all the gay bars in the city boasted regulars in similar leather gear, but these guys wore jeans underneath their chaps—this was a straight bar, after all. Husky rednecks in flannel shirts circled the pool tables, cues in hand, each beer-guzzler intently focused on his next shot.

And the women! The youngest chicks looked pretty and petite, giggling as they sipped tequila sunrises. The remaining female patrons of the Pink scared me a little at first, because they seemed

NEVER GIVE IN TO FEAR

completely devoid of gusto. Most of them shuffled around, hanging their heads or mumbling as they slammed down shots.

Later, I learned that all of these women were junkies—the heroin supply in Monte Rio nearly surpassed that of San Francisco in quality. In fact, the most densely populated area in town, officially named Starret Hill, was referred to by dopers and working citizens alike as "Heroin Hill."

A couple of these chicks, though, shambled around with garbled speech because they'd been savagely beaten by boyfriends in previous years, suffering irreparable brain damage. But, on my first visit to the Pink Elephant, I didn't know any of this. All I knew at that point was that the mushrooms had kicked in.

I leaned in toward Moon. "Are you feeling the 'shrooms yet?"

He nodded emphatically, grinning. "Want to see the gay bars now? I'll give you the tour."

"Okay." Of course I took the Russian River gay bar tour! The gays were the ones who made this place a resort area. Without their money and festivity skills breathing life into the local economy, the only real estate on the River would be a cluster of grubby trailer court/meth labs along the river's banks, or a clot of rundown shacks under the redwoods on Heroin Hill.

After slurping down Stoly-and-grapefruits at several bars with names like The Rusty Nail, and The Mine, I decided to score some coke. Since I was new to town, I had to go through Moon's sources. We tried to get a couple of grams from some friend of his, a gay man in Monte Rio, but the guy was out. "We'll have to use straight connections," Moon told me, "Unless you want to drive to the City."

I shook my head. "No, Moon. No way will I drive to San Francisco." I'd had a lot of experience with psilocybin mushrooms, and the last thing I wanted to do while tripping on them was to drive! After all, the last time I'd operated a motor vehicle on psilocybin was when I lived in Texas. I worked on a survey crew then, staking oil wells, and that particular trip had been somewhat stressful. I'd ingested an enormous amount of psilocybin that night in an attempt to take the edge off the goings-on at a company party.

I'd brought the mushrooms to the party, loads of them, which I'd been picking for weeks. Our crew staked two oil wells in a thousand-acre feedlot off Highway 71, and knowing that psilocybin mushrooms grow out of cow patties, I'd returned to the feedlot with a friend, a closeted gay mud logger from Milwaukee who was willing to trespass with me. We swept through the acreage shortly after dawn and harvested bags and bags of them.

I arrived at the company Halloween party dressed in a devil costume and a pair of red converse high tops. I then played the part of Lucifer—or Lucifera—by liberally distributing the potent hallucinogenic fungi amongst coworkers and supervisors alike, then felt personally responsible when one of the civil engineers, a dude named Billy Bob, flipped out and burned a cross on the front lawn.

Upon hearing the wail of sirens, I felt overwhelmed by paranoia from all the 'shrooms I'd eaten. I jumped in my Toyota Landcruiser, punched the accelerator, and sped from the scene. After what seemed like hours, I finally reached the freeway.

I'd been driving on the interstate a while before I fully noticed that the countryside looked like the scenery in the Wizard of Oz. Munchkin houses and barns sported wriggling, twisting barber pole stripes, in brilliant colors. Everything looked so bright to me that I'd have sworn it was daytime. But it was night, I was tripping, and I knew it. All of this, I assured myself, was temporary.

I leaned back, tried to relax, kept on driving. What did it matter if I was hallucinating, I rationalized, as long as I stayed in my lane? With my rugged four-wheel drive vehicle I could even go off-road if a munchkin cop started chasing me. *Yeah, keep driving.*

I spotted a country store alongside the road and suddenly was aware of how thirsty I'd become. I slowed down, pulled into the gravel parking lot, sat there for a minute, motor idling. *Am I safe to walk in there and purchase a beverage? Oh, yeah, it's cool. I mean, it's Halloween night and everybody's a freak of some kind, right?*

I jumped out, my red Converse high tops crunching on the gravel. I adjusted my horns and tail, then marched on into the store. The guy behind the counter gave off a weird vibe—or maybe it was all in my head, my devil-horned head. I couldn't tell. *How many 'shrooms did I eat, anyway? Dozens of 'em...oh hell yes, dozens and dozens...*

I bought a Pepsi. Smiled at the counter guy. Tried to be casual. "Have a Happy Halloween Mister," I croaked, popping the top and slurping away at the soda in an attempt to reverse the dehydration that seemed to be consuming all of my mucous membrane. "Night!" I stumbled, caught myself before I fell face-first into the plate glass door. Somehow I'd managed not to spill a drop of Pepsi, so I figured I must look pretty together. I pushed the door open, crunched back out to the Land Cruiser.

I jumped back in the car, took the wheel. Steadying my hands, I put the key in the ignition, turned it. Started driving through the Land of Oz again, this time refusing to focus on any of the passing sights, no matter how surreal they might be. My lower back hurt because the corkscrew devil's tail on my costume was digging in, yet somehow I made it to my house. Kansas, Auntie Em, all of that. *Dorothy was so right. There's no place like home! Especially when you're wasted on hallucinogenic mushrooms.*

Once inside the house I kicked off my red high top sneakers and stripped off the devil costume. I put on hiking shorts and a T-shirt, went to the freezer, pulled out my emergency bottle of Cuervo Gold, and guzzled some of it. I closed my eyes, opened them, looked around.

Everything in my house looked like it was covered with feathers—embossed, inlaid with delicate hummingbird feathers and peacock tail feathers, too. The mushrooms had reached a critical mass in my brain. The hundreds of eyes in the peacock feather pattern seemed to be looking benevolently upon me, watching me. That was good. Benevolence is a must when tripping. No way did I want those peacock eyes to turn mean on me! I had hours more to go before the shit wore off.

The feather eyes followed me as I stumbled up the stairs to the loft. I lay down, hoping to relax. But my neck and back muscles had taken on a rigidity that the tequila couldn't counteract. My spine held itself in a tight arch, my neck was so stiff I couldn't turn it at all. Probably due to the effects of the strychnine in the 'shrooms, I figured. I accepted this condition as a side effect, and stoically committed my mind to endure and watch the feather patterns till the mushrooms ran their course.

As I look back on my life, I am amazed at how much twisted discipline and misdirected genius it took to develop the ability— the skills, actually—to procure, distribute, and maintain control while under the influence of the myriad drugs I ingested throughout my dissipated youth. If I had taken all of that ingenuity, tenacity, and strength of mind and channeled it into getting an MBA or a Ph.D...well, I guess these stories would be different ones, wouldn't they?

But back to that night in Monte Rio. Yeah, the Russian River. Okay, as I was saying, Moon and I decided to get some cocaine. We'd been tripping on what was left of the mushrooms I brought with me from Texas, but now we felt a need for some yuppier dope.

Moon started telling me about his straight contacts in Monte Rio. "We'll have to go back to the Pink Elephant and find one of the O'Reilly brothers." He lit a cigarette, inhaled. "They're the only straight people I've ever bought drugs from. And they've got a bad rep, but they've never burned me. Probably because I've never asked for a front."

"Let's go. It's almost last call." I could hardly wait to get some coke up my nose.

Moon started the car. "No problem. Daddy O'Reilly tends bar, and so does the oldest brother, Tommy; they're the ones we're looking for, actually. And if they're not working, there's another brother, Evan, the youngest. He's always holding."

We arrived at the Pink too late for last call, but Moon went up and knocked. I stayed in the car. Moments later he returned, breathless. "They're going to deliver it to us. At my house. This is perfect."

Yes, perfect. After all, Moon's place was right down the street. We could take it easy, have some drinks, and wait. That's what we did, and after about an hour, sure enough, our coke arrived. I heard the knock, but Moon answered the door. A young man stepped inside. I only caught a glimpse of him, because the transaction was swift, but a glimpse is enough when a guy is that pretty.

"Seems like the O'Reillys are a good lookin' family." I started chopping up the coke on a mirror, using one of my credit cards. I divided the cocaine into neat lines. "What are they doing way out here in the wilderness? Come to think of it, what are we doing here?"

Moon didn't answer me right away. He was busy rolling up a twenty. I pushed the mirror toward him; he snorted some, started chatting the way everybody does after they get off on coke. "That was Evan. Tommy's the one I would fuck if I could. He's more reliable, too, so if you're thinking of fucking an O'Reilly, Tommy's the one. Definitely."

"Uh-huh. Okay." But Evan interested me from the start—a magnetic attraction. If I'd been thinking at all, I would have remembered the last time I'd been magnetically attracted to a guy. That irresistible pull came from the dark, crazy, self-demolishing part of human nature, of my nature, an animal force that often made for great sex but always ended up with violence.

My explosive personality constantly swept the ether, searching for someone with common tendencies—a surefire detonator. And with Evan I'd struck oil. He was a petty criminal who came from a family of felons, an unemployed construction worker who liked to set things on fire. And he was only twenty-two.

Mooney and I stayed up all that night, doing coke and talking frantically. The next day we attempted to get some more, but all we could find was some crystal meth. We snorted it and smoked it on aluminum foil...and I loved it! I felt powerful and boundless—so much more in control. Crystal meth made me feel reassured that I could fix my life, and everything would be okay. No other high had ever given me such a payoff. This drug seemed to be tailor-made for my needs. And so began my ill-fated love affair with crystal meth. Little did I know that I would spend years obsessed—chasing, yet never again catching that first wave of euphoric release. When the high receded, I burned to score more crystal. And to score it from Evan O'Reilly, budding criminal and sociopath.

Two days later, cash in hand, I hooked up with Evan outside the Pink Elephant minutes before last call. He wore a red hooded sweatshirt with a San Francisco 49ers logo. I felt so attracted to him physically that, even though he couldn't find me any crystal meth, or even coke, my mind registered only a touch of disappointment. I brought him back to my room at Mooney's place to spend the night. And I fell in love—well, sort of.

I confess my fascination with white trash. I also fell prey to a misdirected motherly instinct. Evan was a few years younger than I was, and I wanted to save him from becoming a punk. Evan aspired to become a career criminal, I could tell. But I figured he'd never get far in the back woods, so I started entertaining the urge to take him to the city with me. I figured I'd spend a little time with Evan, expose him to a bigger world with more opportunity. After all, I was a sophisticated woman, wasn't I? I'd been in Texas!

Mooney left for his place in the city later that week, and he asked me to house-sit the Monte Rio place for a few months. All I had to do was keep the utility bills paid. In exchange, I loaned him my Shell credit card for a spell. Exit Moon.

Enter Evan. Well, not right away. I still did a few comedy gigs here and there, which required driving to San Francisco or San Jose for a night, but I'd always hurry back to the River immediately. My addiction started building, bit by insidious bit. Creeping up on me.

And the dream crept up, too, the first night I slept alone at Mooney's place. There I'd be, huddled up in that Three Bearsy-style bed, with an electric blanket turned up high, two comforters and one thick wool blanket on top of that, shivering. Sure, the weather turned cold. January on the Northern California coast is positively frigid. But I think the chills came from inside my head, where the dream flickered across my brain waves.

I'd been living in South Texas when I first had the dream. The dream first visited in the summer, in late July, on one of those nights when it's 88 degrees at midnight with 90 percent humidity. I didn't have air conditioning in that house, only a window fan. I never had trouble sleeping like a rock for a full eight hours, even in heat like that. Until the dream.

The dream scene started—suddenly—with me looking out the corner of a screened-in porch. The walls of the porch came up about waist high, then the screen part started, so I was crouched down, naked in that corner, peeking outside and down a long dirt road that led away from the house. Huge, tall, evergreen trees lined each side of the road as far as I could see, and the woods on each side of the road was dense. I could smell the forest.

At the moment I smelled the forest, a realization swept over me in the dream, and I knew I was naked, hiding from a mass murderer who held me and my friends prisoner in that house. I knew, in the dream, that he'd already killed my friends and cut them up in little pieces with a power saw. I could hear the saw's motor running behind the house, so I knew the killer was busy, and if I started running down the road immediately, I could possibly make it to the main road and escape. I looked out that window, gauging the time and distance...then the dream ended as abruptly as it started and I woke up, sweating. That was the first time.

The dream reenacted itself every single night for the rest of that summer, until I stopped wondering what it meant; until I grew accustomed to its terror. The purpose of this dream, I figured, was to warn me of some upcoming danger in my life, some thing I must avoid in order to be spared the mass-murderer-and-saw scenario.

Sometimes it haunted me for weeks at a time, then would fade away for a month or more. But it always came back. The dream stayed under the surface for almost an entire year, then returned with a vengeance around the time I decided to move to California. I saw the whole scene more vividly than ever before—every night. I considered changing my plans. I suspected maybe the serial killer awaited me in California, and I should heed my premonition and stay in the Lone Star State forever.

But my hunger for standup comedy, for a chance to truly master the craft, won out finally. I brushed my superstitions aside and relocated. All the same, I'd initially tried to avoid living anywhere with a screened-in porch. As if that'd ward off the psycho.

I hadn't even considered the dream—the tall evergreen trees—when I'd moved up to the River. That first week in Moon's cabin, alone, shivering in the cold, I considered the redwood forest all around me and really got nervous. I slept fitfully, because the dream repeated itself over and over, and this time there was a new part. At the beginning, I was walking through a redwood forest so thick that the branches scraped across my arms, face, and body. Then the woods parted and everything went black. After that, the regular old dream began as always, with me crouched down, naked, looking out the corner of that porch and down that road, the roar of the saw coming from behind the house. The dream seemed so real, palpable now, as if the serial killer hovered closer to me than at any time in the past.

After my third sleepless night, I called Evan and invited him to stay with me. I figured he'd be protection against the serial killer that stalked my sleep. And besides, I liked him and he liked me. We both liked dope, too. So it was a match made in heaven—or hell—depending on which end of the pipe you're on. We spent all our time in bed, except for when we got up to buy more crystal meth. Or when I had to go into the city to do comedy, which was getting to be less and less often since for the first time in my brief comedy career, I started canceling gigs.

The dream faded away for awhile after Evan moved in. We hardly slept. My life with him became a chase for crystal meth, coke, even heroin—whatever we could lay hands on. I'd never planned on getting involved with Evan, but now we shared a monster dope addiction. I'd started bobsledding down the slippery slope of ruin.

Looking back on it now, I have no idea what I found so endearing about Evan. My visit to his parents' place in Monte Rio should have raised a few red flags at least! His mother chain-smoked Marlboros and weed simultaneously. His father had recently suffered a heart attack, but that didn't stop Mrs. O'Reilly from pumping out secondhand smoke, 24/7. Jailhouse tattoos adorned Mr. O'Reilly's knuckles—"L-O-V-E," on his right hand, and "H-A-T-E," on his left.

As we exited his parents' place, Evan told me his Dad recently had suffered a heart attack at work—down at the Pink Elephant, while tending bar. This information caused a fresh wave of misplaced motherly instinct to wash over me. *I can help this poor guy, Evan—he needs me. I'll polish him up, show him a better life. Yeah, I can fix him...*

Lots of women succumb to the dream of transforming a man, of believing that female affection can heal psychosis. I know I'm not the only one who's been sucked under in this manner. My already skewed judgment was now further impaired by drugs, sex, renegade estrogen, and of course, an iron will to self-destruct. As we drove back to Moon's place in my Datsun, I resolved to take Evan with me to L.A. just as soon as I got the money saved.

But how to generate enough quick cash to cover both our appetites for dope as well as first, last, and a deposit on a West Hollywood apartment? My drug-addled brain struggled with this challenge. Gainful employment never crossed my mind. Slippery slope.

I invited Evan to make some suggestions. "It starts rainin' in January," he offered, "It rains real hard for days, and that's the perfect time to do burglaries. Hell, me and my brothers robbed a cop's house last year! We cleaned that place out—even took his badge!" Evan's eyes gleamed when he talked about stealing. "My Pops don' like it when we burglarize. He did time in Folsom for assault. He used to do collections in South City, nights, and tended bar in the day. That's when I was little. We lived in a house then, in Pacifica. Mom liked it better there." Evan started rambling, kind of free-associating, about his childhood and everything. "Back then my cousin James, you'll meet him when he gets paroled next month, he used to take me along on some of his early jobs. He taught me how to crawl in the basement windows, the real skinny ones that only a little kid can get through, and I'd get inside and let 'em in the back doors. It was cool!"

"Mm." I couldn't help but wonder whether cousin James was in prison for those very "early jobs" that Evan spoke of. It struck me that I'd better make the executive decisions when it came to crimes. I'd never been arrested before that, except for once in high school, when I ran away from home and my folks called the police. Oh, yeah, and one DUI arrest in Oklahoma that never came to anything.

I'd been fortunate enough to get hold of a lawyer who reduced it down to nothing. Still though, I'd hung out with ex-cons and active felons while working in the oil field.

"O.F.T.," they call it. Oil Field Trash. The Texas oil field attracts a wide variety of fuck-ups, violent sociopaths, raging alcoholics, junkies, speed freaks, gun nuts, parolees, flash-backing Viet Nam vets, and guys on the lam from almost every state in the union. I'd worked with at least one individual from each of those categories, so I'd become inured to the criminal element.

For a time, I'd worked on an explosives crew. One of the guys, a friend of the field supervisor, had stepped off the bus from Huntsville Penitentiary, possessing nothing more than the cheap, prison-issue suit and some gate money in his pocket. He disappeared a week later, along with the powder truck and our entire inventory of explosives, a value of about 250 grand. But naturally, since he'd been the boss' friend and recommended hire, no one said anything.

I felt I'd seen it all. So when Evan started talking theft, I didn't freak out. No way did I want to risk prison time, though. I figured if we were smart, and discreet, we'd be able to get away with a few sort of "gray area" enterprises. The so-called victimless crimes appealed to me. I considered selling weed, for starters. I knew somebody up in Humboldt County, a chick named Sky, who worked as a caretaker for a very large cannabis operation. I'd met her through my old roommates, the crack-smoking Columbia grads. I got hold of her, drove up to her place on the Eel River, and talked her into fronting me a pound of killer bud, which Evan and his brothers moved very quickly. Profits weren't quite as high as I'd hoped, since Evan smoked a lot of it, but we were well in the black anyway.

I went back to Sky for another pound, but she had no more to sell me, since it was the end of January, the off-season, and stash was scarce. But I made another contact in San Francisco, thanks again to the crackhead Columbia alums. The connect was a couple—Gary and Rachel.

Gary, an actual chemist at his day job, sold crystal meth at night. Rachel, his girlfriend, worked for an escort service, answering the phones. Gary and Rachel had an apartment in the Avenues in San Francisco. Evan and I started scoring excellent meth from Gary and turning it. Gary's dope was really pure, so we figured he was either making it at work or procuring the finest ingredients there.

Frequent visits to Gary and Rachel's for dope revealed their freakiness. Not only were they dope fiends but they were sex weirdos, too. Sometimes they'd rush us through a buy, excitedly whispering, "We've gotta make this quick—we've got a tranny coming over for a three-way in half an hour." They told us they loved to do menage a trois with transsexuals. "Especially if they're thin!" Rachel exulted. "Gary loves thin people, the more anorexic they look, the better! That really turns him on. You know, sometimes I think that, in another life, he must've been a commandant in a Nazi concentration camp!" She smiled at Evan and me, as if searching our faces for a reaction.

I couldn't think of anything to say. I mean, how does one respond to something so ridiculously creepy? Evan spoke first. "Yeah, your boyfriend's Colonel Klink. And I'm Hogan. Gimme the fuckin' dope, will ya Rachel?"

As we continued to score at their place, Gary and Rachel began to behave even more strangely. One night they met us at the door wearing these really cheesy Tarzan and Jane outfits that they bought at an adult bookstore. Evan and I stood in the doorway, aghast. Rachel tried to act flirty. "Hey, you two! Wanna swing with us?"

Evan pushed the door open. "Get outta the way." He strode into the apartment and slapped down our cash.

I drew a sharp breath, then followed him in. "Yeah, we just came for the dope and that's it!" The way I looked at it, dope dealing in itself wasn't depraved. It was business—a job, even. But fucking around with these freaks?? Very, very depraved.

The couple possessed zero sex appeal. Gary reminded me of Heinrich Himmler, but with a pocket protector. Rachel had a shopworn quality that suggested she'd acted out way too many unsavory sexual fantasies. They carried a dark vibe. Under the surface, I felt a sense of moldering danger. It always seemed like the hardwood floors in their apartment concealed a trapdoor so they could snag unsuspecting dope customers and use them for sex slaves.

Either that, or they were flat out aliens from another planet, employing the ruse of drug trafficking to entrap earthlings and feast upon their entrails. I imagined them clad in their Tarzan and Jane fantasy garb, battening down on some unfortunate speed freak, slurping up amphetamine-rich blood and squealing, "Hey, wanna swing with us? Wanna get in a three-way?"

Still, though, they had a quality product. So we kept on going there to make our buys. It's amazing what you can adapt to when you're strung out. We were addicts, experts at denial.

Gary owned the latest in video equipment, which was a really big deal back then, and also very expensive. In order to raise money to cover the cost of camera, lights and tripod, they rented the gear out on weekends, for a fee. Rachel ran an ad in several different types of newspapers to attract customers. They talked about it all the time. Blah, blah, blah.

One rainy dark Friday, Evan and I jumped in my Datsun Sentra and headed south on the 101. We weren't ready to re-up yet, but we'd run out of personal stash early. I was jonesing in a big way. The dream had returned on Wednesday night, only a couple of nights past, so I dreaded crashing. We needed crystal meth, immediately if not sooner, but on this day we lacked cash. In my head, I reviewed the pitch I would use to hit them up for a front. We loathed approaching them this way, since we knew they'd try to get us to trade weird, creepy sex for it.

Evan pulled into a gas station just south of Petaluma. We always stopped there, because it had one of those glass enclosed phone booths, set way out on the edge of the lot. We made our phone calls there, out of earshot. No cell phones back then. Even if we'd had cell phones, we'd never have used them. Wiretapping. Pay phones only.

I dropped the coins in, dialed Gary and Rachel's. Rachel answered, and I told her we wanted to stop by. I indicated that we needed a little credit. "Oh, Gary can't do that," Rachel practically whispered into the phone. "Don't even mention it at all; he's in a bad mood. But I have an idea. Would you like to deliver our video equipment? I mean, just drop it off? It's up in your neck of the woods."

I liked the idea and so did Evan. We drove on down to San Francisco. When we got to their place, Rachel and Gary acted unusually enthusiastic about the video delivery. "It's so cool! This guy's willing to pay triple the price for a weekend rental." Gary rubbed his hands together, then started weighing up an eightfball for us.

Rachel's eyes looked so dilated that the irises seemed to have disappeared, swallowed by glassy pupils. "He's at his lake house in Calaveras County. That's up near you, right? And you'll only have to drop it off there—just one way. He said he'll bring it back to the city here, at his house on Loma Linda. I checked out his credit rating, and it's excellent. Here are the addresses and phone numbers of both places. He's solid. And he's very excited to meet you guys, especially you, Marti. I described you to him. He says he loves pretty ladies. He even wants to take you guys out for dinner and everything. Anyway, his name is Charles Ng. Here's the information." Rachel handed me a piece of yellow notebook paper. She'd written the name on there, "Charles Ng," and the addresses of both houses, in neat block lettering.

I stared at the paper. I felt suddenly tired. "Well, Calaveras County isn't all that close to where we live." I sighed, then turned to Evan. "But I guess we ought to do it. I mean, we need the dope..."

Evan leaned in, took one look at the paper, snapped, "No fucking way! Look at the name. Motherfucker's a GOOK! We're not doin' it."

Evan's bigotry embarrassed me, that's true. And yet, a wave of relief swept over me. *Yeah, fuck Rachel and Gary. Evan's right, although obviously not for the racial reasons. The whole thing just doesn't feel right. It's too bad Evan's so crude and everything, but I can help him to lose his prejudice. He's a product of his conditioning.* I always liked to tell myself I could fix him up, another of my exercises in delusion.

We split from Gary and Rachel's, drove back to the River, and spent a couple of days sleeping. And although I slept all that time, I never had the dream. Not once. The dream never returned after that Friday.

I don't know why, but I kept that piece of yellow notebook paper with the name and the two addresses. Eventually I copied it into my notebook with similar names and numbers. I guess I liked to keep some kind of record of nefarious contacts, in case I'd need them for records, or blackmail or something. I was always paranoid. Speed makes you obsessive sometimes.

A few months later, I happened to pick up a copy of the local paper, the Santa Rosa Press Democrat. The headline caught my attention. The story told about these serial killers, Leonard Lake and Charles Ng, who lived on some property up in Calaveras county, and how they'd captured a number of people and tortured and killed them.

They got caught when Ng and his partner, Leonard Lake, got stopped by a security guard for shoplifting a vise from a discount hardware store in South San Francisco. Ng managed to flee the scene before police arrived, leaving Leonard Lake to face arrest. Lake was carrying identification in several different names, and driving a Honda registered to a man who'd been reported missing for months. And police found a .22 caliber pistol with a silencer in the trunk. The gun was registered to yet another name.

As soon as the cops put him in an interrogation cell, Lake broke down and told them his partner's name was Charles Ng, his name was Leonard Lake, and that he was wanted by the FBI. Then Lake requested pen and paper, to write a letter to his wife, he told them. When the officers left him alone in the interrogation cell, Leonard Lake took a cyanide capsule, which he'd been wearing attached under the collar of his shirt, and collapsed.

Further investigation led detectives to the cabin in Calaveras County, where they found a concrete bunker built behind the house, as well as a tall concrete incinerator. The bunker held two small torture cells. Police began scouring the property for the bodies they suspected they would find on the property, and a frantic search was under way to apprehend Charles Ng.

The article listed the address of the cabin Ng had occupied with Lake in Northern California, as well as another address Ng used in San Francisco, which actually belonged to his father, also named Charles Ng. A front-page photo showed the cabin in Calaveras County. It looked exactly like the one in my dream.

I dropped the paper, ran into my room, and opened my notebook. There it was, in the Ns—Charles Ng's name and the two addresses that Rachel and Gary'd given me. I shuddered. The dream, I believed, had been a warning. I tried to figure out why I hadn't recognized it. I figured the fact that it spooked me enough to bring Evan into my life full time was part of the plan. His ignorance and xenophobia served me well that night. Still, I promised myself I would enlighten him. He simply needed to hang out with me and my friends. In my naiveté, I thought I could change him.

Television reported the Ng/Lake case that night. The news anchor's voice narrated the story: how detectives discovered that the two serial killers rented audio and video equipment from a family—young husband, wife, and infant son—in San Francisco who were now on the list of victims. The husband ran a steady ad in the newspaper offering to rent out recording equipment and camera. *That was one way they'd lure prey to their house up in the woods. They'd answer ads like Gary and Rachel's.* The television camera showed a long, unpaved road leading to the place. Tall evergreen trees lined the road, exactly as it had looked in my dream.

The news anchor continued. The family went up to the remote cabin in the woods and never returned. They shot the husband, killed the baby boy, and kept the woman for sex and torture. Police found videotapes of the torture slayings of several women, as well as human bones scattered around the property, and charred bits of clothing in the incinerator.

Finally they located a mass grave behind the house. Forensics found the bones of an indefinite number of men, women, and children in the pit. However, since these bones had been cut up in very small pieces, scattered and/or incinerated, identification was deemed impossible. On one wall of the concrete bunker at the back of the house, cops found a variety of power saws—*The saw I heard in the dream!*—all of them encrusted with dried blood and remains. Yep, the saw I heard in the dream, behind the house that looked just like the one in the dream.

You might say I dodged a bullet. I think so. I'll never know where that dream originated. But it's mysterious things like this that make me want to believe in angels and demons, unseen principalities and powers. Jesus watching out for me? I hope so. But it is strange. The first Ng/Lake killings occurred in 1984. The dream came to me during the summer of 1979! Partial precognition?

Charles Ng managed to escape to Vancouver, where he avoided extradition for six years, since Canada opposes the death penalty. Police estimated that Ng and Lake had killed at least twenty-five people. Since Lake was dead, Ng would be charged with the crimes. He didn't stand trial for a long time, though. Ng's manipulation of the judicial system slowed the legal process so that his trial is known to be the most expensive trial in California history, even more costly than the O.J. Simpson case.

Strange how addiction drives a person. I was so busy trying to generate cash, initially according to plans to move to L.A., then eventually simply to feed my growing drug habit, that I never once stopped to consider how my lifestyle brought me into contact, or near contact anyway, with horrific psycho mass murderers! The whole serial killer thing didn't even stop me from continuing to do dope deals with Gary and Rachel. I also never thought twice about my relationship with Evan. I mean, he wasn't a rocket scientist, but his looks appealed to me, and I told myself that was enough. Plus, of course, we shared an avid addiction to crystal meth which, to me, seemed like a bond.

So I continued down my path of self-destruction, humming and skipping lightly along the highway to hell, oblivious to the warning signs. Oh yes, warning signs are posted all along that highway, which I believe is actually more of a toll road. You pay as you traverse the distance toward perdition. You pay and pay and pay.

# CHAPTER 2

# ONWARD DOWN THE TOLL ROAD

Right at first I didn't mind paying the toll. I was only starting out. My downward spiral still felt like a carnival ride. And the drug scene still appeared intriguing and exotic to me. I went to great lengths to hustle up a steady stream of quality crystal meth for myself and my boyfriend. We spent all our time together, and most of those hours we were wide awake. Speed freaks have plenty of time to tweak and get into trouble, and Evan and I were no exception. Unfortunately, I can't begin to say that none of these capers were my idea. I definitely precipitated my share of trouble-making endeavors.

"I'll tell you what," I said to Evan one day. "You can be my bodyguard. You know, drive me up there and wait for me. If I scream, you can run in there and kick his ass. Nothing's gonna happen. The guy's way crazy, but no real threat. Let's do it."

Evan rolled his hazel eyes, then leveled his gaze at me.

"Really. Evan! It'll be easy. The guy's name is Franz. How tough can this be? All he wants to do is try on my panties. For cash! And we can keep some of the coke. Plenty of it! We'll get some heroin and speedball. I've always wanted to try that. C'mon." I sincerely believed what I said.

"Okay. But I wanna drive."

Turns out, Evan didn't drive. Not that night anyway. See, I'd gotten Franz's number from Rachel. She occasionally worked for

24

an escort service, answering the phones. Rachel'd met Franz over the escort line, around four a.m. on a Thursday, when all the professional ladies had clocked out hours earlier. According to Rachel, Franz sounded so coked out that she immediately established a rapport with him. One dope fiend to another, right? Franz made some outlandish requests, nothing freaky enough to make Rachel blink, let alone flinch, of course, and they struck up a friendship. Or should I say, "fiendship."

Rachel and Gary told me they'd been up to Franz's estate in the wine country, and they'd even partied with his wife, Helga. And although Evan didn't remember it, I clearly recalled meeting Franz over at Gary and Rachel's apartment in the avenues. Rachel introduced us in the foyer, as we passed one another. Franz was on his way out, briefcase in hand, Evan and I entering, cash clutched in our fists. By my standards, Franz and Helga would be cool.

And tonight I'd be delivering a quarter pound of cocaine to their house on the mountain outside Sonoma. I had the directions Franz gave me over the phone. "You vill be travelink a-LONE? Zis is trrue?" His voice actually achieved shrillness when he said, "alone," then dropped to a guttural bark when he said, "trrue?" Teutonic paranoia no doubt engulfed his soul. "You must come ALONE! I vill be vatching vrom za vindow..."

"Umhmm. No problem. Franz, I gotta go now. What color panties do you want to try on?" For a fleeting moment, I wondered what Helga thought about Franz's naughty little hobby. Did she know he had a fetish for modeling strange women's undergarments? Did she even care?

"Puurple iss nice. Za vones you ah bringink? Zey ah puuurple?"

"Uh-huh, they're purple. Gotta go. Be ready!" I tried to sound perky—brisk and businesslike. *Yeah. Make quick work of this deal. Like Viet Nam—march into the jungle, make your kill, get out.*

Early spring evenings in the Bay area are hypnotic. The air is crisp and fragrant and full of the promise of blossoms. Evan and I looked at the star-studded sky through the windshield of my little Datsun. We made it to Sonoma in no time flat.

As we approached the mountain, Evan perked up. It seemed to me he'd finally stopped resenting our mission. Evan, I knew, really possessed street wisdom, and I'd never have ventured this far without him. I felt safe knowing he'd be there to protect me from harm. Oh yeah, except he'd have to duck down under the dash as we drove up to the place. No way could we risk Franz seeing a man riding shotgun! Not after I'd promised to bring the coke and my puuurple undervear—alone.

We followed the directions, which turned out to be accurate indeed. We snaked around and around the narrow mountain road in the darkness. No streetlights, only security floods mounted on the outer gates of these palaces. In a genuine fancy neighborhood, you can't see the houses from the road at all. Here, you couldn't even see the lights of the houses, the entrance lanes were so long and curvy.

Evan's handsome face lit up. He started talking fast, excited about the prospects of blackmailing Franz. "I mean, Baby, this Franz dude is loaded! We could rob him, but that's not the best payoff. In this situation, blackmail gives bigger returns—way bigger! This could turn into an annual income of …well, fuck!—of a LOT!"

Like I said before, Evan was not a rocket scientist. Immediately, under my breath, I began to make a mental list of the pros and cons of staying with him. And strangely, for the immediate moment, the pros won out. My judgment lacked a certain something, I'll admit.

We arrived at Franz's outer gateway and I punched in the code. A heavily- accented voice over the speaker. Franz, no doubt. "Yas. Who iss zis?"

I identified myself. Moments later, the towering wrought-iron gates swung open. We drove through, Evan crouching down now, eager to conceal himself from view. Evidently he no longer saw the situation as an indignity, but as an opportunity for future criminal enterprise.

The paved road wound its way up a steep incline. The trees on either side of the lane leaned toward each other, their branches nearly connected and forming an arbor, a canopy, above us. I thought they might be live oaks or maybe bay trees. A few stars shone through the foliage.

All of a sudden I saw the house—the castle—where Franz and Helga resided. I parked as far from the front door as possible in an attempt to stay clear of the sentry lights which blazed from strategic points around the perimeter. Not one glimmer of light shone from the mansion, though. *Fucking hyper-paranoid rich coke freaks!* I grabbed my purse, snatched the brown paper bag with the coke out of the trunk, and strode purposefully toward the immense stone house. Silently I prayed that Evan would keep his head down. As I approached the front entrance, I reached for the bell, but the heavy oak door swung open before I could even ring once. Obviously, Herr Franz had been lurking at the entrance, watching me drive up. He waved me inside.

"Mizz? You ah alone?" Franz leaned toward me in the darkness. He was all tricked out in black leather and wool: black leather jacket, black wool turtleneck sweater, black leather pants, motorcycle boots. He'd also pulled a black watch cap down over his eyebrows so that only his Aryan blue irises gleamed at me through slitted eyelids.

"Yeah, I'm alone. Nice to meet you—I'm Marti!" Saying this as perkily as I could, hoping to dispel some of the paranoid vibe with what I hoped was an all-American girl, cheerleader-esque tone of voice. "Shall we do this?" I indicated the brown paper bag I carried, wadded up, in my jacket.

"Ssshhhhh!" Franz glanced furtively over his shoulder. "Zis is not my night, I'm afraid—my vife Helga is on za rampage! Ve must take care vit zis transaackschnnn." He sort of growled the last word in the sentence, and his accent got the better of him. Franz rolled his eyes upward, as if to indicate that Helga was running amok upstairs.

I listened, but couldn't make out even a rustle from above. I began to doubt Franz even had a "vife." Imaginary friend seemed a lot more believable. "Uh, okay, but let's get goin' on this deal, huh, Franz?" I unwrapped my jacket, pulled out the coke. "See?" I waved it in front of his face. "Oh, and here's that pair of panties we talked about. Purple, see?"

I fervently hoped I could get the cash and split. In the first five minutes, Franz had already exhibited several strong symptoms of dope-induced psychosis. No telling what array of unstable quirks might manifest in the next half hour!

Franz reached out for the panties, rubbed them between thumb and forefinger. "Zese ah perfect! I vill need to sample za coke now." He turned, almost goose-stepped through a door on the left of the foyer, motioning for me to follow him, which I did, in trepidation. The room turned out to be a library, or office, with bookcases lining two full walls and a heavy teakwood desk in the center. We sat down in plush leather upholstered chairs.

This room was completely dark except for a tiny desk lamp with a dark green shade. From a narrow drawer in his desk, Franz pulled out a silver letter opener, then passed it across the desk to me, with an expectant look. Accepting the tool, I opened the gallon ziploc that held the product. As I dipped the tip of the silver blade into the powder, I attempted small talk, in hopes of dispelling some of the palpable tension in the room.

"So Franz, where you from? Originally? Me, I'm from Texas. I thought I heard a bit of an accent there, just a touch..." I leaned forward, held a snort under Doctor Cokenstein's right nostril. He sniffed voraciously.

"I vas born in Austria." Then, "Sshh. I hear my vife. Helga." Franz switched off the light, sat back, listening. "Zat bitch hass stolen my stash before. I cannot permit her to steal zis vone." He spoke in a hoarse, agitated whisper.

I had to get him to focus! "Hey, Franz," I spoke in low tones. "This isn't your stash until you pay for it." I stood up. "Go get the money. And I need some lights on to count it." I started feeling my way out of the office and into the foyer, where the light from the security floods spilled in through the panes of beveled glass on either side of the front door. Here I would make my stand, with better visibility and a chance to scream for Evan if Franz nutted up.

Fortunately, Herr Cokerhosen took me seriously enough to pull a small flashlight from the pocket of his leather jacket and head for the dark inner recesses of the house, mumbling, "I hid za moncy. Helga vill never find it. Vait, okay? I'll be back zoon."

While waiting, I ventured a peek out one of the tiny windows. My modest compact car stood silent. Except, I thought I caught a glimpse of movement inside. *Damn! Evan must be getting restless...* I successfully fought an impulse to wave, then turned and stood with my back to the massive door.

Good thing, too, since Franz crept silently into the foyer now, mini maglite in one hand, cash in the other. The guy was giving me the creeps. And where was Helga? I tried to reassure myself that they'd had a squabble and she'd gone off to cavort with her tennis pro. But my instincts told me the Frau wasn't into tennis. I feared that Helga lurked somewhere in the gloom, wearing body armor, brandishing a Luger and a leather truncheon, poised to strong-arm me for the dope I was muling! It seemed to me that Franz, a mere panty fetishist and harmless dope fiend, took orders from Helga, valkyrie and criminal genius.

Franz offered the cash. I took it, began to count the bills. Suddenly Franz yelped, lunged past me, pressed his face up against one of the panes of beveled glass. "I zee zomevone out zere! In your car! I told you to come a-LONE!"

I turned, looked out the window with him. "Uh, I don't see anything. Relax, Franz." But I sensed something was amiss. Time to make my exit. I abandoned all attempts to finish counting. I knew if I didn't leave immediately Evan would somehow be discovered, and then Herr Snortenzee just might be crazy enough to call the cops. Or worse, Helga might burst from the shadows, Lugers blazing, and—well, either outcome would be unacceptable.

I managed a nervous grin, tried to sound breezy, sociable, like I'd finished playing a game of croquet instead of muling cocaine and panties to a certifiable sexual deviate and full-blown dope fiend. "Okay, cool, thanks, but I gotta get back to the City now. Here's that purple underwear. Enjoy!" I opened the front door a crack, squeezed through, and nearly ran to my car. I jumped in the driver's side, stuck the key in the ignition, revved the dinky little hamster-on-a-wheel of an engine, and peeled out.

Minutes later, I took the luxury of taking my eyes off the road to check on Evan. He sat slumped in the passenger seat, his face pale, eyes as big as saucers. We drove in silence till we reached the gate. As I punched in the code, Franz's voice came over the speakers, in an antagonistic tone of voice. Coke creates a false bravado, a boldness. "Ze next time you brink me zomesink special,"—a pause while his greedy Aryan nose snorted up what sounded like a massive rail of blow, then, "Zomesink special vit ze underpants, okay?—Ask Gary und Rachel if Zey can zend me a young teenage boy—zay, tvelve years old? Zoon, okay?" I bit my lip in horror. The ponderous gate swung open just then, as if to disperse us into the world to do his bidding. I shuddered, gunned the puny Datsun motor, skidded over the threshold.

Evan's face reddened. He clenched both fists at his sides. He lowered his window, launched his head, shoulders, and torso up and out. Resting his forearms on the roof of the car, he leaned toward the gate's intercom and screamed, "You SICK FUUUCK!" as we sped away.

Evan lowered himself back into the car. "I shoulda burglarized that Nazi dickhead while you were inside. We definitely shoulda stepped on that coke a lot heavier than we did!! Fuckin' child molester! I knew we shoulda straight up burned that fucker, Marti. Now I GOTTA blackmail him!"

After we completed our descent from the mountain, we parked momentarily on a back street to do a line or two of our share of the coke. After that, Evan told me what he experienced while waiting in the car. I listened, amazed.

It seems that I'd been in there a lot longer than I thought, long enough for my boyfriend to get restless, and with good reason. He'd bought a six-pack of Budweiser on the way to Sonoma and polished off three of them by the time we arrived at Franz and Helga's. It didn't take long for Evan to be hit with an overwhelming urge to take a leak.

Quietly, stealthily, he crept out of the car. Then, as he hunkered down, keeping a watchful eye on the darkened house, he made his way to a secluded path of shrubbery on the periphery of the paved driveway. Under cloak of darkness, he unzipped and began to urinate, confident that he was completely invisible to any observer. But, only a few seconds into relieving himself, he felt the hairs stand up on the back of his neck. "I just sensed somethin'," Evan told me. "An' I turned around, an' that's when I saw 'im comin' at me!"

At that moment, Evan saw a German Shepherd guard dog silently approaching him, crouching low with ears laid flat, obviously in full attack mode. Evan's urine stopped in midstream and he bolted back to the car in terror, the dog right on his heels. He managed to get inside the vehicle and shut the door, quietly, before the beast could clamp its jaws on him. The attack dog left a few tooth marks on the heel of one of Evan's Nikes, but he still counted himself lucky.

Then the siege began. Evan heard the dog breathing just outside the safety of the little Datsun. To his dismay, he heard another dog join the vigil. The urgency in his bladder rose to a crescendo! He tried scooching down, leaning in toward the bottom threshold of the passenger door, and opening it just an inch. He could sense the dogs were close, yet they didn't try to breach the inch-wide gap, so he felt confident about sticking the tip of his penis out, just enough, he figured, to finish peeing.

As soon as he tried to expose enough of his manhood out of the gap in the car door, the dogs were there, snarling, slavering! He whipped himself back in, unscathed, and shut the door, panting wildly. Several attempts at this failed and almost cost him his gonads, when finally, he had an inspiration.

On the floor behind the passenger seat, Evan noticed a thick fashion magazine—a recent issue of Vogue I'd bought at a newsstand. Feverishly, his bladder now near bursting, he rolled the magazine into a cone, opened the door a crack, stuck the narrow end of the periodical out first, then leaned in and peed through the wider end.

The dogs snapped viciously at the end of the cone, so that Evan required both hands to steady the funnel, yet somehow he managed to drain his bladder without injury and without getting pee in the car.

We stopped to throw the shredded, dog-slobber-saturated magazine in the trash can at a Shell station. Evan spoke grimly through clenched teeth as he took one last look at the tattered makeshift funnel. "Coulda been my dick!" Then, "Marti, I'm gonna get my brothers to help me fuck that guy up. While we rob him. And blackmail him." I said nothing in response to his vow. I steadied my hands on the wheel and continued driving home—back to the River.

Later on, after we got back to Moon's place, our de facto residence, and smoked a joint, I resolved to resume my standup comedy career. After all, I had an appearance booked on the premier late night television show, didn't I? Evan and I talked it over and resolved never to do any more dope deals with Gary and Rachel or any of their contacts. But I got no assurances from him when it came to Franz. I could only hope he'd let go of his criminal ambitions over time. *After all, he's young. I can change him.* Yeah, right. Looking back on it now, I can't understand why I didn't simply buy a rundown beach house and remodel it. That'd be something I could actually fix up...and a much better investment.

By noon the following day, I'd managed to schedule a paying gig at a comedy club in San Leandro, California, due to the fact that one of the comics had cancelled suddenly. It was only an emcee spot, but I felt elated to be working in the legit world once more. The pay wasn't bad for emcees back then, and the motel where they put us up was decent. I drove to San Leandro alone, about an hour and a half drive. I felt inspired, and not a little relieved, to be traveling alone. I told myself I needed a break from my relationship with Evan.

After the first night, though, I started to miss him. So I called him, not at Mooney's house, because I wouldn't give him the keys. As if that would stop him from breaking in. Evan had spent time in CYA as well as other branches of California's juvenile detention system, not to mention adult facilities. He'd learned well how to pick locks and jimmy doors.

After calling his parents' number and hearing nothing but rings, I called the Pink Elephant and left a message there with the bartender, a burly Viet Nam veteran known simply as "Doc." Doc dutifully took the message, the phone number, name and address of the motel in San Leandro, then broke the news to me. Connor O'Reilly, Evan's father, who normally worked six days a week at the Pink,

33

had suffered another heart attack on the job. Paramedics rushed him to the hospital in Santa Rosa. Evan and all the other O'Reillys were down there with him. I thanked Doc and hung up the phone.

I hung out all afternoon, then into the evening, waiting to hear from Evan. My distorted motherly instincts had re-activated when I heard about his dad. About fifteen minutes before I left my motel room to go to the comedy club, the phone rang. Evan wanted to come to San Leandro—said he missed me. I told him I missed him too. Of course I urged him to spend the rest of the week with me.

He arrived at my motel after the show, in his old Chevy pickup. We partied—neither of us slept all night. Late the next day, Evan asked me if he could borrow my Datsun. "I need to get some parts for my truck," he told me. "I'll give your car a tune up, too."

"Sure, take it, Evan." I handed him my keys. I loved the fact that my boyfriend worked on my car. It seemed macho and sexy. "Did you call the hospital?"

"Yeah. My Dad's still in there. My grandma's threatenin' to come down from Marysville. Tomorrow." Evan once told me about his father's mother, Katie. According to Evan, Katie and her business partner, Della, were tough old bags who dabbled in fraud, shylocking, arson, and a host of other crimes. Through his accounts of his grandmother, I'd come to the conclusion that the O'Reilly white trash thing went back several generations, at least. Yet somehow I thought Evan was hot enough, and cute enough, to make up for all that—still no red flags in my line of sight. Not yet.

"Okay then." I turned on the television, lay back on the bed. I wanted to talk with Evan about what was happening with his father, all the emotional turmoil he must be experiencing. But Evan never talked about how he felt, except to describe great sex or how high he was. I didn't push it. Drugs pretty much rendered me an emotional cripple as well. "See you later, Evan." I waved. He took off. I kicked back and spent the afternoon napping and watching TV, alternately. When Evan didn't come back by the time I had to go to work, I didn't worry a bit. After all, the comedy club was really close by. The only thing separating the club from the motel was a Sizzler with its adjoining parking lot. I walked to work, walked home after.

I returned around midnight to a dark motel room. I would have started to worry except I hadn't had any sleep the night before, and my day naps weren't enough to stave off total exhaustion. Plus, I'd had a few drinks at the club. I tried to wait up for an hour or so, but failed. I crashed.

I awoke to find Evan beside me. I got up and opened the motel drapes a crack. Sunlight dazzled me. I decided to go out to the motel pool, sit out there and relax. I put on my favorite bikini and slid my feet into my sandals. Then I put on this old white cotton jacket of mine as a cover-up. It had long sleeves and big patch pockets in the front. I grabbed my car keys off the nightstand and put them in the right hand pocket. I slipped out quietly, so I wouldn't wake my boyfriend, and on the way out the door I idly noticed a tall stack of cardboard boxes of varying sizes, piled up against the wall just inside the door.

A blip of rational thought floated across my drug-addled, alcohol-rinsed brain in the form of a question: "What is in those boxes and why are they here?" However, I took no heed. I kept on walking.

Out at the pool, the sun felt good. Of course, the water was way too cold to swim, but I didn't care. I had the whole area to myself. The pool furniture was standard motel stock—aluminum-framed with those thick plastic straps stretched across and heavily weathered. I lay down on one of the chaise lounge models and set the recline slant the way I liked it. Peace and solitude began to heal my hangover.

After about a half an hour, a guy came out and sat down on the recliner next to mine. Annoyed, I opened my right eye a slit, so

I could get a look at him. He was stocky, hard muscles, a couple of scars on his torso, one on his lip. He wore cut-off, frayed Levis and flip-flops. His sandy blond hair looked like he'd gone into Super Cuts back in 1977, demanded a Rod Stewart "rooster" style hairdo, and then had just let nature take its course after that. His hair came just below his shoulders in some places, just to his ears in others. I'm not saying it was a mullet; I'm saying it was worse. I shut my eye.

Now he started talking. "Sun's nice."

"Yeah."

"You stayin' here?"

"Yeah, with my boyfriend."

"My connection's in town here. Wanna get high with me later?"

I opened both eyes. "No, thanks, uh, I gotta get going now. Nice talking to you." I put my jacket on before I stood up. What was with this guy? He was pretty loose, just walking up and talking about dope like that. It made me paranoid, and I wasn't even holding!

I walked the long way back to the room, looking for my car. When I found it, I opened the passenger side door, and checked the interior. I've always been very particular about my cars. I like to keep a clean car. The interior looked good. I shut the door, locked it, and walked around back and popped the trunk. When I saw what was inside, I took a little step back.

At first glance, I felt pissed off. On the right hand side of my trunk lay a bag of green bud. It looked to be about an ounce, and it was just lying there in the open! *Evan made no attempt to conceal it—at all!! And he transported it, then just left it—in my car, that's registered to me. What a bust! I gotta get back to the room and straighten him out. Damn.*

I reached in the trunk, grabbed the bag of weed, and stuffed it into the left hand pocket of my jacket. Good thing the pockets were so big and the jacket so loose. Then I noticed the other shit. In the center of the trunk lay a square, corrugated cardboard box, about a foot square and three or four inches deep, with the lid flaps closed but not fastened. As I swept my eyes over it, I glimpsed something white out of the corner of my eye, something my doper vision zeroed in on instantly. Two bags of white powder, either speed or coke, I figured. They'd been placed kind of off to left; no attempt had been made to cover them with anything. *Fuck. And it looks like quality stuff.*

I leaned way into the trunk, snatched up the bags of white stuff. They looked to be about an eighth ounce each. I stuffed them into the right hand pocket of my jacket. I stepped back, casually, looked left, then right, around the parking lot. I saw no one. *Good.*

Now I turned to the cardboard box in the center, feeling a little shaky. I pulled back the flaps that loosely covered the top and took a look. In my head, I screamed. *What—the—FUCK!* Evan. The gun, I knew, was a Beretta. I thought it must be .32 caliber. I never found out whether it was loaded or not. I didn't want to touch it. The other weapon, a wicked set of brass knuckles, gleamed menacingly. And...in...my...car!

"Now I'm definitely pissed." I muttered this under my breath as I looked for some way to obscure the felonious items from view so I could carry them back to the room to confront my white trash boyfriend. I'd left a couple of sweatshirts and a pair of jeans in the trunk a couple of days before. I figured they'd do. I wadded up the laundry and piled it on top of the box containing the weapons. Then I grabbed a pair of flip-flops for good measure. *Camouflage. Yeah.*

I took a deep breath and started walking back to the room. Evan'd left my car way out on the other side of the motel. As I rounded one wing of the layout, I considered cutting through the courtyard, but instantly thought better of it. If I went that way, I'd be plainly visible from the registration desk, and I felt much too paranoid for that.

So I stayed on the perimeter of the near-empty parking lot. My sandals made a scraping sound on the asphalt. I kept adjusting the laundry items in order to assure that the gun and brass knucks were truly hidden under them. I started planning how I'd confront Evan and demand an apology. I'd keep the dope, I told myself. I'd get high, I promised. I started to feel cheerier. *Yes. Very high.*

My path led me around the parking area that adjoined the restaurant. This motel boasted a restaurant and even made room service available to guests. The excellence of its cuisine rivaled that of the Denny's down the street, which isn't saying much. Anyway they were only open for lunch and dinner, so I thought it strange to see so many cars parked in front of it.

I walked a little further, and finally noticed that all of the cars parked at the restaurant were police cars! *That's weird,* I thought to myself, *What are they doing here?* But alas, I didn't put it together. Instead, I retreated into a state of giddy denial. I reassured myself. *Oh, they're probably just here for breakfast. Donuts or whatever.* I kept on walking purposefully, putting one sandaled foot in front of the other, trying to appear casual as I rounded the corner and headed for my wing of the motel.

I was almost at the glass-doored entrance to my wing, within several paces of it, when I noticed the two blue-uniformed officers pacing back and forth across the hallway. It was too late to turn back, I figured, especially if they'd noticed me. No, I figured I'd better head for the room. I pulled open the heavy glass door and headed on down the corridor. I passed the cops and they never even looked at me twice. *Cool. They're probably here for a domestic. No problem. I'll just go to the room now.*

I slipped the key into the slot on my door, pushed it open, heard Evan's voice sounding dejected. "Hi Marti." I stepped in, and one glance told me everything. Evan lay face down on the floor, his hands cuffed behind his back, and a patrolman stood over him, baton in hand. My motel room was blue with cops! Dozens of municipal police officers stood shoulder to shoulder around the room, their navy blue shirts obscuring the television, the drapes, the crappy motel art. Cops everywhere!

The biggest one, obviously the leader, took a step toward me. He spoke sternly. "Miss, we've arrested your boyfriend here for grand larceny and armed robbery. We've got a list of stolen property from the victim, and in an endeavor to recover said property, we're going to have to search this room, and we're going to have to search you!"

I took another look around the room. All those cops! But not one of them was a woman. Instinctively my mind latched onto that fact. I started to fake crying, maybe for sympathy or something, but it turned into real tears right away. After all, I had good reason to weep. I stood facing dozens of police officers, in my bikini with the white jacket over it for a cover up, bags of dope in the over-sized patch pockets, a box containing a handgun and a pair of brass knuckles cradled in my arms, and blubbered—just for a second, though. Then I started talking fast.

"Oh! I see you don't have a female officer on duty here and I'm so embarrassed! I started my period out at the pool and I need to go in the bathroom and...take care of it! This is...sooo humiliating!" And I started sobbing again.

The big cop softened. Okay, you can go into the bathroom for a second and—take care of your female stuff. But just for a second, or we're coming in there! Sam, let her in there."

I played up the embarrassment thing, boo-hoo-hooing, consciously creating a distraction so I could set the box, still covered in laundry and flip-flops, on top of the stack of cardboard boxes I'd seen just inside the door when I left the room earlier. I ladled on the drama, hoping they'd forget I came in carrying anything at all.

Sam, a young Asian officer, opened the bathroom door for me. Once inside, I pulled the bag of weed out. What to do? If I tried to flush it, there might be traces. I couldn't get away with flushing more than once. They were listening! On impulse, I spun and shoved the weed up under the sink, way in the back, just stuffed it up there, and it stuck. *What the fuck. Okay. Now for the crystal— or coke, whatever. The powder.* I pulled out the two eightballs, held them over the toilet bowl, poised to pour them in. But they looked really sparkly and...so...good! I couldn't bring myself to flush them away.

In a flash of inspiration, I pulled the box of Kleenex out of the tissue dispenser, stuffed the two eighth-ounce baggies underneath the tissues, then popped the box back in place, murmuring the heathen prayers of a junkie.

"Hurry it up in there!" The big cop's voice conveyed mounting annoyance.

I flushed the toilet. Started washing my hands. "Okay, I'm done." I stepped out of the bathroom. "Uh, thank you."

"Don't move," the big cop snapped. The police began to ransack my motel room, rifling through my suitcase, then my purse, and found nothing. Next, they hit the dresser, then the nightstand drawers that held nothing more sinister than a Gideon Bible. After that they searched all those cardboard boxes stacked up against the wall by the door. Upon doing so, the police found every single item on the list that the big cop held in his hand, including the .32 caliber Beretta and pair of brass knuckles I'd found in my trunk. I held my breath the whole time. Miraculously, they never searched the bathroom, so they didn't find the dope. *Whew!*

Evan lay on the floor of the motel room the entire time that all this was happening, and never uttered a word. The patrolmen began tagging and bagging the contents of all the boxes and preparing to carry them away. Most of it was jewelry and guns, as far as I could tell. There were documents in one box. I figured I'd dodged a bullet. The cops didn't seem to want me in cuffs.

Then the big cop, the leader, spoke again. His voice boomed. "There's one more thing. We've got an APB out on the vehicle used in the robbery. The victim got a good look at it. It's a 1984 Datsun Sentra, maroon, license plates G-D-R 447.

"Hey, wait a minute, that's my car!" Now I was pissed. I looked at Evan. "You used my car? Why not your truck? And who did you rob?"

Evan arched his neck up above the motel carpet but his reply still came out a bit muffled. "Aw, Marti, I had to use your car. My truck's got a late registration—you know that."

"Oh. Right. You wouldn't wanna get a ticket on your way to the crime. It'd slow you down." I turned to the big cop and the several officers clustered around him. "I can't believe this! You know, I'm a standup comic. I'm staying here one more night. I'm emceeing at Giggles right across the way. And this is my boyfriend, but I'm not sure what drove him to this. His dad had a heart attack and he's in the hospital—that could be it. The stress or something. He borrowed my car to go to the parts store last night. I mean, that's what he said, anyway." I felt really stupid rambling like that. Like a dumb chick. And why was I trying to make excuses for him?

One of the patrolmen spoke up. "The victim's name is Katy O'Reilly. I believe she said she's your...er, boyfriend's grandmother. She ID'ed him. Says he robbed her at gunpoint, made her open her household safe."

"His grandmother!" Katy, the felonious old grandma that Evan'd told me about. The one he harbored so much resentment against. *So he borrowed my car, drove up to Marysville, and robbed her, not even bothering to wear a mask! And, he brought all the stuff back to my motel room! Fuck! A room furnished by the Giggles booker!* I realized I'd probably never work this club again. I felt outrage, mixed with incredulity. *Wow! I mean, what kind of a grandma has a cache of weapons like that? And what about the dope stash? Did he steal that from ol' granny or did he score the stuff afterwards? Damn.*

The big cop's voice interrupted my reverie. "Alright, O'Reilly, up on your feet. Let's go." All of the police officers, with Evan in tow, started marching out of the motel room. The big cop turned to me. "Okay, show me where that Datsun is." I nodded meekly and followed him out.

When we reached the parking lot, a handful of the cops split off from the group and accompanied me and the big cop to my Datsun. I pulled my car keys out of my pocket and prepared to open the driver's side door. He spoke again. "Miss, I need to inform you that if we find anything in this car that is in any way connected to the robbery, you'll be arrested on the same charges as your boyfriend. Do you understand?"

"Yes."

They looked in the interior of my car, under the seats, and in the trunk, but of course they didn't find a thing. I'd already cleaned it out. They impounded my car, but I paid the fee, and soon I was at the wheel, headed back to my motel room and the dope. I started making plans to bail Evan out of jail immediately. In the meantime, I figured I'd sell the weed and put the money on his books. I figured I owed it to him. The powder turned out to be crystal meth, my favorite, and of course I kept that for myself.

I hadn't learned much of a lesson from all of this. Not yet, anyway. My drug habit still claimed top priority in my life. And I hadn't finished with my white trash boyfriend. But one thing I did learn was never to loan my car to anyone. Oh, yeah, and I always keep a clean car.

I returned to my motel room, did a couple of lines of speed, and got ready for work. I went to Giggles, did two shows, got my check and cashed it at the club. Then I decided to pack up all my stuff and head for the Russian River. I decided that'd be the best place to sell the weed and figure out what to do about Evan O'Reilly. I knew I wasn't realizing my dream of making it big in standup comedy, but strangely, I didn't care as much as I should have. Honestly, I didn't have any idea that it was happening, but I'd begun a metamorphosis. I was becoming one of the River People.

# CHAPTER 3

# DESPERATE MEASURES

November 1985. I decided to go to Japan. The car accident sewed it up for me. My middle class standards were toast by now, after months of cocaine and methamphetamine use and a destructive relationship with my sociopath boyfriend. The point when I really let go of the rope, so to speak, was the day in August '85 when I'd called Jim McCauley, the man who booked me for the Tonight Show, and told him I wouldn't be moving to Los Angeles. "I'm, I'm sick, really sick," I'd told McCauley, "I'll have to take some time out." I'd thought I was lying at the time, but of course it was the sterling truth. I was utterly, hopelessly sick with the disease of addiction.

McCauley, God bless him, had encouraged me to keep in touch. "The small screen needs you," he'd said, "The door will always be open. Call me if you get down to L.A.—or if you're in New York, I can get you on at Caroline's." What a great guy. And what an asshole I was! At that point, I thanked Jim, hung up the phone, and jammed a syringe full of dope into my arm, launching myself into an unending spiral of despair.

I rode my downward spiral. Downward spiral? More like a power dive—events in my life crashed like an avalanche down a very rocky summit and into an abyss. Each day presented a challenge to raise money in order to score and get high, and each day I cared less about what I had to do to get that money, having reached the point where I needed meth in order to function at all in daily life.

So Diane's offer which, months before, when I'd met her, had seemed absurd and unthinkable, now began to look really good. I knew Diane only marginally. I'd met her through a decidedly unstable woman I encountered while walking along Stinson Beach when I first arrived in California. I'd even played around with going on one of her "calls"—she ran an escort service—but I cancelled the whole thing at the last minute.

Later, I'd stayed in contact with her because she paid a good price for Valium, which Evan and I supplied her with occasionally. Diane was blonde haired, blue-eyed, and voluptuous, with a cruel demeanor. I disliked the woman, but that didn't stop me from dealing with her when necessary. As a drug addict, I'd become accustomed to associating with people I didn't like, just to perpetuate my drug supply.

What was Diane's offer? She'd send me to Tokyo to "make a lot of money." According to her, all I had to do was "...fuck some Japanese businessmen..." telling them I was "...a flight attendant or something..." then, in exchange for my services, I'd receive accommodations at a five star hotel and, according to her, ample cash for each transaction.

Depending on how I worked it, she told me, I could expect to bring home anywhere from ten to a hundred thousand dollars for a ten day visit, minus expenses and her commission. She told me she was sending a girl every month. Of course she didn't mention that not one of these girls ever returned, or were even heard from again. That was something I would discover much too late. I didn't think about the obvious danger involved in trusting Diane. I was far too overwhelmed with the danger I confronted in my everyday existence.

Evan had grown more and more abusive. He hadn't hit me yet, but he burst into rages frequently. When we argued, he'd break something on my car, like a rearview mirror or a window. One time he punched my windshield and cracked it. He had become dominating and wouldn't let me out of his sight.

45

My drug addiction wracked my existence. I was broke all the time, scrambling to get up enough money each day to score and get a cheap motel room for one night. I yearned for an escape route, and I was tweaked enough to believe that the Japan trip was the best way out. All I'd lacked until now was a plan—and the means to drop everything and disappear.

I figured I'd accept Diane's offer, go to Tokyo for a few days, make ten grand or so, then fly back to any city in the U.S.A., anywhere except San Francisco. I'd be free from Evan and would start a glorious new life. I would move near my daughter and be able to see her frequently. Maybe I'd even get her back. And I could revive my comedy career. That's what I thought. I didn't realize I was making the same fatal error I always did: I assumed I was bulletproof, that I was immune to any and all danger.

One night a fifteen-year-old boy in his dad's Chevy S-10 pickup truck backed into my Nissan Sentra and badly damaged it. The dad was so eager to cover junior's ass that he settled with me immediately—for a few thousand in cash. I bought a ticket to Tokyo on China Airlines. I bought some new clothes and lingerie, and got my hair done at an expensive San Francisco salon.

After that, I scored an eightball of really good crystal. I split the dope with Evan, feeling a strangely guilty compulsion to placate him. After all, I would never have to see him again after this trip! I reserved a gram or so for myself—enough to get through the first couple of days' jet lag. I figured I would be able to get along for a week or so without it, and then maybe I would quit for good. I needed to kick dope if I wanted to get my daughter back and do comedy again. I filled my head with dreams of how good life would be after I got through this...work...and I made all that money. In my mind, I never called it prostitution. "Work", that's the word I used. As if a generic label would clean it up. Crazy.

I devised a way to conceal my stash while traveling. In spite of the fact that I was using crystal meth on a regular basis, I was an avid fan of vitamins and health foods. I bought a little bottle of acidophilus capsules, which contain a snow white, freeze-dried, powdered acidophilus inside a clear gelatin capsule. The night before my scheduled departure, I sat at the desk in my room at my latest motel residence and with maniacal precision and dogged persistence, emptied all of the acidophilus out of the caps and filled each one with my pure, white, crystal meth powder. I saved enough of the real supplement caps to sprinkle along the top for camouflage. I guess I thought somebody might try to taste one or something. Anyway, it took a lot of discipline to refrain from doing up the dope, and I was kind of proud of my restraint.

Before we go any further, let me tell you that I did check up on Diane, the woman who was sending me to Japan. It was spooky how fast I'd been able to get the necessary papers at the Japanese embassy. I'd only gone in there one afternoon and mentioned the names Diane told me to, and I had my visa. She really had connections somewhere high up, and that kind of creeped me out.

I decided to talk to somebody about Diane, without mentioning that I was poised to begin a visit to Asia in her spurious employ. I knew some old gangsters who were hip about a lot of things in San Francisco. I called some of them and made an appointment to talk.

These guys, it turns out, knew quite a bit about Diane. At first they expressed surprise that she was still around, then filled me in on her "business history." Diane blazed through the San Francisco sex trade like a meteor, establishing herself as a hip young madam who, with her "girls," serviced and partied with all the movers and shakers in the Bay Area. She ran a sex video business, where a client could requisition any combination of chicks—role-playing or whatever—with him or with his wife, and her girls would tape the session. This kind of thing was pretty exclusive at that time, very cutting edge.

So Diane enjoyed wild success—until the IRS caught up with her. She had to go farther underground at that point, and started dipping her tentacles into some riskier markets. It seems she got a thing going with some guards at San Quentin, so that, aided and abetted by them, she could pull off extravagant favors for some very high-profile clients on the inside.

Here's what the madam was doing: she'd send one of her escorts to the guards that loaded the prison supply barges—and that chick would be muling about a pound of cocaine or heroin to the big-shot convict. She'd show up at the guards' gate, they'd help her get as comfortable as possible inside a fifty or hundred gallon drum. Then the guards would do the rest—that is, smuggle the woman and the dope, via the supply barge, to the prison and finally to the designated cell, where she'd perform her service to the client, drop off the shipment, and collect her cash. After tipping the guards, she'd return to the free world.

Eventually the San Quentin guards got popped, whereupon they unanimously caved in and pointed their fingers at Diane. The thing is, she had so much dirt on so many Bay Area judges and prosecutors that she managed to stay out of prison. Rumor had it she placed bribes well and had an extensive video library to use for persuasion. I had to laugh at the thought of Diane waving the master copy of some right-wing republican judge's personal porn flick in his face with one of her hands, then offering "His Honor" a fistful of grease money with the other!

Hearing all of this didn't stop me. I had always wanted to visit Japan. The idea of experiencing a culture so different from mine—a non-Judeo-Christian one steeped in tradition—enticed me. *Plus, it'll be easy to get around. Practically everybody'll speak English. It'll be like Western Europe. No problem. After all, they've got McDonalds and KFC and we've got Sony and Mitsubishi. Once I get there, if I don't like Diane's deal, I'll split and do my own thing.*

The night before I got on the plane, Evan and I stayed in a Hilton by the airport. He tried to convince me not to go. "I don't want you to do this thing, Marti...I don't like it. They're gooks, and you can't trust gooks."

Charming boy...yeah. *This is over as soon as I get on that plane!* "Uhh, it'll be okay Evan, I'll only be there a few days and I'll be back with plenty of money..." I soothed.

———

DID I MENTION HOW I LACKED JUDGMENT? I PURCHASED A ONE-way ticket to a certain airport in Tokyo, per Diane's instruction. I figured a one-way was okay, since I'd buy a return ticket once I'd accumulated sufficient funds to start my new life. "They'll be picking you up at the airport in Tokyo," Diane informed me. "Your contact will be a Japanese man holding a single red rose. He'll hand it to you and you'll drive to your hotel with him. Your accommodations will be furnished, so don't worry about a thing."

"Ooooh, single red rose...very cloak-and-dagger," I grinned. The sarcasm was lost on Diane. I marvel today at my stupidity in following her instructions! She told me to purchase a one-way ticket to an airport that, at the time, was primarily a business airport on the industrial side of town where very few Americans or tourists would witness my meeting with the Japanese contacts. And I apparently lacked the sense to consider how arriving with little cash would render me extremely vulnerable. Also I failed to meditate on the dangers of flouncing off into Asia, abruptly, without notifying family or friends, with no real address or anything of stability in my life. I'd been staying in different hotels and motels for months, living more or less outside the law. I'd morphed into an "unknown transient"—a perfect candidate for total disappearance.

None of those risks crossed my mind as I arrived at San Francisco airport, though. I felt stylish in my beautiful new leather skirt and boots. I carried a bit more clothing in my bag, a convenient carry on. Since I'd be there a week or less, I needed only a few things.

On that morning I carried only three hundred dollars, and I stopped at an exchange booth to convert a hundred into yen. Evan accompanied me to the departure gate and waited with me there. Something looked weird with the China Airlines staff. They were patting down each passenger, running a wand over everybody for weapons and thoroughly searching each piece of carry on and every handbag before permitting anyone to board. I whispered in Evan's ear—"Good thing I hid my dope in those vitamin caps..."

He turned to face me. "Hey, let's turn back now. Don't go. They're searchin' everyone and you're gonna get busted! They've prob'ly got a dope-sniffing dog. And fuck that bitch Diane! Let's get outta here." I couldn't tell if he was worried about the dope thing or me leaving, and I didn't care.

"It's cool. Why don't you go now? Look—I'm next after that couple."

"Okay." He agreed, but seemed reluctant. "I'll step back 'cause I've got some shit on me. But I'll be standin' here watching until your plane takes off. An' I'll be doggin' Diane to make sure she don't fuck you over." *Right.*

So I got through the search okay and down the ramp to the waiting 747. The flight was peaceful and the service gracious. I sat next to a sweet older couple from Beijing who spoke English. Shortly before landing I went to an upstairs lounge and redid my makeup, freshened up.

The flight landed. As we disembarked, I chatted with a couple of corporate sales guys who had business in Tokyo. "Your first visit to Japan?" one of them inquired. I nodded my affirmative. "You'll love it. It's a polite, very elegant culture." He smiled.

We walked a bit further. Then his smile changed to a puzzled frown. "Hey wait a minute. I've never seen this before, and it's my fifth trip!"

Japanese soldiers in full uniform with helmets on and weapons shouldered stood in lines at each side of the ramp we were about to descend when exiting the aircraft. *Oh shit! They're searching bags!* I kept on walking, though, and when I reached a certain point on the ramp, a soldier stopped me. He didn't, or wouldn't speak English, but he made himself clear. Stop. Let's look in your bag.

I smiled at him but it did nothing to soften his expression. I produced my passport and visa. He rummaged in my bag and pulled out...my "vitamins"—those freaking acidophilus capsules where I'd stashed my all-important crystal meth. "What is?" He glared at me.

"Uh, vitamins?" He looked like he didn't know that word. "Um. Health. For good health. Pharmacy." When I said "pharmacy," he got a little jolt of adrenaline. *Oops.*

Now the soldier looked really pissed. "Look, vitamins." I said, and smiled at him. He then opened up the vitamins and acidophilus and smelled them. I guess the smell of vitamins is universal or I have a guardian angel, because he let that go. After rifling through my makeup case for a minute, he waved me on.

Relief washed over me as I strode on. I stood in the airport and looked around. The building was smaller than I'd expected, and as I reached the front of the place, where the entrance and exit doors were, I tried to get my bearings. I looked this way and that for a gentleman in a business suit, holding a single red rose. No such person in sight. Anxiety started to rise in me but I pushed it down with a firm hand. After all, I had two hundred American and however many yen equals a hundred in U.S. currency. That'd at least get me a hotel room and a phone call to Diane. I kept reassuring myself of how streetwise I was.

People here were acting strangely. As they avoided my gaze, I realized I was the only Westerner in the entire lobby. I felt huge and foreign as I approached what looked like a sort of concession stand. An elderly Japanese woman, wearing a scarf over her head that reminded me of a babushka, stood at the counter. *Surely I could get change for the phone booths I'd seen nearby.* I produced my yen note equaling a hundred dollars and offered it to her. "May I have some change for the telephone?" She shrank from me as if I sported two heads, turned her back on me. *Wow. This is strange.*

*All right, I'll go to the phone booth and call Diane collect.* But when I tried that, I couldn't even get an operator of any kind, so I gave up and walked to the glass wall in front where the doors were. I would just hang out and wait for my contact. I noticed that outside the night looked awfully dark; I saw no taxicabs parked awaiting fares, only a bus or two straggling in.

After what seemed like an eternity, I saw him, but it didn't seem right somehow. He glowered sullenly and wore a trenchcoat. The single red rose he gripped in his fist looked wilted, as if he'd strangled it. He shot a glance my way, then shouldered his way through the crowd. Without a word, he glared at me and shoved the rose at me. "Er, thank you, uh, sir, I'm Marti. Pleased to m-meet you?" He grabbed my arm and indicated we should leave now. He tried to pick up my bag but I wouldn't let him. I needed to hang on to everything.

We exited the glass doors. He led me toward a lone taxicab, parked far from the entrance lights. He popped the trunk and grabbed the strap of my carry on bag, as though to load it inside. I hung on tight, but managed a smile. "No, thanks!" The man shrugged then, as if to indicate he didn't give a damn about anything, slammed the trunk lid, stepped around the cab, opened the back seat door and waved me in, slamming it behind me. Not wasting any time, I folded my cash into my passport and hid them in my boot. I sat back and tried to relax.

As he pulled onto the freeway, my driver looked back at me through the rearview mirror but still didn't speak. I determined to remain casual, if only to piss him off. I glanced out the windows as we rode. Tokyo looked enormous, neon-lit, and forbidding. It seemed like I'd landed on another planet.

Finally we arrived at our destination. He parked the car, opened my door, and grabbed me by the arm. I stepped out of the car and decided not to resist as he continued to squeeze my arm so hard that I thought he might bruise it. I allowed myself to be muscled toward a building that was definitely not a five star hotel, but a plush and seemingly vacant apartment building.

I went with him not because I am an idiot, but because I didn't see any rational alternative. The streets were dark and deserted. If I ran where would I escape to? Or would I get mugged or killed or raped on the streets of Tokyo after breaking away from this guy? I felt completely confused as to where I was. I decided I'd have a better chance of coming out of the situation unscathed if I went inside and talked to whoever was in charge. I hadn't fully grasped the fact that I was being taken prisoner. That concept seemed so completely impossible to me—after all, I was an American citizen! *Right.*

We took the elevator to the third floor, walked down a silent, immaculate corridor, and stopped at a door at the end. He unlocked it, opened it for me, and indicated I should remove my shoes, as he did. I complied, but as I stepped out of my boots I pushed the passport and cash down toward the toe to conceal them. He stepped in and closed the door behind us.

I looked around the apartment. It was furnished in the traditional Japanese style, with shoji, tatami mats, antique tansus and tall cabinets made of teakwood, lacquered tables and bonsai plants. It was very quiet here. The thug stepped to a telephone and made a call, spoke a few words in Japanese, and hung up. Then he returned to the door. As he slipped on his shoes, he spoke in barely intelligible English. "He will call you." He gave me a contemptuous, threatening stare. Then he stepped out and shut the door.

I waited a moment or two. Good riddance to him—what an asshole. Give him some time to split. I scooped up my passport and cash and slipped them back in my purse. I grabbed my bag and put my boots on. I wanted to get out for awhile. I'd leave the door unlocked just in case. But when I turned the doorknob it wouldn't open. It was locked from the outside.

"Stay calm." I spoke the words aloud to myself.

The phone rang. I picked it up. A man's voice spoke breezily in polite, lightly accented English. "How was your trip? Are you ready for your first customer?"

"Excuse me, but why am I not at my room at the hotel? I need to talk to Diane...and this door is locked from the outside..." I abruptly stopped speaking. I'd been blurting things out, but inwardly screaming to myself to remain as calm as I could. I knew from my experience in the world of dope that you never show fear, or you attract more things to be afraid of. I struggled to gain some composure. *Relax and play it cool. Play nice. No fear. You're here to make money, and maybe this'll all straighten out later.*

After an eloquent silence in response to my questions, the man on the other end of the line drew a slow breath, then: "Are you ready for next customer? There are only two appointments for you this evening. We know that you are tired."

"Okay," I said. Once I read that Japanese Samurai warriors were always most polite right before killing an enemy. I wondered whether the fact this guy was getting nicer, mentioning how tired I must be and all, might be a sort of barometer of how pissed he was getting. I kept quiet.

"Very nice, then. Goodbye." He hung up. I paced slowly around the room, trying to prepare. Should I sunnily smile and play this off as if I had no perception of any violations and simply submit, or should I hide inside the door and rush the "customer" when he entered the apartment, perhaps knocking him out and escaping? But escaping to where? I was alone in a very foreign country, with no knowledge of the language or where the American embassy was. And how would I knock someone out? With my soft leather carry on bag?

I looked around the apartment for a possible blunt object or whatever, then happened to look up and see a camera mounted discreetly in a corner of the ceiling. I walked into the small half-bathroom adjoining the left side of the foyer. No camera that I could see, but no windows either. While I was checking out the little bathroom, I heard three taps on the front door, and as I ran toward it, the door opened.

My "first customer" stood inside, a mild looking middle-aged Japanese man in a suit, escorted by a big and burly Asian guy. I figured I could maybe take out the wimpier one—but I'd never knock out the big one unless I had a good old American baseball bat and even then, only if I sneaked up on him while he was asleep.

The man stepped in, looked me over, turned to the guard and nodded affirmatively, as if he liked what he saw. The guard turned and closed the door behind him. The man bowed slightly toward me, so I did the same. He seemed to know where he was going, and headed into the only room I hadn't entered yet, which turned out to be a small bedroom, furnished with teakwood shelves, an armoire, and tatami mats on the floor. In the center of the room lay a futon, and in a corner of the ceiling, strategically placed, was another camera. *Great. Now I'm in porn. Or is it surveillance—or both?* I began a verbal protest—I needed to talk to whoever was in charge, etc., etc., and gestured as if to push the man away. He fumed; turned, walked out to the front door, rapped on it twice. The guard opened the door and the man exited.

The guard entered to persuade me with physical pain and intimidation. He stepped up and slapped my face. Then he laughed. He pointed to himself and said, "Samoan. Rugby player!" His next move happened so fast I hardly registered how it could be possible. He suddenly picked me up, grabbed me by my ankles and slammed my head onto the floor, slowing down just before impact so it didn't crush my skull. It hurt a lot. I saw stars and almost blacked out. I couldn't believe the man was so strong! He stood there and held me upside down, shaking me like a toy until I felt overwhelmingly dizzy and nauseous. He kept laughing. He let go of me then; sort of slung me onto the floor in a heap. I sat up, trying to regain some dignity. My neck felt stiff. I moved my head back and forth, to assure myself it wasn't broken.

He grabbed me under the arms and pulled me up on my feet, then stood there, his hands squeezing my shoulders, not hard enough to bruise, but enough to inflict sharp pain. He stared at me menacingly for a minute, smiling. "Take your clothes off." I quickly made it clear that I would cooperate. I took my clothes off. And I did cooperate, but he raped me, entering me brutally and painfully.

Afterward he indicated I should give him head; I began to comply. He pushed my head down on his penis so hard that I thought he was going to dislocate my jaw or break my neck. Finally I bit down on him and he let me go, slapping me several times on the side of my head. He stood up angrily and stalked off. I lay there alone on the floor for what seemed like ages. Finally I recovered myself, stood up, got dressed. My jaw hurt. I tried to swallow and found it difficult; felt pain between my legs.

The demonstration from the Samoan rugby player guard had changed my whole perspective drastically. I didn't feel bulletproof anymore. I knew I would submit, cooperate, perform, whatever it took to get along and survive. I wondered where the Japanese tea ceremonies and cherry blossoms fit into all of this; I'd always thought of Japan as a gentle, Buddhist place—geishas strolling around in kimonos, twirling their parasols...beautiful gardens and kabuki theater. *What the fuck is happening? This is not the Japan I signed up for...*

---

ONCE, WHEN I WAS A FRESHMAN IN HIGH SCHOOL, I'D BEEN reading about ancient Japan and their artwork and had become fascinated with it. I remember coming home one day and telling my father how I really, really wanted to travel to Japan and to experience it before their culture got stamped out by our American input. Dad, a World War II veteran who'd served in the infantry in the South Pacific, had turned to me and spoken almost grimly, "Don't be in a hurry to visit Japan, and don't worry—their culture is still very much alive." I'd had no idea what he was talking about then, but his tone had extinguished my infatuation with Japan for the rest of high school.

Now, here I was in Tokyo, locked in this apartment! And the only people who'd even known that I'd left the States were Diane—who'd sold me down river—and Evan.

After the guard left and I got my clothes back on, the phone rang. The Voice Guy again. "No more customers this evening." Then he hung up. At this point, I was too tired to think. I pushed down feelings of confusion, terror, and violation. I'd trudged past the point of caring about anything except a long, hot shower and about two days' worth of sleep.

A full bathroom adjoined the bedroom of this apartment, and it was very prettily done with porcelain tiles. You could step down three steps into the bathtub, which was narrow, but deep. A tiny shower, attached to the tub and equipped with a built-in tiled bench, offered the option to sit down while showering. I ran some bath water, got undressed again, and slipped into the tub.

The hot water helped with my soreness. I tried not to think—simply sat there in the hot water. After the water cooled, I drained the tub and took a shower, then dried off and dressed again in the same skirt and boots. I grabbed my carry on bag, staggered into the bedroom and lay down on the futon. I stared up at the ceiling and willed myself to stay alert.

A stern and muscular Japanese man, about thirty or so, entered the bedroom. He glared at me. I was still resting on the futon, fighting sleep and contemplating whether or not I should break open one of my vitamin capsules filled with speed, when he spoke. "Excuse me. Diane has given me a message for you."

There was no door between the bedroom and the rest of the apartment, only a shoji screen, which I'd not even thought about closing. Smiling coldly, yet acting as if we'd met in a tearoom or a library, he politely motioned for me to join him in the main room, adding, "And of course, we need to talk business. Call me Kato-san. And your name?"

"Marti." Introductions finished, we knelt down opposite each other on the floor of the main room. "But I can't talk business with you till I've heard from Diane. She's my boss, and she sent me here, and..." My fatigue prevented me from speaking any more, which was just as well. My tone was getting sharp, and I felt jumpy. Everything was wrong with this situation, and though I didn't tell him, I'd already made a furtive attempt to call Diane on the telephone before the "first customer" arrived, yet hadn't been able to get a line out. I'd hit "00" for the overseas operator, but had drawn a blank there. I figured there was prob-ably a code or extension to get an outside line, because both of the phones—there was one in the bedroom also—looked like hotel front desk telephones, with all kinds of different colored buttons.

Kato-san was talking at me again, sounding faintly contemptu-ous now. "You must speak slowly. I do not understand." Of course he did understand, obviously, and his tone seemed to be telling me that the only person talking tonight would be him, and that I would listen if I knew what was good for me.

"Okay, what's the message from Diane?" I sighed pointedly. Now I was through playing around. "When do I talk to her?"

---

HE SAT UP STRAIGHTER, IF THAT WAS POSSIBLE. "SHE'LL CALL you in the morning. She wants you to rest now. You sleep in your room, I sleep here in this room."

He made a dismissive gesture, then turned away. I watched for a moment as he began unfolding and setting up a privacy screen and rolling out a thick sleeping mat. He would be lying there between me and the door, blocking any egress.

I gave up trying to figure things out—they were way beyond my control. I did as I was told. I went into my room, slid the shoji screen doors closed, undressed and collapsed on the futon. Unconscious-ness arrived instantly.

Somewhere bells were ringing. No, it was my alarm clock. Wait a minute, hotel wake up call? Finally I remembered where I was. The telephone in my room was ringing. In the pitch-blackness I reached for the sound. "H'lo?"

"Marti, it's Diane."

"Diane! Hey, what the fuck is going on?"

"Listen, I only have a few minutes to talk and besides, it's expensive. If you relax you're gonna be all right where you are. Don't panic. Your body won't end up in the bay." *What is she talking about?* I hadn't even thought about my body getting dumped anywhere!

I tried to interrupt, but she went on, "Marti, be aware of some things. You're in Japan, and Japanese men value a girl with a nice manner. That's what they call it, a 'nice manner.' If you raise your voice to an Asian man, it's a dishonor to him, and he has to protect his honor. With these guys, the situation could get dangerous for you. Understand? If you lose it or throw a tantrum, they'll get rid of you."

*What did she mean by, "...get rid of?"*

She rapidly continued, "But cheer up. So far, they're happy with you, and that's good. Some girls they send away immediately...to... some other place...to work. So just relax, and keep saying, 'I love Japan!' They like to hear that. And keep working—I'll call you soon. Bye." That was it. She hung up.

*The Bitch! I never even got a chance to say anything.* Tears started coming to my eyes and I felt terror rising up, but I somehow managed it by trading it in for anger. *Fuck her! Fuck her!*

Then suddenly my thoughts became lucid. Anger and fear are counter-productive, I realized. I knew I was on my own and I would have to play to win. I determined to never consciously think about the danger again, not to allow myself to think scary thoughts.

I saw an image of myself sidling along a narrow ledge, hundreds of stories up. If I wanted to survive, I couldn't look down or I'd lurch, arms pinwheeling, and plunge into the abyss. I'd only look straight ahead and sidle around until I found a window to safety. I would imagine myself on solid ground and rest easy. Whistle if I had to. Keep things casual. That's what I'd do.

With this metaphor, I grasped an emotional attitude, a posture, a place from which to make my stand. Hope flooded my mind. Somehow, I would escape this situation I'd gotten myself into. *I'm going back to the U.S., and that's my reality. I refuse to accept the things that I see in my outer environment. No matter what happens, I will perceive that all events are going my way.*

I lay there in the dark and started to drift back to sleep, promising myself that if I'd been sold into slavery, they only had my body, and even then, only temporarily. I aspired to be the best woman that I could be, spiritually, intellectually, and emotionally, in my conduct with these men. Something would happen to open the way out. *Yeah. That's how it would be.* In that alpha wave state right before sleep, self-hypnosis programmed my unconscious mind and fended off the panic so that I slipped into oblivion.

I don't know what time it was when I awoke, because I hadn't reset my watch. But sunlight streamed into the room through the shoji on the windows. Jet lag bore down on me, and I didn't feel like moving a muscle, but then I glanced to my left and saw a newspaper printed in English beside my pillow, entitled, The Japan Times. I sat up and pulled on jeans and a shirt. I crawled on hands and knees to the screen at the entrance to my room, then slid it open an inch. I peeked out and saw the Kato-san guy had left. One more time I tried the door, and of course it was locked. I swore at myself for never learning how to pick latches! Evan had numerous burglaries to his street credit, and I'd not even bothered to ask him to show me the art of breaking in—or out.

On returning to my futon, I picked up the newspaper. Along one side of the front page's letterhead was a brief "bio" of the publication itself, which stated that the Japan Times was the first English speaking newspaper printed in Japan. It went on to say that it was founded in 1945 by a society formed by the wives of occupying American officers and enlisted men.

The front-page story, about a power blackout the day before, caught my eye at once. As I read, I learned that "...leftist rebels supporting the overthrow of the Marcos regime" had brought Tokyo to a standstill for a full day by blowing up the computer in the main transit terminal. Traffic had been deadlocked for eight hours and all mass transit had failed as well. The leftist rebels staged the bombing to demonstrate to Japan they meant business.

I figured that Japan must be to the Philippines what the U.S. was to many Central American nations—a rich, paternalistic neighbor. But that's only what I figured—who knows? At least this explained why there were armed soldiers present when I debarked from the plane, and it told me why the city outside the airport had looked so eerily dark when I'd arrived. The bombing had occurred while my flight was en route, and fortunately for me Tokyo was beginning to get back on track when I landed.

Another article, entitled, "Going to Japan," seized my attention, and its importance to me personally eclipsed that of the former piece. The title, it said, referred to a slang expression in Korea. When a girl was considered to be heading down a path to moral and personal destruction, the article explained, people would say she was "going to Japan." The expression had originated because of a long and sad tradition in Korea—that of impoverished or desperate young women leaving home with a dream of making big money in glamorous careers as models or nightclub hostesses, then ending up as sex slaves and never returning home.

The article continued to say that ads soliciting girls, promising careers in "modeling" or "entertainment," constantly ran in newspapers and magazines, not only in Korea, but in the Philippines and Thailand. Young women would answer these ads that promised riches and glamour, scrape together the money for passage to Japan, reach the contact, and be sold to sex traders.

The article also covered the story of a courageous young girl from the Philippines who had been seduced by such an ad and imprisoned in a brothel, but had escaped and was now causing an international clamor by coming forward with her story, etc.

I dropped the newspaper, feeling slightly nauseous. I was getting a glimpse of what I was up against. I had landed in the Japanese flesh market at what seemed to be a higher level, by the looks of this apartment. This industry obviously had many rungs on its ladder, each one descending lower and lower into a bottomless pit of degradation and misery. Best to perform well at this level, so as not to be demoted to something far more awful! Adapt or perish.

Strangely enough, drowsiness slipped over me, and I started to doze off. I suppose that exhaustion overwhelms fear in some cases. I figured I may as well sleep, that I'd be needing all my strength to survive.

———

KATO-SAN JOLTED ME TO CONSCIOUSNESS, BARKING, "GET UP! Now! Very important person is coming here to see you! Move!"

I wrenched myself awake, muttering, "No, I'm very tired. I need sleep..." Then as if struck by lightning I remembered everything—Diane's phone call, the article in the Japan Times, all of it. I sat up suddenly and asked him to leave the room so I could dress, then rummaged in my bag for a tiny sniff of the speed I'd brought along...a little chemical assistance with my jet lag. I'd bathed the night before, so I hurriedly brushed out my long straight hair, washed my face, and put on a little lipstick and mascara. I chose a conservative dress. I changed in a corner, away from the camera.

Kato-san hissed at me through the shoji screen, "Hurry up! Very important person to see you."

Kato-san stood in the center of the living room, looking stern and dangerous. He knit his brows and glared at me, and again he seemed contemptuous, snappy. *Brother, this guy is intense.* The situation was almost surreal. But this watchdog guy, this Kato-san, truly intimidated me. He chilled me to the marrow.

At that moment, Kato-san unlocked the door to admit entry to a Japanese gentleman in suit and overcoat. He smiled at me, and bowed very lightly in my direction, then stepped forward. He carried a paper bag in one hand.

"This is Mr. Saito." Kato-san glared at me. "He has brought you something to eat." Saito handed me the bag, which contained pastries. We sat down and made small talk while Kato-san sat stiffly and shot menacing glances at me. I tried not to eat too fast—no small feat, since I was starving! Mr. Saito spoke with heavily accented, very limited English and somehow he came across as nonthreatening, even friendly. He seemed to approve of me. Kato-san definitely picked up on the vibe, because all of a sudden his attitude toward me improved ever so slightly.

———————

WHEN I TOLD HIM MY NAME WAS MARTI, HE INSISTED ON CALLING me 'Martina.' Well, with his heavy accent it sounded more like "Mahtinah." I think I'd managed to charm and amuse Mr. Saito, which had to be a good thing, since he was, as Kato-san put it, "...a very important man."

Once Mr. Saito left the apartment, Kato-san began instructing me in what would be expected of me during my stay there. At the moment, he seemed less cruel as he spoke about "...girls that have a nice manner..." and how I could behave like one of them.

"I like a nice girl," he said in clipped accented English, "Nice girl is very sweet, and speaks softly." The plan was for me to greet the customer and offer him a seat on one of the pillows in the living room. Then I was to offer him something to drink, that is, coffee, green tea, sake, or beer. He'd furnished all these beverages for me, he said, then indicated where he'd stored them. It was now my responsibility to stock the refrigerator with beer each day, and to wash all the laundry that was used.

Kato-san showed me a little stack washer and dryer set at the back of the kitchen, then remarked that I would be using a lot of towels, since after making the customer comfortable, I must look toward the floor, shyly, and say, "Ofuro?" Ofuro means bath or shower in Japanese. This was no doubt supposed to be the cue to start things rolling. After that, I was expected to lead my customer into the bathroom and shower with him, etc., etc., helping him to towel off, and then moving on to my room. Each of my visitors were allowed about one hour with me. After each customer exited, I would be allowed a space of time in which to shower, change clothes, and fix hair and makeup for the next one.

Kato-san recited all of these rules stiffly and sternly, then asked me if I was ready to begin working. I sat silent for a moment or two, weighing whether or not to argue. I chose to cooperate. The way I considered it, compliance was my safest path for now.

Every time I asked him why I was locked in, or how to get the phone to call out, or why I wasn't staying in my promised room at the five star hotel, his eyes would practically glaze over and he'd stare off into space, growling, "You must speak slowly. I do not understand."

My first day of work lurched into motion. Kato-san departed; to where, I had no idea, but I'm sure it wasn't far away. He probably lounged in the apartment next door, observing me through those cameras. Obviously his task, besides intimidating me, was scheduling, or at least announcing, appointments each day. Kato-san manned the phones, alerting me to the arrival and appropriate departure time of each visitor. The phone would ring, I'd pick it up, his accented English in my ear. "Next customah for you!" He loved to use that word "customah."

How can I describe that first afternoon and evening? I suppose I could call it intensive, but that's too nice. Wave upon wave of cruelty, that's what I experienced. I endured rape and physical abuse. I had to service a man every hour, and the workday lasted till after dark. In between appointments, I constantly felt watched, monitored, assessed, threatened. I felt eerily surrounded by unseen captors. The whole thing grew more and more surreal as the hours marched on.

I didn't have the faintest idea what time it was until I saw the sun set over the building directly across from the one I was locked into. I'd closed the blinds in the living room earlier, but they were very sheer. My bedroom had drapes, and I kept those drawn all day in an attempt at privacy and some control over my environment.

Inevitably, I grew irritable and panicky, and I thought for awhile that I might lapse into hysterical screaming. After all, underneath every conscious thought, suppressed deeply, lay the realization I'd come to the night before when Diane called and warned that, "...if you lose it...they get rid of you."

On hearing her say those words, I'd known I was in deep water, that these people were Japanese organized crime, and for all I knew they were going to kill me or sell me off or whatever. I couldn't permit myself to think these things aloud or I'd panic and nut up, go ballistic. And that'd be the end of me.

Keeping my morale and my spirits up had become essential to my survival. As I struggled to recapture an emotional foothold, I fixed my gaze on two of the striking Japanese prints on the wall. They were disarmingly beautiful artwork—depictions of black dragons, some with red markings on them. There was something disquieting about these dragon prints—they looked forbidding, dangerous.

After the last appointment, I simply shut down. No use fighting this, I figured. I went in my room, slid the paper screen shut, and sat on my futon.

At the end of that day, and all the others to come, Kato-san brought food for me. He ignored me otherwise, and I ignored him. I'd given up trying to ask questions. I feared the Samoan guard—or something worse—might be resorted to again.

I urgently needed to get a phone call out to the States. I grabbed the phone by my bed and started punching in the numbers for overseas operator. Nothing. Then I tried calling any old bunch of numbers. On one attempt, a woman picked up, speaking in Japanese, sounding like a phone operator. I tried to talk to her in English.

"Help me," I whispered into the mouthpiece, "I need to reach an overseas operator and I can give you the number here..." I started reading the number on the phone to her, wildly hopeful that she understood me, but all I got in answer was an abrupt click. *Fuck it! I need some sleep anyway.*

I gave up on the phone idea and tried to wind down so I could relax enough to sleep. I opened my luggage and looked at my cash, then checked my hiding place for my passport. I started snooping around the room, very quietly sliding drawers open to peek inside. Nothing—except in one bottom drawer I found a little gold necklace; nothing expensive, but recognizably American. I'd seen something like it at Nordstrom's in San Francisco. The piece was in a style popular then. It sported a very slim little gold chain with several tiny gold hearts strung along it. And there in the same drawer lay a paperback book, the kind you get at an airport. Gorky Park, the title read in English. A spy novel of sorts. Okay, at least I had something to read besides the Japan Times.

I considered for several minutes the girl who'd occupied my room before I'd arrived. *Who and where was she?* Then my exhaustion overtook me and I fell asleep.

# CHAPTER 4

# THE TWO SAMURAI

FOR THE NEXT FEW WEEKS, KATO-SAN AND I KEPT UP THE SAME routine and schedule. Isolation reduced my world to a very limited cycle. He'd call in the clients, and I'd receive them. I did what I was told. I relinquished control over my body, but not over my mind. I repeatedly—and unsuccessfully—attempted to reach an overseas operator on that damn phone. I looked out of all the windows in search of an escape route from the third story apartment which had become my prison, but the building had smooth sides all around with no ledges at all, and not one fire escape visible.

Days or nights, whenever I had a moment alone, I kept watch toward the building across the way, but never saw a living being at any of the windows. Until one night. Between appointments, right after dusk, I saw a woman, lithe and young, silhouetted in the window directly across from mine. She stood behind the translucent blinds for a moment, as if looking back my way.

I opened my window and leaned out, thinking I might signal or call out, but then I saw her turn away as a male figure joined her. They embraced and kissed. I closed my window and sat on the floor, peeking out at them. The couple started having sex standing up, and from where I sat it looked like they were dancing—slowly and rhythmically.

I didn't indulge in this voyeurism long because the phone rang and Kato-san announced my next "customah." And I never again saw any sign of the woman across the way, or her lover.

I imagined she was just another girl, shut up in an apartment identical to mine, and exploited.

———————

ONE EVENING AFTER WORK, KATO-SAN ACTUALLY SMILED AT ME, sort of, and announced, "Tomorrow morning, I am taking you to the New Otani Hotel. They have traditional American breakfast—eggs and bacon!" He paused, as if expecting a show of gratitude. Perhaps a Denny's Grand Slam breakfast is considered exotic in Japan. I attempted a gracious smile, while inwardly, I gagged—I hate bacon and eggs. But of course, Kato-san never asked me what I liked to eat.

The breakfast trip the next day was very strange. I couldn't believe Kato-san was taking me outside the apartment. I dreaded what fate might await me. At first I briefly entertained fantasies of making a run for it, down the sidewalk and out into the city. But I rejected the idea of escape after considering that I probably wouldn't get far before being captured and returned to the Samoan for reprisal. I put my head down and followed Kato-san out of the apartment building and into a waiting taxi.

We rode in silence to the destination. "The New Otani Hotel!" Kato-san announced, in an attitude of sweeping grandeur. He grabbed my arm, pulled me out of the cab, and propelled me across the lobby toward the restaurant, eventually easing his grip when he realized I wasn't going to attempt a hysterical bolt for freedom. Kato-san selected a table, motioned for a waiter, and ordered. We ate eggs, bacon, and toast, then sat around for a few minutes drinking coffee. The hotel was shiny and lush, filled with well-dressed corporate types, all of them Japanese. That morning I never saw a European face, never heard anyone speak a language other than Japanese.

A party of three sat at the table adjacent to ours. One of those seated was the scariest Japanese I'd seen yet—which is significant, considering the thugs I'd been subjected to. He was a fierce middle-aged guy, clad in a big trenchcoat over a dark pin-striped suit. And he looked hulking and muscular—like the Samoan. He wore a pair of dark sunglasses. His manner and attire reminded me of the quintessential comic book villain. Everything about him suggested he was the capo in this situation.

There was another tough guy, a lot younger than the capo and nearly as intimidating. He also wore a trenchcoat over a dark three piece suit. He wore his hair slicked back, no sunglasses. A woman sat between them. She looked to be in her mid-forties; very beautiful, in a Dragon Lady sort of way. She wore a black dress under her trenchcoat. Her glossy, straight black hair hung about an inch below her shoulders. She looked stylish and cruel. In fact, all three of them looked pretty ruthless.

Kato-san had entered the restaurant with his cashmere wool coat over one arm. After selecting our table and seating himself, he'd carefully folded his coat over the chair adjacent to his. Now he reached for the fold of the coat, pulled a paper bag out of it, and set it on the floor at his feet. He immediately stood up, motioning for me to follow; and I did, hating myself for being so meek. But I was terrified of displaying even a ripple of the defiance I felt. Just as we got to the exit, I looked back and saw the Trenchcoaters standing up and leaving. The younger guy with the slicked-back hair stepped over to our table and grabbed the paper bag. So it was some kind of payoff. I figured they must be the yakuza connection. I hurried out the door and followed Kato-san to the taxi.

Back at the apartment, I prepared for another day of work.

---

ALTHOUGH I SELDOM SAW ANY OF THE PROFITS FROM THE SALE of my body, some of my visitors grew fond of me and gave me cash gifts. I learned to stage the exchange covertly, out of camera range. I applied my creativity to find ways to hide the money in different places around the room. So far, I'd been successful in hiding my passport and the three hundred dollars I'd brought with me from the States. Now I began to build an escape fund. I had no idea how I'd get out—but I held fast to my mental image of returning to spend Christmas with my family. Since I'd arrived in November, I felt like I had some time to figure out a plan.

Kato-san would leave in the morning, but I never knew where he went. Somehow, he seemed omnisciently aware of everything I did in the apartment. Whenever I watched him leave, I saw that Samoan guard at the door. My neck and jaw still felt sore from my initial encounter with the guard, and I couldn't risk another injury. So I never tried to escape out the door.

The windows in my bedroom didn't open. Only one window in the apartment did open, and it was in the main room, where Kato-san slept at night. I tried opening it one afternoon, and, in spite of my intense fear of heights, I leaned out to take a look. I saw a big Asian guy in dark glasses, trenchcoat, and hat, standing on the nearest balcony, a balustrade some distance down, between apartment blocks to the right, and he was facing my direction. I hurriedly closed the window. I sat down on the tatami mats to await my next call from Kato-san.

The phone didn't ring. Instead the door opened and the Samoan guard and the trenchcoat guy came through the door. The Samoan grabbed me and held his hand over my mouth. The guy in the trenchcoat crossed to the window, flung it open, and turned to join the Samoan in dragging me to the window. They pushed me out the window from the waist and held me upside down by my legs. I didn't scream for fear they would drop me,

71

and besides, no air could've escaped my lungs anyway. My heart seemed to freeze up inside. I've been afraid of heights all my life. I started to cry.

They pulled me back inside and left. The phone rang and I picked it up. It was Kato-san. He was laughing. "'Nothah customah for you." He paused, then added, "You stay busy, out of trouble." On shaky legs, I walked to the bathroom to fix my face for the next intruder.

---

THE REPEATED TRAUMA OF MY AVERAGE DAY OF WORK, COMBINED with isolation and fear, started to wear on me. I'd used up almost all of my meth stash during the jet lag period, my first five or six days, but I'd held onto a bit of it. I only used the dope very late at night, to enable myself to stay awake a little longer and have time to myself, or very early in the morning, to get started; never during the day when Kato-san was awake. I'd been opening the little capsules and putting the speed under my tongue. Sometimes I'd sniff a tiny bit. I was saving one last hit for a rainy day.

One evening, around dusk, between appointments, I decided I needed to get high for old times' sake. I felt so listless and depressed. I decided to smoke that last bit and have done with it. I found some matches and a thick aluminum foil container in the cabinet. What I'd wanted was some thin aluminum foil to smoke the crystal, but the container thing, although far too thick for my liking, proved adequate. I got the powder burning and watched it bubble up, then inhaled it before it all turned black on the aluminum.

Hurriedly, I ran the burnt container under the kitchen faucet to cool it down, then dumped it into the kitchen wastebasket, burying it deep in the trash. I shuddered to think what they would do if Kato-san found evidence of drug use. Suddenly, a rush came on.

I hadn't expected it. I realized I hadn't used for days and my system was clean, so I had no tolerance.

I walked quickly to my room to get my perfume, planning to spray some on my hair and clothes, as well as in the kitchen, to cover up the smell of smoke. The phone rang and I rushed to pick it up. I'd set the phone on the floor at the head of my futon after the last visitor, so I kind of bounced across the padded surface from foot to head, intending to crouch down and grab the receiver.

But smoking the meth, combined with fear of getting caught in the act, had affected my coordination. I stumbled and stepped right on top of the phone. My nylon-stockinged foot slid back and forth on the keyboard and I almost fell. But I caught myself, looked down, and saw that a couple buttons at the top, which I'd never been able to activate or get a dial tone with, were now lit up and flashing.

I grabbed the phone off the hook, got a dial tone, and quickly punched in the code for overseas operator. This time—miracle of miracles!—I got through! The voice on the other end of the line wasn't speaking Japanese. She was speaking English, American accented English! I got so excited I started shaking. "Hello? Is this the overseas operator? I need to get a call through to the U.S.A. Can you help me with that?"

"Sure I can. I'm right here in the good ol' U.S.A., hon," she said.

I wanted to cry for joy. I struggled to stay cool. "Oh, that's so good! I'm calling from Japan and I haven't heard an American voice in a long time. Well, except for my own voice, that is." I heard the operator laugh good-naturedly. "Listen, I've been having a lot of trouble getting a call through to you and I am afraid if we get disconnected, I won't be able to get you back, and I have two calls to make. They have to be collect, and for one of them I need to call information to get the number. This is really important. Can you stay on with me to keep us connected and help me with this?"

"Yes, I can do that. Let's call the information operator first, okay, and I'll stay on with you." I simply could not believe how kind this woman was! I hoped it wasn't a trick.

I decided I needed to get a message to Evan. He was the only person who knew I'd gone to Japan, and who'd sent me, and I hoped he might be able to help. I planned to leave the number of the apartment, which, incredibly, was printed on a sticker on the telephone. Back in those days, phones in the U.S. were issued by telephone companies to the account holder with the number emblazoned on the unit. I guess that was the policy in Japan, also. Still, I was surprised—and thrilled—that these guys had neglected to remove the number from the unit.

"Thank you. The number I need is in California, in a town called Monte Rio. It's a bar called, 'The Pink Elephant.'"

I feared she would hang up on me because my request must've sounded ridiculous. But she didn't. She connected with the information operator, got me the number, and rang the bar. I held my breath. It rang three times, then the bartender known as "Doc" answered it. "Pink Elephant," he said.

The operator said, "This is an international collect call from Japan, from 'Marti.'" She continued, "Will you accept the charges?"

"Yes." Another miracle! I'd known Doc since I'd first arrived at the River. He was a friend of Evan and all the other O'Reillys, so it was perfect. Doc was a Viet Nam vet, and I believe he identified with a distress call from anywhere in Asia. But for whatever reason, he took the call!

"Go ahead," the operator instructed.

"Doc, I'm calling from Tokyo. I don't know how long I can stay on this phone—I might have to hang up any second now. I need to get a message to Evan, or any of the O'Reillys."

"Just a minute." I heard his deep voice ringing out into the bar. "Hey! Anybody know where any of the O'Reillys are at? It's MAR-ti callin' from TOK-yo. It's an emergency." After a beat, he returned. "I'll find 'em."

"Doc, tell Evan where I am, and that things are bad. I have a phone number for him. Here it is..." And I recited the number from off the telephone's plastic-plated face.

"Right. I got it." He read it back to me. "I'll tell him."

"Thank you, Doc."

Next I gave the operator my parents' phone number. I wasn't sure what I would say. I simply knew that I had to make contact. The phone rang. My Dad answered and agreed to accept the charges. "What are you doing in Japan?" My father's voice sounded very calm—and sorrowful. "Why didn't you tell us you were going there?"

Where could I begin to explain what I'd been planning on doing when I came to Japan—how I got into this mess? I started talking in a rush. "Dad, I only have a minute here, maybe seconds. I'm somewhere in Tokyo, and this is probably the only chance I'm going to have to call you. I want you to know I love you, and Mom, and I love Annie so much..." I took a breath, felt a lump in my throat. "And Dad—everything you told me about Japan is true. I made a big mistake coming here. But I'm planning on getting home for Christmas. And if you don't hear from me by then... Dad, can I give you the number here?"

"Sure, honey." He sounded stoic. I knew he must be worried. I hated that I was doing this to him. I gave him the number and he wrote it down. "Okay, sweetie. I'm not going to tell your mother about this call. She'll only worry. I'll look forward to seeing you at Christmas."

"Okay. I have to go now. I love you, Dad. Goodbye." I hung up the phone. I picked it up again and tried to get a dial tone, an operator, but nothing happened. And although I tried many times afterward, I never got the phone to call overseas operator again. I'd had my chance to try to call the U.S. embassy, or Japanese police. I doubted that either of those authorities would help me. I didn't try to tell my Dad what was going on. I was ashamed, and afraid to hurt him. Now I feared that Kato-san, or somebody, was listening on the line, or that all calls were being recorded. *I don't know what I thought I'd accomplish. The number on the phone was probably useless.* Moments later, when the phone suddenly rang, I jumped. Kato-san called to announce the last appointment of that day.

The next few days I walked on eggshells. I feared retribution for the phone call out, but Kato-san never said anything. He'd apparently never known about it. What had happened was a freak accident—or a miracle.

A few days later, Mr. Saito made an appointment to see me. He treated me with kindness and showed respect. He began to see me rather frequently and sometimes bought up two hours at a time. I was not unhappy to see him. He spoke almost no English, only a few words, but he spoke a little bit of Spanish, and so did I, so between us we were able to patch together little conversations. Eventually he brought in a Japanese-English dictionary for me to use to talk with him. He used to hold his hands over his heart and point to me, saying, "Mahtina, my haht," as though trying to express affection for me. I hoped maybe someday I might be able to convince him to help me escape.

After a few more days, I met an ally. One morning Kato-san called and announced a "very important customah" had bought up three hours with me. I wearily prepared myself, expecting an ordeal with some old creep. I felt really down. When the guy came in, I stood with my back turned and refused to acknowledge him. I couldn't bring myself to face this one. Then I heard him speak in accented but excellent English.

"Sorry I'm a little late. I kept looking for a parking space. It took me forever because I'm so stoned!"

I didn't move. I rolled my eyes, figured him for a drunk. *Great.* Without turning around, I spoke to him. "Aren't you worried about drinking and driving?"

I heard him laugh. "Not drunk, stoned."

I whirled to face him. "What?" He looked to be around my age, with longish dark hair, tall, lean and muscular. He wasn't classically handsome, but was definitely appealing; I liked his face, his smile, his eyes.

He sat down cross-legged on one of the silk floor pillows, then reached into his jacket pocket and pulled out a joint. "Want to get stoned?"

Now I smiled. "Yeah!!"

He smiled back. "Ah! You are All-American girl!"

I sat down on another of the floor pillows, facing him, and we smoked that joint. I actually began to like him. He'd been to San Francisco and knew some clubs and hangouts there. We talked about rock n' roll, and he knew what he was talking about. He knew about Stevie Ray Vaughn, Tom Petty and the Heartbreakers, the Pretenders, the Ramones, the Clash, Tina Turner, AC/DC.

The apartment had a stereo and some vinyl albums, but they weren't to my taste: George Winston and—for Pete's sake!—Frank Sinatra; also some Elton John, which was okay. He insisted on playing some of the music, and really loud, while we talked. He made it clear to me that he pumped up the volume in order to be absolutely certain we weren't being listened in on. At this point, I felt thrilled to be conversing in English with someone besides Kato-san. And I liked this guy's attitude—he impressed me as being on my side.

The three hours sailed by. We talked about things; he told me he owned "an import-export business," which I found encouraging, since it was a universal code name for smuggling where I hailed from. Toward the end of our time together, he led me over to the corner which was out of range of the camera and slipped me a wad of bills. I was glad to see he was aware of the surveillance lens. "Take care of yourself and hang onto this," he said. He told me that he was going up into the mountains for a week or so but that he'd like to see me again when he returned to the city. Then he handed me a piece of paper with a phone number written on it. He told me his name—Yuji Ihara. Finally, I felt as though I had a friend in Tokyo, and this renewed my strength to carry on and stay hopeful.

Sleep evaded me that night. I kept trying to relax and drop off, but thoughts of possible escape, interspersed with fears of what might happen to me if I didn't escape, swarmed and whirled through my brain. I refused to allow myself to think about my daughter or my father—I knew if I did my heart would break or even explode. In my dysfunctional way, I felt fiercely protective of my little girl, and I believed that to allow thoughts of her into my mind while I was caught in this hell would be to somehow expose her innocence to danger and damage.

Suddenly the phone, which I'd placed beside my pillow, began to ring. I grabbed it instantly, interrupting the first vibration of that bell. I didn't speak, took an instant to listen first for the sound of Kato-san stirring, moving around in the next room. To my tremendous relief, profound silence filled the apartment. "Yes?" I whispered into the mouthpiece.

"Marti?" Evan's voice.

I'd been running from my boyfriend when I came to Japan, but now I felt relieved and happy to hear his voice. Compared to the terror I experienced here in Tokyo, memories of my life with Evan back in San Francisco seemed like sunshine and lollipops. I exhaled quietly, then spoke as quietly as possible, telling him about the situation.

He told me he'd fixed my car. He offered to torch Diane's house or to rip her off. I forgot all the things he'd put me through. I warmed to the idea that he was making a fuss over me in the only way he knew how. As with all women in abusive relationships, I possessed a considerable capacity for altering my perception of the abuses to accommodate my partner. I told him I wasn't safe talking for more than a minute. I didn't like admitting how scared I was, so I didn't say that aloud. What I did say was that I "might not get out of Japan alive." He offered to do anything he could to help me.

"What day is this?" I asked.

"Tuesday."

"Can you call me in a week, same day, same time, so it'll be night here? I need it to be in the middle of the night, so I don't get caught. Check out the time difference, and whatever you do, don't call during the day."

"Okay. I think it's around noon here. I'll check the time and I'll call you same time next week. I miss you Marti. Let's get you home."

"I've got to hang up now."

I lay there in the dark, listening to the silence in the apartment, the muffled drone of city streets beyond. I knew, but would not allow myself to think about the fact that no one—not Evan, not my Dad—would be able to help me get out. I knew Evan wasn't smart enough or strong enough to intimidate Diane into cutting me loose. I knew Diane had sold me to a Japanese criminal organization, that I was only one of many women she had trafficked, and that she would probably continue to engage in commercial exploitation of women after I was dead or sold elsewhere.

Nevertheless, a feeling of elation sprang up inside me. A tenuous thread of communication now stretched from my imprisonment in Japan to freedom in the good ol' U.S.A. I felt connected to—possibilities!

I fixed my mind on shutting down and getting some rest. I began the process I engaged in every night. I focused on going home, visualized it, believed it emotionally, programmed myself to accept no other outcome. I would be home for Christmas. I would see my daughter. I didn't need to know how, I only needed to know.

Evan called a week later, in the middle of the night. We talked for less than a minute but I felt safer knowing he was keeping in touch. Yuji returned from the mountains. He came to see me a few more times. We began to develop a relationship. He always bought up at least three hours with me so we could spend time together. With Elton John turned up loud for cover, we talked about travel and places we loved. He confided in me that he traveled to Peru and Colombia on a regular basis. "I buy emeralds in Cuzco," he said. I figured if he dealt in emeralds they were a sideline and cocaine was his true export.

He went on to tell me he loved San Francisco but could not re-turn there because he "got busted with a load of fake Rolexes." He told me his "brothers" in Hong Kong had connections for excellent fake Rolex watches and "lots of other stuff." I mentioned that he might like to meet some of my friends in Humboldt County. His eyes sparkled. He laughed, so I laughed too.

I wanted to motivate him to help me escape. I could return the favor with green bud. Of course I didn't propose right then and there that he help me. I could never be that overt. I maintained my cool—simply let him know I knew people. He suddenly indicated we should talk about these things later and changed the subject. I determined I would bide my time. If nothing else, Yuji bought up lots of hours to spend with me, and in so doing, rescued me from the others that traumatized me daily. And he gave me lots of yen notes every time he visited. By now I was starting to build up a good amount of Japanese currency in my carry on bag.

Evan called on Tuesdays, same time, and I clung to my slen-der thread of hope. During the long workdays I made an effort to be charming and polite. Some of the customers continued to show appreciation for me with gifts of cash, which I continued to accept.

I stashed the money away and guarded it closely. The money'd been mined from my misery and I would die before I let anyone take it from me. I felt resentment that someone was getting rich from exploiting me—or any other woman. The only thing I could do about it was to hoard what money I gleaned in gifts and look forward to seeing Yuji.

Over time, Kato-san began to treat me with less contempt and a bit of deference, as though I'd increased in value. One night, as we sat eating some sushi he brought in, he informed me the customers were paying extra money to be with me. "They pay more money for a better class of girl." He rubbed his hands together as he said this. I contemplated stabbing him in the eyes with my chopsticks, but decided against it. If I maimed him, what good would that do? I'd then have to contend with another attack from the Samoan. I set down my chopsticks. "Your father—what is he—in America? His work?"

"My father is an English professor."

"Ah, a professor. Good home. So this is why customahs like you. They know quality."

I said nothing, picked up my chopsticks, and resumed my meal.

"Next you will go to Osaka. I think they will like you there."

I froze. *Osaka? Oh hell no.* "When?"

He smiled, enjoying his power. "One day." He shrugged.

That night, I couldn't sleep at all.

Next morning I cleaned the apartment, as I did each day. Maybe I dusted and scrubbed so fanatically due to an urge to cleanse myself of the trauma I experienced daily. I could not bear to feel dirty. So I washed my body and my linens obsessively and scrubbed every surface I came in contact with. Besides, engaging in routine household tasks helped me dispel my fear. If I gave in to fear I would start screaming and never stop.

The phone rang and Kato-san announced a "customah," a gloomy looking man in his thirties, dressed in a business suit. As I did at the beginning of every session with a customer, I prepared tea and served it in on a tray as we sat on the silk floor pillows in the main room. I kept a Japanese-English dictionary on the floor beside me to help me get a bit of conversation going with each of the men who visited. If I could accomplish this, I thought, I could establish myself as a person, a human being, and the session would be more manageable. The man reached toward me and took one of my hands in his. He pointed to me and said, "Dorei." Then he picked up the dictionary and thumbed to a page, passed it to me, resting a fingertip on one of the entries to mark the place he wanted to show me. The word, "dorei," was there in print, with the English counterpart, "slave."

I felt a chill. I straightened my spine and looked him in the eye. I shook my head, pointed to myself. "No dorei."

"Dorei." He stated this matter-of-factly.

I slogged through the hour with him. He didn't want to act out bondage roles or dominance games, so I couldn't attribute his pointed use of the Japanese word for "slave" to that sort of thing. Of all the horrors I'd endured since being shut up in that apartment, this one ranked high in its power to disturb me and knock me off balance—the nonchalant manner in which he categorized me as "slave." I fervently hoped he would not return.

One of my frequent visitors was an old man I thought of as "The Nazi." He would buy up two hours at a time, and he loved to talk. He spoke English. "Notice that I can pronounce my Rs very well," he'd say. He remarked that although his English was limited, he pronounced the Rs well because he spoke fluent German. He told me he "...spent a lot of time in Germany during the '40s," then moved to Argentina. That's why I thought of him as a Nazi. Back and forth between Germany and Japan during the Axis years, then on to Argentina? Sounds Nazi to me.

The old man liked to talk about Swiss banking systems and Swiss finance. I listened and nodded. He told me about New Year's traditions in Japan, and how they change the shoji each year in a ceremony for good luck. He also said the Japanese line up at the Buddhist shrine near the Emperor's palace in Tokyo each year— that the line stretches for miles, and people get blessings and make prayers for the coming year. He said all the people standing in line sing Beethoven's "Ode to Joy," in German, every New Year's, while they're waiting to get to the shrine.

He told me he had a house in Nepal. We talked about Tibet. Lazily, he stretched out a hand and stroked my hip and thigh, saying, "I will take you to my house in Nepal. I will keep you as pet." His tone, his attitude, one of casual acquisition—alarmed me.

I made no response to the comment. I hoped I was acting as if I hadn't heard him. I don't know if I can adequately describe how squeamish his words made me feel. I began to be afraid that one of these customers might have an option to actually purchase me from the gangsters. Surely it would have been possible.

I began to focus my efforts on deliverance at the hand of either of the two most friendly ones—Yuji Ihara or Mr. Saito. Both of them treated me well enough that I thought of them as friends. Still, I had no idea what they thought of me. I knew almost nothing about Saito, and there was a language barrier. I decided I could not trust him. Yuji was different. He seemed like a genuine friend to me, and I knew he was an outlaw—that is, someone I could trust.

On Yuji's next visit, I restrained myself from sounding desperate. I hinted at the fact that I might be going to Osaka at any time. When he heard this, Yuji's forehead wrinkled. "When?" he asked.

"I don't know. The only thing he's said is that I will be going. I don't know anything more. I'm afraid to ask. I...well, I'm just afraid to," I said lamely, hoping he would get the idea of what I was up against, if he didn't know already. But, I decided, he must know. I thought I could tell by the look in his eyes, even though Yuji maintained a bullet-proof cool at all times. Certainly cool is what it takes to succeed in his line of work.

"I'll ask to spend the night with you. We'll be together—and have time to make a plan."

"I still have my passport," I confided to Yuji. "I've been hiding it, along with some money in tips. It hasn't been easy."

"It's okay now." He put his arm around me. I put my head on his shoulder.

Later the next day, Kato-san announced that "very important customah has paid for all night. Tomorrow night." He rubbed his hands together, no doubt an unconscious expression of his avarice.

When Yuji arrived for our overnight, he brought some excellent Chinese food with him: abalone, scallops, and vegetable dishes. We sat and ate with chopsticks. He brought some cool music too—some classic Bob Marley and a new album by Dire Straits, called Brothers in Arms.

———

"A GIFT FOR THE HOUSE," HE STATED WITH A BRIGHT SMILE. He put the Dire Straits on the turntable and cranked it up loud. "I know some people in the record business," he began, "I know a lot of reg-gae musicians in Jamaica and stuff like that. And I used to do a lot of business with a recording studio in Louisiana."

At that, I lost some of the reserve I'd intended to maintain. Maybe it was nostalgia for the States, and my life beyond this apartment prison cell. I leaned forward. "I know Louisiana!" I piped in. "I love it—got some friends there. I used to live in Texas, and I worked in the oil field. We did some jobs in Louisiana."

He took my interruption in stride. Nothing ever rattled Yuji. He always acted as if he moved within an eternity, a river of time, in which he could float languorously. He always looked amused and happy. "You worked in Oil? What did you do?"

"Well, I ended up surveying with a civil engineering company for several years. But I started out setting off explosives." I included a mention of my limited experience with dynamite charges because I hoped it sounded glamorous and intrepid.

"Explosives? Really? Can you buy them?"

"Well, I don't think so, but I'd be able contact someone who could." I stopped then, unsure of whether to engage in discussion of explosives. Better to persuade him I could be useful in some other way. I felt compelled to establish myself as a damsel in distress who had the power to repay the rescuing hero and square all accounts. I sat up straighter. "So...you were saying? About the recording studio in Louisiana?"

"I flew into New Orleans with a musician from the islands. I had sixty thousand bucks on me and customs confiscated it. We had a lot of other stuff to think about, and I was concentrating on that, so I forgot about the cash. See, where I'm from we don't have to declare cash, but in the U.S. you do, and this was one of my first visits to the States. I didn't know. Anyway..." He paused, smiled, pulled a joint out of the breast pocket of his shirt, lit it, took a hit, passed it to me. He exhaled and continued. "Anyway, the big stuff made it through. But I lost the sixty grand. And I'm not allowed into the port of New Orleans anymore."

I exhaled my hit. "Wow, that's terrible. I wonder if I might be able to help you out there. I have this old friend from the oil field—he's almost family—and he married a chick from New Orleans who is an international lawyer. They live in the French Quarter. Her father is an international lawyer. They're an old New Orleans family and I bet they have some influence." I smiled meaningfully. "Louisiana is very corrupt, you know."

Yuji smiled his bright smile. "That's very interesting."

"Yes," I said, "And if I could get back home for Christmas, the first thing I would do is call them. I'd love to call them now, but my address books are at home in San Francisco. You know, I really miss all my friends. Especially the ones in Humboldt County."

We talked everything over very casually—we had an entire night. I enjoyed hanging out with him. We made love, and as always I noticed the network of pale scars on his torso. They looked to be marks left by very old wounds—a web of slashes laced his back, sides and midriff. I took the utmost care not to appear as if I noticed the scars. I didn't want to make him uncomfortable. I wondered how he got them, but never asked.

Yuji brought out a small amount of coke. We did lines so we could stay up all night, alternately plotting, making love, and listening to Bob Marley or Dire Straits. He mentioned to me that if I wanted to, he could arrange a means to transport heroin "...in shipping containers, concealed in some other legal import item, such as silk kimonos..." If I could handle moving some of it, I could possibly get into the business. I neither agreed to nor rejected the idea. He again expressed an interest in California green bud.

He assured me he would buy my return airline ticket and get me to the plane. "We will need to be careful," he warned. "Don't act happy like you are now. Act like you don't like me. I'll buy us a chance to go outside of here—say, a trip to the Imperial Palace Gardens, shopping in the Ginza district—during an afternoon, and I'll bring you back here. Then a few days later I'll get in here and take you to the airport. When we do the shopping trip I'll tell you the day you fly so you can be ready."

"Can we stop at a bank that day? I'd love to change my money." I showed him my cash stash I'd been hiding from Kato-san.

He stood up and reached for his backpack, unzipping it with a flourish. "No problem!" He laughed, then pulled a huge pile of money out of the pack. The bills were in bank bundles. "What would you like? I have German marks, Swiss francs, Japanese yen, British pounds, American dollars." He riffled through the bundles eagerly, laughing, then suddenly lost his grip on the mass of cash. The money dropped to the floor between us.

I dropped to a crouch and started picking up the money. "Here. Be careful." I began handing him the bills as I scraped them up.

He reached out and grabbed my hand, pulled me up to my feet, making a dismissive sweeping gesture. "It is only paper." He laughed again. He exchanged my yen into dollars, gathered up the remaining cash from the floor, and zipped it back into his pack.

Early in the morning, Kato-san returned and Yuji left the apartment. I took care not to reveal the tremendous relief and anticipation bubbling inside of me. I asked Kato-san for the day off, but no such luck. Another workday began. It was an especially rough and painful day and Kato-san treated me with contempt and antagonism. But now I had hope.

A few days passed and I heard nothing about any shopping trips. Kato-san acted hardhearted and derisive. I had a lot of difficulty sleeping. Finally, Kato-san announced that a "very important customah" was going to take me out into the city for the afternoon, with "security" following, of course. Next day I left the apartment with Yuji. I'd stuffed my passport into one of my knee-high leather boots. In my purse I carried all of my accumulated cash. I was ready for anything. We walked past the Samoan, took the elevator to the ground floor, and stepped into the street. At first I thought we were clear, and I squeezed Yuji's arm. I wanted to make a run for a taxi. Then I caught sight of the "security."

Two sullen thug types followed not far behind us, making no effort to conceal themselves. I glanced at the goons one time only, then ignored them. They wore three piece pinstriped suits and black sunglasses. One of them actually sported a fedora. They looked like a cliché from a gangster movie. I thought it was ridiculous. Later,

I learned that the yakuza like to dress in such garishly obvious attire in order to demonstrate their rebel, outsider status, and the effect is intimidating to citizens.

Yuji and I walked to the Imperial Palace Gardens, the part which is open to the public as a park. He told me that at New Year's, the emperor and his family leave the estate and go to their summer palace, and that while they are away, the rest of the grounds, as well as the palace itself, is open to viewing by the people of Japan.

Yuji took me to a Buddhist shrine. Ceremonial drummers performed in the area, clad in traditional costumes. Speaking in low tones, Yuji told me he would see me in a few more days. "Do the same thing you did today. Be ready for your adventure." At the shrine, he helped me to purchase a Zen Buddhist relic, blessed by a priest. It was encased in a bit of embroidered silk. "This is for health and life," he told me.

Then he led me to a beautiful stone well, which reminded me of a classic fairy tale wishing well. Yuji handed me a Japanese coin. "Toss in the coin and make a prayer—or you might call it a wish—for your future. It's a tradition in Japan this time of year." Feeling stronger and healthier knowing I held the Buddhist relic, I tossed in my coin, closed my eyes and prayed/wished: to see my daughter—and for her to have happiness in her life. Then I added one more: to get to do standup comedy again.

Yuji walked me back to the apartment building with the thugs trailing us. We stopped at two little shops on the way back. I bought some Christmas presents for my loved ones—jewelry, pink pearls for my little girl, a pearl tiepin for my father, and some beautiful little porcelain cups for my mother.

Yuji returned me to Kato-san at the time agreed upon. I went back to play my role for a few more days. The next day was a workday like all the others, except for one thing—Saito came to see me. He'd bought up three hours. He carried a beautifully wrapped gift in his hands. In broken English, he communicated to me that the gift had been "made special," and "much work to find."

He knelt down and set the package on the floor between us. His hands trembled as he began to unwrap the paper and remove its contents. I watched him set up a tiny, black-lacquered wooden platform. Behind the platform he placed a finely crafted miniature ornamental screen. And finally, he pulled a clear-lacquered shell from the gift box. He opened the shell and it fell into two halves in his hands.

Each half of the shell was delicately painted in lovely colors, and the bottom edges of the shells had each been dipped in gold. "Twenty-four karat," he indicated the gold work with one of his index fingers, then pointed to himself. "I do this." Gently, reverently, he set each of the shell halves on the tiny display platform, then sat back on his heels. I stared at the delicate artwork in the shells. One shell's depiction showed a courtly Japanese lady in a crimson kimono, sitting in a house. The house was portrayed in a style from the romantic era. The colors sang. The other shell showed a continuation of the scene, beginning with the edge of the house, depicting an expanse of pastel green with a few tiny scarlet flowers painted in—a pastoral background. And in the foreground, two samurai knights, in black kimonos with red decorations, sat on the painted meadow beside the house, with swords drawn and laid across their laps. They looked absolutely alert and ready to defend the lady against any threat. All three of the figures faced the viewer. They seemed to come alive as I gazed at them. I looked at Saito, trying to figure out how to express gratitude for such a gift.

He held out his hand as though to indicate I shouldn't try to speak yet. Then he presented me with a scroll of creamy paper. I unrolled the scroll. On the larger sheet of paper the writing was in Japanese, but another sheet of paper contained a translation into

English. Saito gestured with hands in a rolling motion, as if to say, "go ahead, read it."

I held the page in my lap and read. The paper told the history of the shells. It said that in ancient Japan, before the Chinese arrived on Japanese shores, they had no written language. At that time, they used common seashells as a sort of currency—that is, they were used as receipts or declarations. They recorded important events, intentions, or thoughts by painting on shells the ideas they wished to commemorate. The tradition was that no two of these shells are alike, and that one of the halves will only fit the other of that same shell. The shells they painted conveyed a spirit of unity, fidelity, loyalty, etc., in that the two halves are one. After the Chinese came and the Japanese adopted their system of written characters, the Japanese continued to use the shells for very important events. Eventually, the painted shells became a tradition with aristocrats, who sometimes gave them as gifts to courtesans—to express high esteem. For a courtesan to receive such a gift was the highest honor. In some cases, it said, the courtesans played a game with the shells, like tarot cards, to read each other's destinies or predict how their love lives might fare.

I finished reading. I looked up at Saito. "Arigato." I only knew a few words in Japanese; I figured if I fumbled around I might spoil the moment. This demonstration of human respect touched my heart. The fact he saw me as a lady moved me deeply. I could see he was feeling some intense emotions also.

"Keep them with you," he said in his faltering English, "In your room. They are blessed by Zen Buddhist priest and will guard over your love life." Then, he drew a business card from his suit jacket and handed it to me. It was printed in English. "My real name." He laughed softly. On the card, it said his name, and the name of his jewelry store. Then it listed locations: Rome, Tokyo, Paris, New York. Carefully, he took the shells off the platform and wrapped them up. Then he returned all the pieces to the box. When he left I packed them into my carry on bag, feeling a deep sense of gratitude for the blessing of a Zen Buddhist priest. Lord knows, I needed it.

Late in the night, I lay awake and tried not to worry about getting sent to Osaka. I feared that Saito somehow knew I would be going there immediately, and that was why he delivered the shells and gave me his card. Perhaps he intended for me to contact him if things in Osaka became too awful for me to bear. I didn't know, but I determined to keep the card and try to call him if Yuji's plan failed and I found myself Osaka bound.

# CHAPTER 5

# OLD SCARS AND THE STORIES THEY TELL

THE NEXT MORNING, KATO-SAN INFORMED ME THAT "VERY important customah," would be returning to take me on a shopping trip to the Ginza district. "He wants to buy you present." Kato-san betrayed no emotion, his eyes dead and dull as a shark's.

On my last morning in Tokyo, Kato-san left the apartment as usual, and announced "customahs," as usual, but at noon he called and told me that the remainder of my workday was reserved for "very important customah," to take me out of the apartment.

Much earlier that morning, alone in my room, I prepared to go home. I dressed in my tall leather boots, my jeans—not a skirt, I might need to run—and a cashmere sweater. I put my passport into my left boot, along with as much cash as I could fit in there. I stuffed the other boot with bills. In my small leather carry on bag, which actually looked like a large handbag, I put the remainder of the cash, the shell gift from Saito, the Christmas presents for my daughter and parents, a change of lingerie, my hairbrush and makeup.

I sat on the living room floor with my bag on my lap and boots on, waiting. Yuji came through the door smiling but looking very alert. The second I saw him, I sprang to my feet, my heart pounding in my chest. I slipped my bag over my left shoulder, reassured that it felt so lightweight. Yuji took my right hand. The door hadn't closed behind him, and I could see the Samoan standing outside in the hallway. Yuji and I exited in step, taking our time, Yuji making small talk all the while. I forced a smile and nodded, trying to conceal my trepidation as we advanced down the hall toward the elevator.

Yuji pressed the button for the elevator and stood waiting. A moment later, as the doors opened, Yuji signaled me to walk to the left, further down the hall and around a corner. He led me to a staircase. We walked downstairs to the ground floor and stepped outside into a narrow alley, then out of the alley toward a group of three black Mercedes-Benz sedans, each with its engine idling. Suddenly, three tough looking Asian guys jumped out of one Benz, and four out of another. For an instant, my knees almost buckled from terror, but then I noticed they were smiling. They were Yuji's guys! Yuji was propelling me toward the front vehicle, which sat empty. His friends greeted Yuji with jubilant high five gestures. One of them wore a sweatshirt with University of California emblazoned across the chest. Yuji jumped into the lead Mercedes' driver's seat as the University of California-sweatshirt-wearing-guy helped me around to the passenger side seat and shut the door. All of this happened in seconds.

Yuji pulled the car around the corner to the main thoroughfare and edged into heavy traffic, the two identical cars right behind us. Yuji picked up a car phone receiver and said something in Japanese, or was it Chinese? I decided I couldn't tell, and didn't have time to care. I tried not to look around for the security goons, tried to stare straight ahead and look casual. "We're not going to the airport right away," Yuji said smoothly, reaching into the console and pulling out a joint. "I'm going to show you around the city for a bit. We've got plenty of time before your plane leaves. First we are going to a big subway station, then to a bus terminal, and then you go to the airport. It is better this way." My rescuer kept his eyes on the road unflinchingly, yet, with a gallant flourish, he lit the joint in the cigarette lighter, lifted it to his lips, and inhaled deeply. He passed it to me.

"I, I can't get high right now, Yuji. I'm...too..."

"Take it—I insist," he urged. "You need to take it easy. C'mon, now."

"Okay." I took a hit, only a small one, and tried not to hold it in long enough to get stoned. Weed, at times, made me paranoid and now, I figured, was likely to be one of those times. *No kidding.* I was nearly in a state of paralysis from fear!

But the weed tasted sweet and mild, and I felt myself easing into a very tranquil state of mind. Yuji passed it back and I took another, deeper hit. I began to feel better—no, that's not quite it. Maybe I simply got so stoned that I couldn't concentrate on the danger any more. I decided this was better for my adrenal glands anyway, and took a third hit. "Whoo." I looked at Yuji meaningfully, as if that conveyed everything—my apprehension, my gratitude to him for this escape attempt, compliments on the weed, everything.

"Good weed, isn't it?" He tossed what remained of the joint into the ashtray, then glanced in my direction for an instant. The car phone speaker, or radio, whatever it was they were communicating through, crackled, and I heard dialogue-not-in-English once more. Yuji listened, replied tersely, returned the unit to its cradle. Calmly, he took an abrupt turn in the heavy Tokyo traffic and we nearly collided with a truck or bus—some large vehicle that had a flashing light on it. Unruffled, he continued to drive, regularly glancing in the rearview. I supposed he was checking to make sure our rear guard was still with us. I hoped he wasn't checking out Kato-san's security thugs on our tail. I never looked back. I clasped my forearms around each other and made an effort to think happy thoughts. Yuji resumed speaking. "I think it is excellent weed. It's grown in the mountains in the Philippines, by some friends of mine who hide out up there. I do a lot of business with them." I nodded and smiled, incapable of making any audible reply. I'd suddenly developed a bad case of cottonmouth from the bud.

As if instantly anticipating my every need, Yuji produced an exceptionally large, flawlessly formed apple from somewhere on his side of the vehicle and handed it to me. I noticed he had one for himself as well. I bit in, savoring its juiciness and flavor. "These apples are grown here in Japan. It is a new breed of apple. Each apple tree is attended to by a dozen or more workers all season, right up to harvest, to assure the finest quality." He took a bite, chewed slowly, swallowed. "Japan will soon be selling these on the international market."

I appreciated all of Yuji's anecdotes. He kept me entertained and distracted so I wouldn't stress out. After we finished eating the apples, we drove along in silence for a time. Yuji stayed on the phone with his friends, running interference on the route we took, changing directions often. We stopped at the subway station, where we never got out of the car, but swung back into traffic, and drove around some more. "When you get home to California, do you plan to live in San Francisco? Or L.A.?"

"I don't know," I said. I hadn't told him about how I'd run away from a bad boyfriend, and how I wanted to resettle in the Midwest, near my daughter, where I could quit drugs, and everything that came with the drug scene. "Maybe I'll go to L.A.. It might be safer."

"I think you should stay in San Francisco." He kept driving, but looked my way for a moment. "I know a woman, a friend of mine, who lives near there. You remind me of her. I think you will like her." He passed me a piece of paper with the name, "Lisa," and a telephone number written on it. "Call her when you get to the States. Tell her I sent you. When you see her, show her this." He pulled a single bill of currency from his jacket pocket. It was a 5,000 yen note. "See how big it is? That's the way they used to make them. Show her this, and she will know what she needs to tell you."

I nodded. "I will." I folded the yen note and the contact info and slipped them into the pocket of my jeans. Yuji continued navigating expertly through traffic, changing routes and maintaining communications with his crew until we arrived at the bus terminal. Yuji accompanied me into the building. He presented me with a printed sheet of paper which was my ticket—Charter Tour, it said—the rest was in what I figured must be Japanese.

Yuji helped me check in for my flight at the bus terminal. His friends, for all I could see, had disappeared. I believed they were still running interference, or posted on look-outs. I never asked Yuji any details, or why he was helping me, or if he feared reprisals from Kato-san—or rather, the organization he worked for.

"We will sit here and wait for the right bus," he told me, "It's only a short way to the airport from here. This is much better for us." We sat down together on a bench in the middle of all the hustle and bustle. He reached into a pocket of his jacket and drew out an envelope, then handed it to me. "Holiday card for you." He grinned, then shot me a serious glance. "Go to the women's room, open it in there, and read it in there."

I went into the restroom, entered a stall, closed the door. I opened the envelope, and pulled out the card. On its face was a photo of a Japanese Buddhist temple nestled among evergreen trees. I opened the card, which bore no message—at least not in writing, anyway. A clear plastic baggie of cocaine, which I figured might be over a half gram or as much as a gram, clung to the card by a piece of tape. I couldn't handle doing coke under the circumstances! Rattled, I closed the card and returned it to the envelope, which I slipped into a pouch in my carry on bag. I rejoined Yuji a few moments later. "Wow! Thanks!"

"Did you read it?"

"Uh, no, I...I can't read that fast, if you know what I mean." I glanced around the terminal. "Maybe I can read it when I get home."

"No, no...read it now." He pressed my hand. "Go back there in a few minutes. You have to read it now. Before you get on the plane!"

I went back to the restroom and snorted a nice-sized line of the coke, which had been put through a strainer and did not need chopping. It was excellent quality. I took another snort. I should have flushed it down the toilet, but the addict in me couldn't resist trying to hang on to the remainder of the dope for a little while longer.

Back on the bench, Yuji greeted me with, "How did you like the card?"

"Beautiful. I love it." I felt invigorated and full of the false bravado that comes with a coke high. "I haven't finished reading it yet but I will soon. How much time do we have before my bus leaves?" I had no idea what was going on in this place. Even before I snorted the coke I'd felt like I was on another planet. Now I felt like I'd crossed into an alternate universe. I was totally overwhelmed by the adrenalin charge of escape and the car chase. Now I'd introduced a stimulant narcotic into my system.

"We have some time." He squeezed my hand, spoke reassuringly while his eyes scanned the terminal for—what? Finally I gave up trying to figure out what was going to happen. Yuji'd gotten me this far, I figured, so I'd lean on him the rest of the way. "Your bus just left, but another one will be coming. I'm watching for the opportune moment." He smiled, kept watching.

We sat together there on that bench, and I realized once more how comfortable I felt with Yuji. I liked his company, and I believe he felt the same way about me. In the terminal, in the middle of a crush of people, with so much noise and haste, and in the uncertainty of my situation, I felt enveloped in a cocoon of strength and safety.

"Another bus, we'll let it go on...You will see your family for the holiday?" He asked while fixing his eyes on something beyond me.

"Yes," I said. "How about you? Will you be with your family for New Year's? Your parents?"

He looked at me, his face impassive. "I never knew my parents. They died when I was very young. I grew up on the streets. In Hong Kong."

"Oh." A surge of emotion for him, warmth and concern, rose up in me. There were so many things I wanted to say, to ask, but I needed to be cool. Yuji's pervasive calm demanded that of me. Now was not the time to show emotion, or do anything else which might attract attention. I was probably already highly visible because I was a tall, blonde foreigner. And I was running from Japanese organized crime. "Do you have brothers or sisters?" I asked.

"Brothers. My brothers raised me. On the streets of Hong Kong." He looked out into the terminal. I decided I wouldn't ask Yuji anything more.

We sat in silence until at last he stood up and said, "This is the one—your bus. I can't go with you, but it's okay. Stay on till you get to the airport. From there you can ask assistance to find your gate..." He put his arm around me and walked me to the bus.

I turned to face Yuji, touched his shoulder. "Thank you." That was all I said. I stepped up to get on the bus. When I turned to look back he was gone.

Aboard the bus, I sat down beside a loudmouthed Canadian businessman in a trenchcoat who kept talking about how good the Tokyo nightclub scene was. Glad for the company, no matter how obnoxious, I kept him talking till we got to Narita International, then asked him if he would mind accompanying me to an information desk so I could ask about the boarding gate for my charter flight. The businessman got me that far and then marched off to the nearest bar.

I found out my flight's scheduled departure time and the gate from which it would be leaving. I needed to hurry! I made it down to the boarding area and felt dismayed when I took in the scene there. A large crowd of people gathered at the gate, pressing toward the airline officials, shouting in some Asian language, holding up handfuls of cash and gesturing wildly. To this day I have no idea what was going on at that gate. I felt terrified the crowd would prevent me from boarding, or that one of them had bid on my seat and bought it out from under me. I hesitated, then noticed a couple of American corporate types in suits looking my way. I strode over to them and asked if they were on the flight. They told me they weren't.

"Any idea what's going on over there?" I asked them. "Excuse me, but I'm trying to get out of here. Um, I wanna be home for Christmas and I'm on that flight, I think…I mean, this is my ticket, I guess…" I showed them the sheet of paper. "Do you think it's legit?"

One of the men smiled at me. "I think you're legit," he laughed, "…and all you need to do is glide over there on those long American legs of yours, throw your shoulders back and push on through that crowd like you own that plane."

Encouraged, I did exactly as he said. I jostled my way through and boarded the jet. An attendant welcomed me and told me to find a seat. I stumbled in and found myself a seat in the back of the plane beside a sleepy looking Latino guy. Shortly after I boarded, the attendants instructed everyone to fasten seat belts. The pilot announced takeoff. Moments later the plane taxied down the runway and lifted off.

Once we were in the air, I remembered my "holiday card" from Yuji. I'd forgotten to finish "reading" it! Suddenly I heard a collective shout from the midsection of the jet, where a large group of American servicemen in fatigues were seated. One of them yelled, "U.S.A. here we come! Whahooo!" *My sentiments exactly*. I noticed the attendants coming down the aisle, taking drink orders.

I reached into my boot and pulled out a couple of hundreds. When the attendant stopped at my row, I asked if I could buy a round for the plane.

"I had a very rough trip," I said, handing her the money, "I'm so happy to be going home that I want to celebrate it with everybody here."

"I think we can do that." The attendant took the money and smiled at me. After I bought that one, the soldiers started buying rounds for the plane. The attendants obliged, then finally one of them stood up at the front of our section looking flummoxed and said, "This is a Pan Am jet! This is not a roadhouse! We cannot allow any more rounds for the plane, okay?"

We stopped in Manila for what seemed like a long time to me. I didn't get out. I went in the restroom and snorted a little more of my coke. I got a scary dizzy rush, though, and decided not to partake of any more of it. An American man in a suit and a big overcoat loped onto the plane, clutching a briefcase to his chest with both hands. He slumped down in the seat to my right and started talking very fast. "I'm with Asian Studies—barely made it—can't wait to get out of Manila! It's crazy out there!" He set the briefcase on his knees, slapped the top of it a couple of times. "Look what I got in here!" Wild eyed, he clicked the locks on the attaché case and flipped open the top. "Check it out! Want some?" I recoiled, fearing it might be heroin or guns. Then I looked. The briefcase was brimming with—vodka. Those little tiny individual bottles you get on the airlines.

"Uh, no thanks." I turned away from him and pretended to sleep. I figured he must be drunk or crazy. The plane took off again.

The sleepy Latino guy on my left awakened after a while. He sat up straight, turned to me, and said, "Want a Valium?" He opened one fist and showed me about a dozen of the little blue 10 milligram pills with the "V" punched out of the center. We used to call them "flyin' Vs." I accepted one of them, then asked him if he'd like some coke. "I need to get rid of it," I explained. I shared my coke with him and we talked. He started telling me about how he'd been up in the mountains in the Philippines, working with rebels against Marcos. He told me wild stories of how he worked as a trainer for strategic military, *paramilitary, more likely*, and that these rebels were working hard to overthrow the corrupt Marcos regime. Seems like they succeeded, too—Marcos' rule ended a few months later, in early 1986. My newfound friend showed me several snapshots of his rebel friends. As I looked over the photos, I wondered about what Yuji'd told me of his "friends in the mountains" in the Philippines, the ones who grew that kickass weed. Were they financing their revolution with weed? I would never know. I took a Valium and went to sleep for the rest of the flight. I awakened hearing the pilot's voice announcing our descent into San Francisco.

When we landed and I got off the plane, I almost kissed the ground. At first, exuberance and relief flooded me—freedom at last! But my jubilation didn't last long. The instant I began walking through the airport I experienced the terror I'd never allowed myself to feel while in the control of Japanese organized crime. A wild whirlwind of fear threatened to knock me off balance and slam me into...catatonia or oblivion. I took a deep breath and kept walking. Somehow I managed to suppress panic.

Outside the airport, I got a taxi to a nearby Hilton and checked in. On the phone in my room, I called Evan's cousins in Richmond and left a message for him. I also left word for Evan, and the hotel number, at the Pink Elephant in Monte Rio. I sat down to wait. I tried to think calmly, to sort out what had happened. I told myself how lucky I was. No doubt about that. Yet how very stupid I'd been...I thought about that, too. But I couldn't really concentrate on any train of thought for long. And I couldn't get myself to feel even the slightest bit safe. My heart skittered in my chest.

The date was December 22nd. I'd been in Japan since the second week of November. I had now come full circle. Here I was, searching for the sociopath I'd been trying to run away from. For some reason I felt compelled to see him before I went home for Christmas. I thought I could somehow connect to a kind of normalcy through contact with the familiar—even if it was miserable and chaotic—and that would quiet my shattered, turbulent mind and emotions. I slumped onto my knees beside the bed and laid my head on the bedspread.

Then I thought of my daughter Annie and stood up. I'd missed her birthday on the 17th, but I would damn well be there for Christmas! I picked up the phone again and called United Airlines. I reserved a flight to Indianapolis, leaving on the morning of Christmas Eve. *Good. There.*

I felt a pounding in my chest—my own heartbeat. I realized I needed to talk to someone who would understand something about me. I wanted to call Yuji's number but didn't think I could get an international call out on the hotel phone. Besides,—irrationally—I feared that Yuji's line in Tokyo would be bugged by the yakuza and they'd somehow trace the call, find out where I was, then come to the Hilton and kill me. Suddenly I remembered—Yuji's friend Lisa. I sat down on a chair beside the bed and reached into my jeans pocket for her phone number. I felt terrified to call, yet compelled to do so immediately.

I grabbed the phone, punched in the numbers, and listened as it rang several times before Lisa picked up. "Hello."

"Excuse me, I'm looking to speak with Lisa?"

"I'm Lisa. Who is this?"

"Lisa, I'm Marti. I'm a friend of Yuji's. I just got back from Japan. Yuji told me to call you. He wanted me to show you something, he

said if I show it to you, you'll know what to tell me. It's a yen note."
I fished the note out of my jeans and unfolded it, smoothing it out
on the quilted motel bedspread. "Listen, Lisa, I have to go to the
Midwest for Christmas with my family. I'm pretty tired and...well, I
can't wait to see you in person and show you this thing. Would you
mind if I describe it to you over the phone? Maybe that would do
it." I finished talking and took a breath, hoping she was still listening. *I must sound crazy.*

But Lisa was still on the line. "Yeah, let's give it a try. Any
friend of Yuji's is a friend of mine. Hey, tell me, what's this yen note
look like?"

I studied it. "Well, it's a 5,000 yen note. And there's a guy's face
on it...and it's big." I figured I must sound so lame!

"It's big? Bigger than the yen notes they have now, right?"

"Yeah, Yuji gave it to me and said, 'See how big it is?' And then
he told me to show it to you when I got back to the States."

Lisa hesitated. "Oh, I know what's going on," she said, then
asked me, "What do you think of Japanese men?"

I felt affronted, scared all of a sudden. I was ashamed to say
anything for fear I'd reveal the circumstances—and the terror—of
my stay in Tokyo. I fumbled for an answer. "Uh, well, they're very
polite, and uh..." But Lisa interrupted me—fiercely.

"I don't think they're polite. They're sadists—they're cruel,
and..."

No longer hesitant, I chimed in. "Yeah, they are! They were. I
was in this apartment, and I couldn't get out...they had guards. But
then..."

"Marti. Hey." Lisa spoke quietly as though trying to soothe me.
"Then Yuji came along, didn't he? Oh, here, let me tell you. That
yen note...they stopped printing those about five years ago, when
they introduced the newer, smaller currency. Five years ago—
that's when Yuji got me out of Japan. I was a prisoner for three

years—ended up in this, this really awful brothel after I tried to escape. As punishment for the escape attempt, they dropped me out of a second story window and I broke my shoulder and my arm and really screwed up my neck. But none of that matters now because Yuji came along and rescued me. Somehow he's got a sixth sense for damsels in distress. He really knows when and how to zoom in and save the day!"

We talked a little while longer. She elaborated on the horrors of the Japanese underworld—their exploitation and mistreatment of women. As I listened, a profound fatigue overwhelmed me. I asked Lisa if I could call her back some time. She said that'd be okay. I hung up, lay down on the bed, and fell asleep in my clothes. I awoke to the sound of a phone ringing—Evan calling from his cousins' in Richmond, telling me he'd be with me soon. I felt relief at the prospect of company. Regardless of how desperate I'd been to end the relationship with Evan, I now eagerly anticipated his arrival.

———

EVAN SHOWED ME MY CAR, HOW HE'D STRAIGHTENED THE FRONT end. I thought it looked okay; I mean, it was thrashed—but it looked a lot better than when I left, and the engine still worked perfectly. He'd brought my coat and some other articles of my clothing with him. I asked him to drop me off at the airport for my Christmas visit. My brain reeled from what I'd experienced in Tokyo, but I still clung to the hope that I might be able to move to Indiana near my little girl. Of course, I didn't say anything about not returning to California. Evan brought some meth with him and we did some of it. Now I was back in the same old cycle. The dope increased my agitation, but I told myself it'd help me shake off the fear and suppress the all too fresh and vital memories of the trauma I'd been through.

I attempted to compose myself for the family Christmas visit. I called my parents' house. My dad answered it. I told him my flight number and time of arrival. He agreed to meet me at the airport in Indianapolis.

When my plane landed, Dad was waiting for me. I hugged him and he hugged me. We walked in silence through the airport and out the exits. The icy wind blew fiercely. Freezing rain stung our faces as we made our way through the parking lot to my parents' car. We got in and sat down on the front seat. Ice glazed the windshield, obstructing visibility. Dad started the engine and turned on the defroster. Finally one of us spoke.

"Well, dear, a lot of people have been very worried about you," Dad said, deliberately looking straight ahead, "...and I am one of those people, of course." My father studied the windshield as he continued. "After you called me that night, I spoke with my friend Sam Takahashi. You remember meeting him, don't you?"

"Yes, Dad." I faintly remembered only the name. I listened as my father explained about Dr. Takahashi, a colleague of his at the University who'd emigrated to the U.S. with his wife, prior to Pearl Harbor. Dad told me Dr. Takahashi was a member of a venerated family of Zen Buddhist priests.

"Sam's family is highly regarded in the diplomatic circle, and I knew that he was planning to visit Tokyo for a conference at the time. I called him, told him my concerns, as well as the phone number you gave me, and asked him if he might be able to help us out in some way. That was all I could think of to do. I—I'm glad you're here."

Dad glanced my way for an instant. In all my life I have never seen tears in my father's eyes, but now I could see them glistening, beginning to collect on the lids and lashes. He looked away quickly and began tinkering with the dashboard. "This darn defroster—it's really irritating my eyes!" He wiped thumb and forefinger across his eyelids, then put the car in drive. "Well, we'd better get going. Your mother will worry if we're late." Dad maneuvered into traffic.

We drove home in a profound silence broken only by bits of small talk. I was relieved that he didn't question or scold me. If he had, I would have jumped out of the car and never stopped running. I thought about the Zen Buddhist blessing on Saito's gift to me, and the Zen Buddhist relic Yuji helped me obtain at the shrine. Then I considered the idea that my father's colleague, descended from Zen Buddhist priests, must have been offering up prayers on my behalf. I could only conclude that the Japanese have some serious juju going on with the Zen thing. Unfortunately for me, I never took it any farther than that. A healthy soul would have endeavored to study Zen meditation at that point. But of course, a healthy soul would never have ventured to go to Japan under such risky circumstances.

What a weird Christmas! I felt estranged from the whole human race at that point, so it's no surprise I had difficulty connecting with my family. I saw my daughter Annie; Dad let me borrow his car to go pick her up at her paternal grandmother's house. My little girl's innocence and beauty comforted and amazed me. I made a tremendous effort not to feel sad, dirty, and desperate in her presence. I'd failed her in countless ways, yet she still loved me. I decided I didn't deserve her unconditional love.

Annie must have known something was terribly wrong with me. I desperately tried to masquerade as a happy mom. I exulted in being able to spend time with her. She shared some of her dreams and hurts with me, and I felt privileged to be included. Annie told me how she longed for a horse of her own. Her paternal grandparents owned show horses, as well as a stable for them, on their wooded acreage in Indiana. Annie was now living there with her father and his new wife. On hearing this, I thought of a way I could make a small difference in my child's life. I could buy her a horse—not a show horse, but some kind of horse—couldn't I?

I took a third of the money I'd escaped from Japan with and deposited it in a savings account for my little girl. My father agreed to be cosigner for her. I wanted Annie to be empowered to use that money any way she liked. If she could get her grandparents' permission to board a horse in their barn, then she could use the money to purchase one, and there would be enough left over for some riding lessons, I figured.

I banked the money as a parting gift. Despite all my good intentions and hopes, I ultimately despaired of moving to Indiana and starting over. I felt too ashamed, too afraid, and too angry to follow through on my wish. I let my addiction and my self-destructive urges win out. That night, I booked a return flight to San Francisco.

On my last night at my parents' house, I rummaged around in one of the upstairs bookcases for a book to read. I found a tattered old paperback about secret societies. I don't remember what the title was, but the book described the Knights Templar, the Masons, and similar groups around the globe. One of the chapters covered various crime organizations, one of which was the triads in Hong Kong. A triad is a Chinese street gang or secret society. The triads have existed as criminal organizations since the early 1900s. There were many triads throughout the Chinese underworld, functioning independently of each other. Something that struck me in the text about the triads was an example of an initiation rite.

According to the book, triads recruited members as young as eight years old from the throngs of orphans living on the streets of Hong Kong. The rite involved marking the bare torso of the initiate with countless slashes from knives, then abandoning him, wounded and stark naked, at a challenging location—for instance, a street corner in a territory hostile to the gang. The aspiring triad member would be left—weaponless, naked and bleeding—to fend for himself for 72 hours, after which senior members would return to the designated location. If the initiate survived the test, without asking anyone for help, or compromising the secrecy and security of the gang in any way, he would be welcomed into the triad.

As I read the account in the old paperback, my mind flashed to Yuji and the webs of pale scars which crisscrossed his torso. I became convinced that my friend and rescuer had attained membership in a triad by enduring that selfsame test on the streets of Hong Kong. After all, didn't he tell me that he grew up on the streets of Hong Kong? And didn't he tell me that his brothers had taken care of him? His brothers in the gang. So this was why Yuji'd been able to deliver me from Kato-san and the other gangsters! Yuji worked with an organization of his own.

I had hinted to Yuji Ihara that I could repay him for helping me escape. I fully intended to make good on my implicit promise. The next day in the airport, en route to San Francisco, I called my friend the international lawyer in New Orleans from a payphone and spoke with her briefly, laying the groundwork toward obtaining assistance for Yuji with his $60,000 customs problem. After I landed in San Francisco, I followed through, connecting Yuji with my lawyer friend, who assured me that with minimal litigation, they could obtain a $60,000 favor for him in the Port of New Orleans.

At that point I felt certain that I had repaid his kindness. I still halfway intended to conduct business with him—that is, if I could get my friends in Humboldt County on board. But it didn't take long for me to figure out that I was far too traumatized and jangled to get into the flow of international drug trade. When I thought about what a terrible mother I was, sorrow flooded my heart and ached so fiercely that I regretted being born. I sensed an impending breakdown and doubted that I would even survive the year 1986. The way things unfolded, my fears were nearly realized.

# CHAPTER 6

# HANGING BY A THREAD

I FELT ASHAMED TO TURN TO MY FAMILY FOR HELP AND TERRIFIED of going to the authorities about what had happened to me. I knew that the Japanese underworld was present in the San Francisco club and street scene, and I believed they could easily hunt me down and kill me. I despaired of being able to make a new start and quit dope and felt overwhelmed by everything I'd been through in the past month, so I resumed the only coping pattern I knew. I went back to my unhappy relationship with Evan. I flew back to San Francisco, leased a cheap studio apartment for the two of us, and paid up the rent for six months. The apartment, a tiny studio with puke-green carpet, was furnished with a Murphy bed, a hideous stuffed chair, circa 1950s, and a battered old mismatched wooden end table and dresser. The microscopic kitchen discouraged any true culinary activity, but we were speed freaks, so we hardly ate anything anyway. The apartment boasted a large bathroom with a huge claw foot bathtub and porcelain tile. I spent a lot of time soaking in that tub, a feeble attempt to calm my torn psyche.

I hoped to be able to basically hang out and subsist on the money I'd managed to escape with until a better strategy presented itself to me. And I was so freaked out, traumatized by all I'd endured in Japan, that I felt desperate to stay awake in order to fend off the nightmares which now plagued me. Every time I ran out of crystal meth, I'd finally drop off to sleep and be sucked down into the realm of terrors. The worst of the nightmares was a recurring one, where I was forced to confront a human face, entirely enclosed and locked in a rusty iron mask. I felt horror and pity for whoever was trapped in that mask, and I drew closer to try to break the lock and release the prisoner. But as I drew close I'd realize with a shudder that the sufferer in the iron mask was me. At this point I'd struggle to the surface, gasping, sometimes screaming. Then I'd jump up, get dressed, and go out for coffee and crystal meth, not necessarily in that order. But on that morning we had plenty of dope, so we'd been up, sitting on the bed in my tiny apartment, talking and looking out the windows, watching the lights of San Francisco fading, then extinguishing, giving way to a sunrise unabashed by morning fog.

I hated that Evan was still with me. But I felt like I needed him, too. He was the only person on earth who knew what happened in Japan, who knew the bitch that sold me down the river, so to speak. I clung desperately to a visceral feeling that he could, and would, protect me and help me to get my head straight. Of course, I now understand that it was ridiculous for me to demand so much from any one human being, let alone a twisted dope addict like Evan. Besides, at this point Evan had morphed from boyfriend to tormentor and financial burden. On several occasions he actually woke me up from my tortured slumber saying things in my ear, in a hokey Japanese accent—things like, "Nothah customah fo' you!" Needless to say, it caused me intense discomfort. He could be such a dick.

I was still supporting him, along with both of our dope habits, which continued to grow exponentially as we spent my cash on more and more crystal meth. We'd both started shooting up, too. The day our relationship exploded, it didn't exactly come as a surprise to me. It's how badly he beat me up that truly shocked me.

At around eight a.m., we got a call from Evan's friend, Jerry Mueller. I liked Jerry. Of all Evan's friends I felt safest with him around. He was a middle-class boy, raised a Catholic, like I was.

He'd even endured the horrors of Catholic elementary school, just as I had. So I felt a kinship with him. Jerry, like Evan, grew up in Pacifica, a suburb of San Francisco. Pacifica is a beach town, and it's beautiful. Good thing the surfing there rocked, because from everything else Evan'd told me, life in Pacifica wasn't suburban bliss, especially for Jerry and his brother, Karl.

It seems Jerry and his little brother Karl grew up with a domineering father. Mr. Mueller, an electrical engineer of proud German heritage, was a fervent advocate of discipline in all aspects of life. One of Mr. Mueller's top priorities was to keep his family's German heritage alive—by forcing his sons to wear lederhosen on holidays. Good ol' Pops ordered the Tyrollean outfits from the old country, sparing no expense. Then he frequently terrorized his young sons into actually wearing the gear. Imagine the Mueller boys' torment as they were turned out into the neighborhood, sent out to play with the other kids, say, on Christmas Day, wearing matching leather hiking shorts with suspenders. Obviously, as young boys, they frequently got their asses kicked. When the ass-kickings started, did Mr. Mueller relent and burn the lederhosen? No. He was a stubborn, tyrannical patriarch—never budged an inch. But he did send Jerry and Karl to karate classes. So by the time Jerry reached high school he'd earned himself a black belt and a reputation as a badass street fighter. Nobody fucked with Jerry.

Jerry'd only very recently completed his parole from the State of New Hampshire, where he'd robbed a rare coin store with another guy. I don't have any idea what he was doing so far from California. They must've been high out of their minds to hit a rare coin store! Common sense tells you that antique gold coins would be nearly impossible to fence, yet extremely easy to track. And that's exactly how it went. Jerry and his pal robbed the store, then headed out on the road, unloading the loot for whatever cash they could get, trying to stay high along the way until three weeks later, when a horde of cops swooped down on them in a New Orleans bar.

When he got to the penitentiary, Jerry found out that the rare coin store he'd robbed just happened to be owned by the godfather of the local crime family—an old don who was currently doing time there, along with a bunch of his associates. Jerry spent his first day sweating the situation. On his second day inside, he steeled himself for a confrontation. He went to the old gangster and apologized. He told the mob boss that when he'd done the job, he'd had no idea who owned the store. The old crime boss, no doubt impressed with Jerry's courage, befriended him. After that, they met twice a week to play chess.

When the phone rang at eight that morning, Evan and I'd been up all night, wired to the tits on crank, as we often were during those weeks after I'd returned from Asia. We always kept the phone on the end table, within reach, just in case the dealer called. Evan picked up the phone on the first ring. "Ah, Jerry! What's up?" Evan listened a moment then immediately started laughing. "You hit that fucker going how fast? Hey, I didn't know they were full of sand! Damn! Okay, bro, c'mon over. Right, Pine and Powell. We're on the fifth floor. Stand on the corner and yell when ya get here. We'll toss down the keys."

The front doors of our apartment building stayed locked night and day, and our landlady was a nosy old bag who insisted on delivering each tenant's mail by herself, which is essentially illegal, but for some reason we all put up with it. Evan and I didn't like to wait out front for our visitors, and our building lacked the buzzers and intercoms found in better-maintained apartments, so we'd tell our friends to shout at our fifth-floor windows from the sidewalk. Then we'd throw the keys down to them and they'd come up. We'd stay in our studio behind closed doors, which we preferred to do whenever possible.

We'd met precious few of our fellow tenants, and from that sampling we'd come to the decision to stay isolated. One fellow tenant we frequently encountered in the elevator was a woman named Delores. She looked to be in her seventies and always wore one of those clear plastic scarves, the kind you never saw on any living soul except for senile, bus-riding, old ladies. Delores, a real extrovert, doggedly insisted on engaging Evan and me in conversation, even though her speech was completely incoherent.

One day Evan returned from a cigarette run, bright-eyed and breathless. "I been talkin' to ol' Delores in the elevator, Marti, an' she's partly makin' sense today. I tell you that ol' lady's a gold mine! She got run over by a Muni bus! That's why she's so fucked up. An' she's suin' the city for a couple million. Even if they settle outta court, she'll get half of that. An' she told me she's not as old as she looks. I think she's kinda hot for me. Hey Marti, maybe I oughta play ol' Delores, get the dough, then give 'er the ol' pillow treatment?" Evan lit up a Marlboro, chuckling.

"And the, um, pillow treatment entails...what, exactly?" Evan truly annoyed me at times like this. He could be such a dickhead.

Evan took a drag on his cigarette and stared at me, then erupted into gales of laughter. "What, you jealous, baby?" Then he walked over to the bed, snatched up one of our pillows. "Y'know what I mean—sneak in there while she's nappin' an' smother the old biddy."

Of course I'd known what he'd meant, but I guess I needed to hear him say it. Deep down, I must've realized I'd paired myself with a sociopath. Yet still I insisted on cloaking myself in layers of denial which I stubbornly clung to. Until this one particular day— the day that everything blew apart.

Okay, back to eight a.m. Jerry called us. He needed help. He'd wrecked a car on the freeway around six a.m. and didn't know where to turn. So, we invited him to take refuge with us in our tiny, puke-green carpeted apartment. Not much of a sanctuary, but no doubt he was desperate.

Jerry arrived flustered and still a little drunk and began to recount his tale of woe. He'd ridden out to the airport late the previous night on the express bus, simply to pass time. Somehow he'd managed to rent a car from the Avis counter. He knew a chick who worked there and I guess she was sweet enough on him to let him rent for cash—on a suspended license, yet. Jerry'd picked up his rental car at the Avis lot, headed out on the freeway, then made a beeline for his dealer's house in Pacifica. He tried to get a front for enough weed and crank to drown his sorrows, but Big Al, his dealer, refused to do any creative financing.

He went back to the car and decided to drive around for awhile. "I was drivin' around to relax." Jerry quit looking straight ahead and started staring at the floor. "And that's when I slammed into the goddam thing—y'know, one of those big round plastic barricade things; they always set 'em up on the medians near road construction. Plastic! Fuck—they're plastic on the outside! On the inside they're full of sand. Fucking thing felt like an oak tree when I hit it."

"So, how'd you get here?" Evan lit a Marlboro, passed one to Jerry.

Jerry took the cigarette, shrugged. "It runs. It's just...the body's all dented up. Fuck, it looks like it's been through a war. I can't take it back to Avis like this! The chick—the friend of mine—she'll get fired, at best. I can't do that to her."

Evan leaned back against the old bed's rusty metal headboard. "Okay, bro, here's what you do...you call that chick, your friend at the Avis counter, an' tell her the car's been stolen."

"Hey," Jerry said, "Did you hear me? I can't just fuck her over like that."

"Oh, man." Evan said sorrowfully. Suddenly he brightened up, like he always did when he contemplated something convoluted and illegal. "All right, then how about we call Ron down in Daly City? We'll take it down there and see what he can, y'know, do."

I stood up. "I'm going for coffee. Anybody else?" All this talk about cars irked me; definitely threw up a red flag. I knew Evan well enough to foresee that this tweak talk would culminate in some sort of felonious activity. I wasn't sure exactly what criminal venture I was poised to become an accessory to, and I didn't want to know. All I really knew was that I needed coffee and methamphetamine—in that order, and quick.

Neither Evan nor Jerry wanted coffee, so I walked down to the corner shop, got a large double espresso to go, and returned immediately to my little tweaker pad. There I found the guys still further discussing possible solutions to Jerry's rental car problem. None of these plans sounded clear-cut. My uneasiness mounted with each moment.

Evan and Jerry came to the conclusion that the only chance they had was to go down to Daly City and enlist the help of Ron, a buddy of theirs who ran a chop shop. I insisted on going along, because Evan wanted to do up our remaining supply of crystal meth before we departed. This, I knew, would leave me with nothing to keep me awake through the night. I dreaded falling asleep and being tormented by the inevitable night terrors. And, after what I went through in Japan, I feared being alone. So I figured I'd better accompany the guys to the chop shop, even if they didn't want me there.

As we grabbed up our stuff and prepared to leave, I suggested we stop at our dealer's and stock up on speed, just in case. Evan said we should wait and score in Daly City. He said he could get some really good stuff in that town. So I backed down and let him win. I figured it'd be okay. Evan knew how I dreaded crashing, so I figured his priorities were the same as mine. That's what I expected from him. Okay, call me naive, fucked up, whatever. I was guilty of all those things. Everything sucked.

There I was, adrift on the high seas with Evan like an albatross around my neck. I'd lost my rudder, had no compass, and couldn't see any stars. Yet I clung to the illusion that I was a woman in control of every situation I found myself in. Of course, a lot of this I can lay at the feet of my drug habit. It filled me with steely denial. In order for me to find my way out of trouble, I'd have to admit I was lost. In order to admit that, I'd have to come to grips with my addiction. And that, back then, was impossible. It was like the real me—the brains, the will, the heart and soul—was bound, gagged, and locked up in the trunk. And my addiction was driving.

Okay, so Jerry, Evan and I left the apartment and headed down to the elevator. I pushed the down button and we waited for a minute or two. Then the doors opened. Delores stood in the elevator, wearing a shabby old coat with a fur collar, and her signature plastic rain scarf. Her eyes lit up when she saw Evan. She batted her eyelashes. "Oh!" She said brightly, and motioned us inside.

We all stepped in and pushed the lobby button. Delores turned to Evan. "Are you going down to Minneapolis? Or up to Excelsior?" Delores, I figured, must've come to California from Minnesota, and now that the bus had run over her, she occasionally got confused and thought she was back there. She must've suffered one hell of a concussion. A fucking bus, man—it ran her down in the middle of Market Street, for Pete's sake.

The elevator landed on ground floor, and the doors opened. Jerry, Evan and I walked out into the lobby. Delores preferred to stay in the elevator, though. "Up to Excelsior!" She chirped, as the doors started closing and the elevator ascended again.

I shuddered. Somewhere in my meth-addled consciousness, I grasped the fact that I actually had a couple of things in common with that crazy old woman. Apparently we both found Evan attractive. Also, each of us hailed from the Great Plains: I was born in Kansas, and poor old Delores originated in Minnesota. Delores had been maimed in the bus accident, while I'd been blind-sided by all that shit that happened in Japan! We were both casualties! Of course, she was twenty or thirty years older, I told myself. Didn't I have plenty of time to get myself together? I felt uneasy. Silently, I prayed I'd never end up like Delores, riding a creaky old elevator somewhere in the Tenderloin district of San Francisco, squawking out names of Midwestern cities.

Evan, Jerry, and I left the apartment building and crossed the street to where Jerry's rental car sat parked. The battered rear quarter panel appeared pristine compared to the demolished front end. Jerry was right. It looked like it had gone through a war—a nuclear one. "Hmmm," Evan walked around the vehicle, surveying the damage, "Looks like we got our work cut out for us."

"Yeah," Jerry said, "I knew that." We all piled into the car. Jerry started it up. "At least it still runs."

When we got to Ron's garage, Jerry pulled the car in and Ron shut the doors. Jerry and Evan told Ron their sad story—how Jerry cracked up the rental car and had to return it later that night or face big problems. I'd never met Ron before, but he seemed like an okay guy. His rolled up sleeves revealed jailhousey-looking tattoos on his forearms. He listened sympathetically, then came up with a possible solution. The rental car was a very common model, he said—lots of 'em parked around Daly City.

Ron explained that the quickest solution to the problem would be to steal one of these cheap little vehicles, one identical to Jerry's rental. Then they'd remove the steering column, dashboard, and driver's side door, which have the vin number stamped on them, from the stolen car, and replace them with corresponding parts from the rental. After that, Jerry would be able to drop off the car at Avis and split. With a little luck, Ron reasoned, the rental car company would never get around to checking for the vin number on the block and bell housing.

"Problem solved." Ron stated this firmly. "We can do this in less than three hours if Evan can still go out there and bring back a fucking car as quick as he used to. I can't spare any of my guys to do it right now."

Evan answered with a grin, then pulled his Marlboros out of the inside pocket of his jacket. He lit one up, took a deep drag. "I think I can find another piece o' shit identical to this one. Just get us some crank will ya? My girl can stay here an' wait."

Now I was starting to get annoyed. I hated it when Evan acted all street and macho. He swaggered when preparing to commit one of his stupid crimes, and this situation was no exception. It also pissed me off that I now would be doomed to spend the day in a garage.

I've never made any effort to learn about cars, so all of this bored me tremendously. But I definitely didn't want to go along on a foray into auto theft territory. I felt content to be a simple drug offender.

Evan and Jerry took off in one of Ron's cars. I stayed behind, hoping that the dope would arrive quickly. Ron went out for a bit. I looked around for something to read and finally settled for a grease-stained copy of Easy Rider. Then I sat down on a dusty old couch along one side of the shop.

I felt so nervous and out of place! And that was beginning to make me angry. What would I do if I couldn't get enough speed to keep me awake? I'd be forced to sleep and experience those trauma dreams. Fuck that!

Ron returned with a couple of six packs of Budweiser and two fifths of Cuervo Gold. He offered me a beer. I took one, just to be polite. Then he went back to work on some car part or other. A carburetor, I think he said.

119

Jerry returned about twenty minutes later, looking relieved. He told us they found the right car—parked in a strip mall. He said Evan was on his way back with it. *Okay, then, when is it cool for me to ask about the dope?* I felt anxious, tense. I wanted to run around the block, to blow off steam, but I was wearing high-heeled pumps, silk slacks, and a sweater. I always tried to dress up when I went out. Too bad!

Really, who wants to run in high heels? Drag queens, maybe, but not me. I determined to sit it out. Somehow I managed to regain my composure. I told myself that all I'd have to do was hang out for a few hours and it'd all be over.

Just then Evan burst through the shop's side door. A Marlboro dangled from his lips, and he flipped open his lighter. "Okay, open the gates, I'll pull Jerry's new vehicle in." Ron raised the garage doors. Evan drove the little replacement car in. He jumped out and strode across the concrete work area toward us. He stopped, sat down on the couch beside me, and put his arm around me. "Didja miss me, Baby?" Acting cocky again.

"Yeah," I answered sarcastically, "but not as much as I missed the dope we were supposed to be getting." But the moment I spoke those words I regretted it. It was a mean thing to say, and I'd had way too much meanness in my life lately. I needed to be sweet, I admonished myself. So I said, "I'm sorry, Evan, I didn't mean to say that. It's just that I'm worried about coming down. Y'know?" I gave him a meaningful look that, I hoped, would communicate my feelings of urgency in the matter of meth procurement.

Evan turned to Ron. "What's the word on the crank? Thought you were a crankster gangster. What's up?" Ron explained that the connect wasn't home, but he had it in good confidence that he'd be back in a few, and no problem.

"Meanwhile, let's get to work on this job." Ron jumped up, walked over to Jerry's wrecked rental and opened the driver's side door. After grabbing a Bud each, Evan and Jerry joined in the labor.

I sat on the couch and paced back and forth, alternately. I thumbed absently through the worn out biker rag till I thought I'd die of boredom. In my opinion, all of this shit was completely unnecessary. This was tweaker behavior to the nth degree! Everybody knows that if you wreck a rental car, you simply turn it in and the company eats the cost. I figured Jerry was overreacting, and Evan was more than happy to reinforce Jerry's paranoia, most likely because Evan welcomed any opportunity to steal or strip cars.

As I sipped my Bud, I recalled how one night, when I first got together with Evan, we were driving back from San Francisco and one of my headlights grew dim. I wanted to pull into a gas station and buy a replacement for it. But Evan insisted we stop at a MacDonald's off the freeway first. I thought he might be hungry for some fries or something. As we entered the parking lot he said, "Park here, Marti." Then he murmured, "...Be right back." And he ducked out of the car and ran off into the darkness.

Evan returned in minutes, clutching something under his right arm. He slipped into the passenger side, quietly closed the door, then looked at me and smiled beatifically. "I got you covered." Chagrined, I drew a sharp breath. In his right hand he held a headlamp assembly, snatched off some unsuspecting motorist's vehicle while he sat inside buying his kids some Happy Meals. How pathetic.

"Hey, take that back! I don't want stolen parts." He gave me a hurt look. "Okay, then, I'll take it back," I said. "Which car did it come off of?" But then I'd realized I couldn't return it. I mean, what could I do? Stroll up to the victim, hand him the headlight, smile and say, "Hey, did you lose this car part? I found it in the parking lot." No, that wouldn't be cool. I decided to make a run for it instead. I fired up the engine and exited MacDonald's.

A couple of exits down the freeway, we stopped again. I figured I'd better let Evan try to replace my dimming headlight with the stolen one. It turned out that the purloined headlight didn't even fit my car. I felt awful, but I'd told myself I could change Evan, show him a better way to live. Today, I can't imagine how I felt qualified to do that, considering what a fucked-up life I led then.

I finished my Bud and reached for another. The beer tasted good to me. I looked around the garage. Evan and his friends crouched around the cars, working furiously.

The phone rang. Ron wiped his hands on a cloth, walked over to the desk, and answered. I heard him mumble a few words and hang up. "My dealer. He's on his way." He picked up one of the Cuervo bottles and broke the seal. He gulped some, then passed it around. We all took a swig.

The tequila must have been the tipping point for me, because I honestly can't remember much more of the events leading up to my fight with Evan. I remember the dealer came by the shop and dropped off some crystal. We consumed it immediately—the quantity and quality were inadequate, but no one complained. I did my share and returned to the Cuervo. This was a big mistake. The tequila delivered a roundhouse kick to my consciousness. My cerebral cortex sort of rolled over and took a nap.

I'm able to recall only shadowy snippets of the remaining hours at Ron's shop. Perhaps that's because the combination of crystal meth, tequila, and beer slammed into my brain like a Mack truck. Of course, my fatigue due to protracted drug use didn't help much, and neither did the emotional damage caused by my recent POW-type experience in Tokyo at the hands of Japanese organized crime.

I have no idea what I said to Evan in that garage, but I'm pretty sure that my comments were clever. I remember getting laughs from everybody except Evan. The things I said were most likely derogatory toward him, directly or indirectly. But they must've been funny. Or at least I thought so at the time.

My memory of events in the car on the way home is much clearer. I remember Jerry asking Evan to drive. Evan took the wheel, Jerry sat in the back seat, and I sat in front. The car seemed to be handling kind of funny, maybe because of how fucked up they were by the time they installed the steering column. Jerry asked us to go back to my place, pick up my car, and follow him out to the airport to drop off the rental. We agreed to do it.

Evan and I kept arguing loudly the whole time. I remember Jerry attempting diplomacy from the back seat, vainly struggling to reconcile us. I clearly recall Evan screaming at me, calling me, "...bitch." The next moment is preserved in my mind's eye like one of those prehistoric insects in amber. I leaned over toward Evan and slapped him in the face, and he responded by punching me in the nose, so hard that I heard a crunching noise followed by a snap.

I reacted instantly, although not rationally. He had to slow down to hit me, so I opened the door on my side, leapt out onto the street, and started running away from the car, high heels be damned. I ran for a block or two, then cut through a half-deserted parking lot. In all the confusion I barely noticed that I'd bailed out of the car on Folsom south of Market—a pretty rough neighborhood and a long stretch from my place. Still, I kept running. I wanted to run—from my fear, my desperation, my drug habit, and my crazy-ass boyfriend.

Abruptly I realized that the sun had gone down already. *Strange, I thought this was afternoon. Damn. I can't believe it took those guys all fucking day to switch that car out.* I felt something wet and viscous running down my upper lip, dripping off my chin. Thinking it was snot, I reached up to wipe my nose on the sleeve of my sweater.

I pulled my sleeve away, soaked with blood. I ran faster, or tried to, anyway. High heels truly suck for sprinting.

Suddenly I heard footsteps pounding the asphalt, only a few dozen strides behind me. I started to cry then. "Evan, leave me the fuck alone!" I sobbed, but didn't dare look back. Just then my pursuer overtook me.

He grabbed my shoulder. "Marti, it's me, Jerry. Stop, will ya?" I stopped gladly. I don't know how much further I could've run, truth be told. I'd taken up smoking only a month before, upon returning from Japan, and my stamina, my wind, already suffered for it. I rocked slightly on my high heels, gulping breaths.

Jerry sounded a little wheezy, too. He smiled ever so slightly. "Too many Marlboros, huh?" I stopped crying, nodded, almost smiled back. "C'mon," he said, "I'll walk you home."

"Yeah." Good thing I'd clutched my purse under my arm. I had my keys on me, some cash; I'd be okay. "Thanks." I smiled at him. It hurt to smile. "Do I look okay?"

Jerry looked at me. He reached out, gingerly touched my nose. Grimaced. Then he said, "Yeah, Marti, you're okay. We'll get some ice on it. Let's go."

So we hoofed it all the way to my apartment. I felt a little dizzy, but Jerry grabbed one of my arms and steadied me. I wanted to ask him about the rental car thing, if he still had time to return it without suspicion or consequences, but the words escaped me. We walked in silence, feeling the cold San Francisco night air.

We reached the apartment, finally. I suggested we take the stairs, because I was so embarrassed about how my face must look—like a horror show—all bloody. But Jerry didn't think I should walk up five flights feeling dizzy. So we took the elevator. Thank God, Delores ceased her imaginary trips to Minnesota in time for the evening news. We had the elevator to ourselves.

Once inside my apartment, Jerry found a washcloth, wetted it, then went to the freezer and wrapped some ice cubes in it. He told me to lie down, then handed me the ice pack. "Keep that on your nose." I held it to my face for a couple of minutes, then sat up.

"Jerry," I couldn't stop myself from asking. "Jerry, is my nose broken?" No way did I want to look in the mirror. He walked over to me, examined my face closely.

"You're turnin' black around the eyes. Yeah, I think it's broken. But you gotta keep that ice on there, okay?"

"Okay." My voice sounded strangely nasal. I lay down and closed my eyes. The ice felt so good. Then I heard rattling, and a scraping noise. I sat up in time to see Evan standing out on the fire escape, pulling one of the windows open. He stepped through into my apartment.

"Don't say nothin.'" Evan said and stared at me. "If you say one motherfuckin' word I will fuck you up." He turned to Jerry as if to resume a conversation that had been rudely interrupted. "Where were we, bro'? Oh, yeah, I'll take her car an' follow you to the airport."

"No, dammit!" I shouted. "Not my car!" I dropped the ice pack, stood up. "You're never gonna drive my car again! Get outta here!" I stomped over near him and gestured out the door. "Get out."

"Fuck you, bitch," he muttered, and took a step toward me. I figured he expected me to cringe but I stood my ground.

"No, fuck you..." I murmured under my breath.

Evan started laughing, a forced laugh, but just as humiliating as a genuine one would have been. He pointed at me and smirked. "Don't you look nice. Really fine." He looked at Jerry for reinforcement. Jerry didn't say anything, just stood there, eyes on the floor.

A rush of heat climbed up into my chest. My face felt like it was on fire. I couldn't control my rage. The anger developed into a separate entity, overthrowing any remaining reason or rational thought.

I dove at Evan, got in what I thought was a pretty good punch. He came back with a fist to the side of my head. Everything went black for a second. Then the lights came on in my mind again, but with limited focus. I remember a kind of dim tunnel vision—a red glow at the end of a very dark spiral. *Maybe this is what they mean by 'seeing red.'* All of a sudden I'd entered this crazy rage zone where violence bitch-slaps survival instinct into a corner. And a surge of adrenaline gave me a rush, deceived me with a visceral feeling of capability.

I swung at Evan and he punched me again, in the nose, for a second time. That punch landed high on the bridge of my nose, more like right between the eyes. I staggered backward into the Murphy bed and fell down on it. I still had those fucking high heels on, but that didn't stop me from jumping up and trying to give as good as I got. I remember hearing Jerry's voice, far away, saying, "C'mon, man, don't do this." I didn't know whether he was talking to Evan or me.

I remember Evan pushing me down on that creaky old bed, then throwing all of his weight on me, and punching me on the side of my head again. Jerry pulled him off me. I got back up and went after Evan again, knocked him down. I don't remember whether I did any damage, but I remember Jerry pulling me off of him. Jerry's voice sounded so distant! He kept saying, "Stop...oh, man, stop this..." Then everything went black.

That dim red light at the end of the tunnel switched back on and now I heard a woman screaming, "...Stop! Stop!" I realized that I was the woman screaming. I became aware that I was lying on my stomach on the bed, with my head turned to the left. I could feel the texture of the blanket under my right cheek—it felt scratchy. Evan lay on top of me, no, it felt more like he knelt on my back. He'd pinned my right shoulder to the bed—he felt so heavy—and his fist pounded into my left temple, my left cheekbone, over and over.

I remember wondering where Jerry was, then thinking he must be, he had to be, trying to pull Evan off me.

Suddenly I heard voices outside my apartment door, saying something like, "Somebody's killing a woman in there!" Then another voice yelling, "The police are on their way!"

Evan wouldn't get off of me. He kept hitting me, but Jerry finally dragged him off. Then the cops came through the door and Evan tried to get out via the fire escape, but they grabbed him. They closed in on Jerry, but I told them that if he hadn't pulled Evan off me I'd be dead. I guess you might say that left Jerry free now to return that bogus rental car to the airport. One of the cops cuffed Evan. Another asked me if I needed an ambulance. I refused it.

I don't remember much of the aftermath, probably because of my injuries. I experienced partial hearing loss and couldn't walk in a straight line for a couple of days. I fell asleep right after the cops cleared out and woke up a few hours later. I struggled to stand up, went to the mirror, and gasped when I saw my reflection.

Both eyes were black, my nose had swollen twice its size, and I noticed a huge blue-black bruise spreading over my left temple. My entire face looked swollen and tortured, and my upper lip had turned black. When I carefully lifted my lip, I discovered that the underside of the lip was black, as were my gums, all the way down to where the gumline meets the teeth.

I grabbed the phone and called Greg Smith, an agent—and friend—in San Francisco who'd booked me for some commercials when I first arrived in California. Greg lived in an apartment above the City Lights Bookstore in the North Beach. He took a taxi to my place. He helped me get to the hospital.

The physician I saw in the ER told me I had a concussion and a broken nose, and that from what he could see of my blackened and bruised gums, it was a miracle I still had my front teeth. He told me he'd like me to come back in a day or two so he could re-break it.

I decided to take my chances on healing up without the re-break. After all, I had no health insurance; it would have to be cash and, sadly, I wanted to save my money for dope. I returned home and waited for the dizzy spells, blurred vision, and rushing sounds in my ears to cease. And eventually they did, thank God, but not for months.

I stayed in my apartment. I never pressed charges on Evan. I figured I didn't need to. He had several outstanding warrants, one in Contra Costa County for a grand theft conviction—the one he got when he borrowed my car and did an armed robbery during the previous year. He'd failed to turn himself in to do his sentence for that. And it turned out Evan had four old bench warrants in San Francisco from before I met him. *Maybe a little jail time will help... give him some time to consider. Yeah. Maybe while he's in there he'll think it over and decide to leave me alone.*

Funny how somebody like I was at the time, living on the fringes of society, an unemployed dope fiend and victim of domestic violence, would invest such faith in the California justice system! How naive to think he'd even stay locked up at all, let alone rehabilitate. My denial had grown to enormous proportions! Oh well, aside from my drug habit, denial was all I really possessed.

Okay, I still had my car. And my crummy apartment with the puke-green carpet. My teeth didn't fall out, another thing to be thankful for, I told myself. And it seemed to me that once the bruising and swelling cleared up, I'd still have my looks.

A day or two after the fight I called Jake, a former boyfriend. I'd met Jake when I worked in the oil field in Texas. Jake and I had something real back then, we loved each other for awhile, and he'd been my last love before Evan.

I didn't entertain the notion that he could do anything to help me, but I felt strongly motivated to talk to him, to tell him everything, see how he'd react. To be honest, I think I felt like I'd done something to deserve that beating, and I wanted to get a second opinion. I know now that all victims of domestic violence feel as though it's their fault. It took some effort to muster the courage to call him.

Over the phone, I told Jake about the events leading up to the fight and about how badly Evan had beaten me up. I heard nothing but silence on the line for about a minute. After the silence, he said, "You need backup." That's all. Jake seldom spoke more than three or four words at a time. Then, unbeknownst to me, he booked a flight to San Francisco.

Jake's flight landed in the wee hours. He caught a shuttle and checked into a hotel. Then he called me. "I'm here."

"Jake? What, you're here? In San Francisco? But you hate California!"

"Yep."

"Well, um, thank you." I felt thrilled to have an ally, somebody in my corner, but I didn't dare to hope that Jake came to help me. And I didn't want him to see me all beat up, strung out, unemployed, and living in a shabbily furnished, puke-green carpeted, efficiency apartment! "Why'd you come? Business?"

"Backup. Gimme your address."

I gave him the address, then waited for him outside, on the corner, even though a heavy rain pounded down from slate-gray skies. It started storming the night Evan beat me up, and hadn't let up for a second. We'd been experiencing a very rainy January and now, a week or so into February, it seemed like we'd never see the sun again.

Pretty soon, Jake stepped out of a taxi and loped over to me, holding a newspaper over his head in a futile attempt to repel the downpour. He took one look at my face, swore under his breath, then took me by the arm. We walked together into my shitty apartment building and approached the elevator.

Then I saw old Delores standing there, resplendent in her plastic rain scarf and old coat, pushing the up button and waiting for the doors to open. *Oh, fuck no. Not now. Delores and I have never been so much alike as we are now, dizzy, half-deaf, and battered-brained!* The bus-bashed old woman turned, saw me, tilted her head to one side, as if trying to recall whether we'd been properly introduced. "Excuse me, dear," she spoke in her quivery old-lady voice, "Are you going up to Minneapolis? Or down to Excelsior?"

"Uuhm, neither," I said, grabbing Jake's arm and steering him to the staircase. Jake was so cool to be with. He never made any judgments about me and my fucked up life, or at least if he did judge he kept it to himself.

We entered my apartment. The message light on my answering machine blinked on and off, a red glow. It reminded me of my tunnel vision and "seeing red" episode. *Wrong color...gotta get a new answering machine—soon!* I tapped the "repeat" button and the message played back. A disembodied voice informed me that this was a collect call from a correctional facility. An attempted call from Evan! Probably trying to get me to bring him money for cigarettes or some fucking thing! I unplugged the answering machine in disgust.

Jake spoke then. "When's visiting hours?" He asked, sounding almost casual. Almost.

"What?"

"At the jail." At that point Jake uncharacteristically engaged in what was, for him, a conversational splurge, a verbal spree. He explained, "We're goin' down there an' we're gonna visit the asshole that did this. I wanna walk in there, stare him straight in the eye and tell him, 'You better take a good look at my face, punk, because if you ever touch Marti again, my face is the last thing you're ever gonna see.' An' believe me, he'll get my meaning."

Jake narrowed his eyes, added, "After that, I'm goin' back to Texas. But if that punk ever comes near you again, call me and I'll come to town. An' I'll find that fucker and give him what I promised him." I didn't say anything in response. He'd stunned me into silence. We looked up the number for the Bryant Street Jail, where Evan was being held, and got the skinny on visiting hours.

At the appropriate time, we headed down there. Up to that point in my life, I'd been lucky enough to have seen precious little of jails, so the experience shocked me a bit. The Bryant Street Jail is old, cold, crumbly and overcrowded—and that's just the lobby.

Jake and I took our places in the long line of visiting hopefuls. From where I stood I caught a fleeting glimpse of a couple of inmates, really butch-looking drag queens in fishnet stockings, pacing to and fro. But I hadn't been trying to see in there. I felt so self-conscious about the damage to my face that I hardly looked around much at all. Instead, I kept my head down and looked at the floor.

After what seemed like a century, some guy in a white shirt, dark pants, and a badge—I guess he was a guard—came out and said something I didn't catch. The beating left me with only partial hearing. But, from the reaction of the crowd in line, I figured he announced the beginning of visiting. A couple more guys in white shirts and dark pants came out and stood around. I had no clue to what was happening, but Jake seemed to. He stepped out of line, approached one of the white shirt guys. I saw him lean in and converse briefly with the guy, then slip him a couple of twenties.

I never did find out what Jake said, but after that, things moved faster for us. We moved up in line a little. When our turn came, we told the guard my name and he went to "...call the inmate down." Turns out, Evan was up on the third or fourth floor. Jake and I waited for what seemed like ages to me. My ears kept ringing, and the clanging and cacophony of the old lockup made the ringing escalate to an unbearable level.

When they finally told us Evan was ready, we stepped into another area, a shabby, dimly lit room with a sort of ledge along two of the walls, and above the ledge, a glass barricade and phones at regular intervals. On the other side of the glass, wooden stalls had been constructed, with corresponding phone receivers for the inmates to use. I pointed Evan out to Jake as soon as I saw him. Evan had turned to the side, so he didn't see us. We started to approach him together, then I hung back, let Jake go ahead of me. My pride hindered me. I loathed giving Evan the satisfaction of seeing how much damage he'd done.

Jake stepped up to the glass window, blocking my view of Evan's face. I saw Jake pick up the phone but I never heard what he said. My hearing only worked when somebody was talking to me face to face. But that doesn't matter. The entire interaction went swiftly. When Jake hung up and turned around, Evan was long gone.

"He ran and hid like a little girl." Jake looked irritated. "But he got the message."

I started shaking. I felt glad for Jake's backup, but I knew I had to keep on living my life completely alone, and that scared me. I understood that it would be weak to try to cling to Jake, or any guy, at this point. My problems made for tremendously heavy emotional baggage, and the only way to keep a clear conscience would be to shoulder that baggage alone. We had dinner in Chinatown, at a restaurant renowned for its excellent food, but I hardly tasted any of it. I felt like everybody was staring at my black eyes and broken nose.

I took Jake to the airport in my car and dropped him off in time for him to catch his red-eye flight. Driving back to my place in torrential rain, I faced the reality of being alone. I knew I needed to acquaint myself with my difficult circumstances, try to figure a way out. My survival depended on it.

Finding a parking place took ages, since the driving rain made it almost impossible to see, but I finally scored a spot. I steeled myself to go home—well, to my apartment, which wasn't exactly home— with its dilapidated furnishings and puke-green carpet. I figured the sound of the rain might enable me to go to sleep for the first time in days. I would face down the nightmares, I told myself. I couldn't run from them forever.

As I lay down on the same mattress where I'd almost been beaten to death a few days before, I promised myself that as soon as I woke up in the morning, I'd flee San Francisco. I'd call my favorite dope dealer, a guy known as Doug the Mug. Doug lived up at the Russian River, and he always carried a consistently high quality product. *That'll be cool, yeah, that's exactly what I need...*

# CHAPTER 7

# FLOODED

WHEN I WOKE UP THE NEXT DAY, THE RAIN STREAMED DOWN out of the clouds. I felt groggy and spaced out, so I ran down to the corner to get my customary double shot of espresso. At the coffeehouse, I picked up a copy of the San Francisco Chronicle. The headline read, "RUSSIAN RIVER ON RAMPAGE." *Whoa. Doug the Mug's up there! And so is the dope I need!! Damn! I gotta hurry.*

I ran back to my hellhole of an apartment and dialed Doug's number. He answered it. I started blabbering, "Hey Doug, it's Marti, I'm here in San Francisco and the paper says, "RUSSIAN RIVER ON RAMPAGE!" Hey, are you all right? I'm..." Doug interrupted me then.

"Oh, man, I can't believe the phone still works!" Doug sounded out of breath. "I mean, I'm standin' here in water up to my chest. We're staying up at my upstairs neighbor's place, an' I just came down here to get a coupla things set up high—we don't know when the river's gonna stop floodin', and Deanna, you know Deanna, she's stuck here with me and Jane and she's past her due date, I mean, I hope she doesn't go into labor...hey listen, I'm carryin' my lock box with me, y'know, on top o' my head, just to keep it dry, and it's real heavy—I gotta go now."

"Oh man,—Doug—I'm coming up there! I'll be there as fast as I can. Hey, keep that lock box dry!!"

"Yeah, hey, it's my livelihood..."

I hung up the phone, adrenaline coursing through every cell in my body. Doug had told me his lock box was too heavy to hold on his head! This news electrified me, since I knew that he kept his crystal meth, cocaine, and heroin stash in that lock box. By implication, my dealer had revealed to me that he was, as they say, "holdin' heavy," and I found that information alluring indeed.

I'd already intended to drive the seventy-plus miles up to the River in order to score, and it made no difference to me that a natural disaster was in progress. I wanted, no, needed to rescue my connection—and his stash—for several reasons besides the obvious one: that I was a drug addict.

One reason I felt destined to go was that my life had spun so far out of control—I welcomed an environmental cataclysm. My problems seemed Lilliputian to me in comparison to nature's fury unleashed. The idea of a record-breaking flood reduced my beat-up face, psychological trauma, and drug addiction to mere annoyances. This provided a sense of relief from my private desperation.

Another reason, and not the least of my motivations, was that I knew Doug's girlfriend Jane and her sister Deanna, and I liked them. I felt certain that if I drove fast, I could make it to their place in time to get them out to higher ground.

Underneath all of my conscious reasons for launching this quest lay the fact that I was responding to the growing effect of the Russian River itself upon my psyche. At that point I still didn't fully grasp that I was now almost completely transformed into one of the River People, and that's why I felt such a wild urge to drive up there.

It wasn't the dope—not really. I mean, I had dope connections in San Francisco, San Rafael, Concord, all over the Bay Area. No, it was the River. I'd become a part of it, of its nature, its culture, and now I was heading home to like-minded associates, the other River people. And I really did like the idea of rescuing the pregnant chick.

Okay, I started getting ready. I grabbed my umbrella and my tweed coat, which would be useless as a rain repellant but would at least keep me warm. Upon awakening that morning, I'd looked around for something to wear and chosen a short skirt, sweater, tights, and high-heeled boots of Italian leather. I selected this ensemble because these clothes were the only ones I had left that were clean. Everything else I owned I had stuffed into trash bags and stowed in my trunk. I planned on doing my laundry up at the Russian River after I scored some speed from Doug.

There was no time to launder clothes and come up with a more weather-ready outfit. *No, time is of the essence.* I ran out to my car, jumped in, fired it up, and peeled out of my parking space. I sped through rain-soaked streets of San Francisco and across the Golden Gate Bridge. Powerful gusts of wind knocked my little Datsun Sentra to and fro, but I kept it between the lanes.

Just past the Golden Gate, as I approached the Rainbow Bridge and prepared to enter Marin County, a wicked blast of wind blew one of my windshield wipers off. But it was only the passenger side wiper, so I kept on going, madly continuing on my rescue mission.

I got up to the exit for River Road and turned left toward the tiny town of Monte Rio, where Doug the Mug lived. Occasionally, I looked to my right and saw the Russian River, its waters swollen beyond belief. The churning sediments gave the river the appearance of chocolate milk, swirling in a blender, churning. Through the sheets of rain I could make out the shapes of huge chunks of trees, tossed along in the current like matchsticks.

But River Road was still passable, if one didn't mind plowing through huge puddles of water from time to time, and I didn't care. In fact, I embraced the opportunity to come within arm's length of self-destruction. I was crazy, and I would soon be high as well as crazy if my luck held out.

And my luck held. I wheeled into Monte Rio and pointed my car toward Doug's street, which I saw at a glance was already partially under water. But two streets over, one road stood on high enough ground to navigate. I parked there and walked down to where I stood parallel with the house where Doug rented the downstairs level. I called out, "Hey! Is anybody there?"

That's when I saw them—Doug, with his stash box perched on his head, Jane beside him, waving her arms over her head, and Deanna, looking my way also, her hands placed protectively over her bulgingly pregnant belly. They stood on the balcony of the upstairs level. A guy I didn't recognize had his hands on the railing, looking down at the rising floodwaters. I figured he must be the upstairs neighbor Doug had mentioned. "Hey! Over here! Help us!!" They all screamed this in unison. I realized they hadn't recognized me yet.

"I'll be right there! It's Marti!" I started running to my car. I wasn't sure what to do. Just then, I looked down toward one of the houses that were partially submerged and saw a canoe tethered to a tree, just within reach, floating there all alone. I waded over to it, grabbed it with my umbrella, and pulled it close. I jumped in and grabbed the paddle, untied it, and made my way around to the front of that nearest house. I pounded on the partially submerged door with the paddle and screamed, "Hey! Can I borrow your canoe for a minute?"

I heard nothing in response but the pounding rain. Then it dawned on me. No doubt all the normal people had evacuated before the water started coming down the street. Only the crazy, paranoid, or desperate types had tried to stick it out and wager on the hope that the river would stop rising.

I borrowed the canoe and ferried them out, one by one, starting with Deanna. Miraculously, all four of them fit into my little car. Doug rode shotgun, clutching his stash box to the top his head, high and dry, so to speak, and the others squeezed into the back. I gunned the little rubber band in my Datsun motor and peeled out down the road. The rain poured down and the wind gusted again and the windshield wiper on my driver's side blew off. That's when Doug and I had to roll down our windows, stick our arms out, and wipe away the water by hand as we braved the storm.

First, we headed for Guerneville, a tiny resort town down the road. Doug told me that local residents always set up a flood rescue center at the Veteran's Hall there, so we figured that'd be the best place to get help for Deanna. I pulled my car into a parking space along the street, relieved to be able to quit windshield-wiping with the sleeve of my now sodden tweed coat.

Jane helped her sister Deanna out of the back seat and into the Vets Hall. Doug leapt out of his side of the front, took a deep breath, adjusted his grip on his stash box, and lunged after them. I followed, the upstairs neighbor guy, Cory, right behind me. The rain pounded us all as we skirted the puddles and ran across the parking lot to shelter.

Once inside, we took stock of the situation, our collective paranoia escalating. The place was crammed with rain soaked, agitated people. Everyone seemed to be shouting or crying or loudly discussing strategies for survival. The noise really put me on edge. I looked around at my companions and figured they felt the same way.

"Well, it's not raining in here," I offered, trying to sound positive. "Let's find Deanna a place to sit down." We shouldered our way through the throng until we found some empty folding chairs against the back wall and then slumped into them.

Doug the Mug shifted in his seat. Jane sighed, turned to Deanna. "They must have a helicopter or a boat—some way to get out of here!"

I stood up. "Fuck it, I'll go see. And if they don't have transportation for you, Dee, I'll take you outta here in my car. I got in here, didn't I?" I wanted to believe that within me beat the heart of a hero, but deep down I knew that my motivation came from my gargantuan jones! I simply could not sit still while nearby, only two folding chairs over, sat Doug the Mug with his heavy lock box full of dope. Once we got Deanna to a safe haven, I reckoned we'd be free to go about the business of methamphetamine consumption, my favorite pastime.

I turned and walked toward the front entrance of the Vets Hall. I saw a guy standing by the door in coveralls and hip waders, wearing a rain slicker. I approached him, flashed what I hoped would come off as a dazzling smile despite my still-healing black eyes and broken nose, and asked, "Hey, do you know who's in charge here?"

He turned, pointed a finger at an officious-looking, fulsome woman who sat at a large oak desk, barking orders at men in camouflage pants and blindingly yellow mackintoshes. "That's her." Reaching for one of the door handles, he looked back. "Her name's Brenda." He opened the door and plunged into the deluge.

I made my way toward Brenda's desk—her throne, from the vibe she radiated. Clearly she relished her power. "Um, excuse me, I heard you're in charge here. Brenda, right? My name's Marti." I smiled, but only tremulously.

Damn, Brenda scared me a little. She whipped her head around and glared at me. "Yes?" She made that one word sound like a death threat. Brenda wore very thick, distractingly bright red lipstick, that brash shade of lip color sometimes referred to as "cocksucker red." Her hair was jet black, almost too black to be real, and shiny—waxy looking, like maybe it was a cheap wig. She wore it in a style frighteningly similar to Doris Day's in those old movies she did with Rock Hudson.

"Um, yeah, well, I arrived here a few minutes ago with this friend of mine, and she's nine months pregnant, real close to her due date, and I was wondering if you can help her get to a safe place, like in Santa Rosa where there's a hospital? I mean, is there a helicopter or something?"

Brenda snorted. "A helicopter? Well, not yet. We're waiting for some National Guard trucks to arrive, but that won't be till later. Where's your friend?"

I shifted nervously from one foot to the other. Brenda had a knack for intimidation. I turned, pointed sheepishly in Deanna's direction. "She's over there."

"Hmmph. Okay, send her over to me and I'll talk to her." Brenda folded her meaty arms across her ample chest. She couldn't restrain herself from adding, "You poor people!"

I turned and walked back to Deanna. "She says she wants to talk to you. Good luck." Jane helped Deanna to her feet and accompanied her to Brenda's desk. I sat down on one of the folding chairs and wished my coat would dry out faster. The Vets Hall felt drafty from people coming in and out its big front doors. I shivered, glanced at Doug and Cory, who looked pretty miserable, too.

Doug the Mug shifted in his seat and adjusted his lock box. "Fuck playin' refugee! This shit makes me even more paranoid than usual! As soon as my old lady's sister gets on her way to the hospital, we're gettin' the fuck outta here. We can survive this flood without the Red Cross and shit, right?"

"Well, yeah, I guess so." Anyway, I hoped so. I'd never witnessed a river overflowing its banks—not first hand. I'd experienced numerous flash floods in Texas when I worked in the oil field there. But back then I drove a four wheel drive. I wondered how my tiny little Datsun Sentra would react to a full-on flood situation.

Cory spoke up. "I'm stayin' put. I'm a refugee and that's that."

Doug grimaced. "Man, Cory, you always were a pussy."

Just then a woman's voice rang out. "Doug! Hey!" We looked around, expecting the worst—that Deanna's labor contractions had begun. But Jane and Deanna stood at Brenda's desk, engaged in a discussion.

"Doug! It's Mary! Over here!" Doug swiveled his head around in the direction of the voice. I followed his gaze to a plump redhead standing along one wall. She waved her arms frantically. Another chick stood beside her, leaning against the wall. She glared at Mary, obviously annoyed, then grabbed her elbow and led her toward us.

The women joined us. "Man, be cool!" Doug admonished them. "I'm in pocket." Then, "Hey, this is Marti. She's a comedian from Texas."

"Um, hi." I felt ridiculous being introduced as a comedian. I hadn't done any comedy since way before I went to Japan. Besides, my face still looked like I'd been hit by a truck—or a truck driver, anyway. And at the same time, in a strange way, I felt exhilarated. *Maybe I'll start doing comedy again. It's not too late. I'm still funny...*

Doug interrupted my reverie. "And Marti, meet Mary and Whispering Linda." Both women smiled at me. Mary said, "Hi." Linda mumbled something so faintly that it sounded like tissue paper rustling. They didn't seem to be judging me for my beat up face, anyway. I began to feel more like myself than I'd felt since I'd returned from Tokyo. *Fuck Evan. I'm never going back to him.*

Minutes later, Jane and Deanna returned from talking with Brenda. They had a promise of an incoming National Guard transport for those most in need of assistance. Jane would accompany her sister for support.

We all dug in and waited for things to happen. I quickly got restless and started milling around the place. I felt adrenaline-charged and ready for action. I stepped up to Brenda's desk. She narrowed her eyes. "Now what?"

"I'd like to volunteer," I said. "I can help. I've been in flash floods in Texas. I know how to fill sandbags and stack 'em. Where do I go to sign up?"

Brenda stared at me and blinked dully. I noticed one of her false eyelashes was on crooked. She spoke in an exasperated tone. "Well, hooray for you and Texas. But honey, this is California, and we don't use sandbags! We just let the river keep on rising. So go on back and sit down with your scrawny friends and wait for the National Guard trucks. And don't come back to this desk, y' hear me?"

"Yep." I returned to the folding chairs and people I could hang out with. Criminal types. People I could trust. "Brenda's got a burr under her saddle," I said. "She's on a power trip." I sat down, trying not to concentrate on how cold and wet I felt.

Doug leaned forward, speaking in low tones, addressing our little group of junkie survivors. "Look, I've been in three floods on this river. Every time, I got washed out of my house and ended up in one of these refugee centers. They always treat us the same way—like shit. This time, I wanna do things differently. I wanna get outta here while we still can and find a place to hang out till it's all over. Anybody got any suggestions?"

Mary answered him first. "Um, Chuck, Whispering Linda and I are waiting for Nick. He's coming to meet us over here and we're gonna take off with him up to the mines. Guy Valdez is up there, he's got it all stocked up to last us two weeks."

I interrupted. "Er, what mines are you talking about? Sounds crazy."

Doug explained. Seems that way back in the nineteenth century, when the first settlers arrived in Guerneville, they started cutting down redwood trees and annihilating the indigenous people, that is, the Pomos and Miwoks. But that wasn't enough for them. They also started fucking up the land by mining.

The founding fathers of Guerneville had come to California in search of gold and settled for raping the land of redwood timber and cinnabar. Cinnabar is the raw ingredient for quicksilver, which is a quaint term for mercury. Anyway, up in the hills above Guerneville, the occupants dug out a network of mine shafts and processed the ore in the spring-fed streams that flow into the Russian River. Of course, all of this eventually caused freaky health problems, so they shut down the cinnabar mines toward the end of the nineteenth century.

The mines were now federal land, surrounded by chain link fencing, with signs posted prohibiting trespassing under penalty of federal prosecution. As I listened to Doug expound on the topic of local abandoned mines, I grew uneasy. For one thing, I'm no troglodyte—not even a spelunker. I've never found underground exploration appealing in the least. And I've always been afraid of the dark, not to mention falling!

I spoke up. "Hey, uh, I'm not so sure I wanna drive up there. I mean, we could be risking a federal beef, and besides, it'll be cold and creepy, won't it?" I shuddered inwardly at visions of tweaking around in a dark, abandoned mine, closed since the turn of the twentieth century. Eeeeooooh! Plus, there had to be a toxic risk involved. *Fucking mercury?*

"No, hey, Guy is really organized! From what I hear, he's lined a couple of tunnels with heavy-duty plastic sheeting, and tarps, and he's got Coleman lanterns and stoves and everything. It'll be cool," Mary replied. Whispering Linda provided her with barely audible rustles of agreement. Both women stared at me earnestly.

Mary continued, dropping her voice to a conspiratorial whisper, "Also, Guy's got a big load of dope, and he's got food and water to last a month or so. It's an open invite."

Doug reached up with both hands, brought his stash box down and set it on his knee momentarily. "Hmmm, it could be a way to weather the storm, but I'm paranoid about trespassing on government land. Like Marti says, it would amp up our bust potential to federal proportions."

I breathed an inward sigh of relief. We could skip the mines. *Whew!*

We all sat in silence then for what seemed like hours but was probably only twenty minutes. The Vets Hall continued to fill with stragglers, locals who'd endured multiple floods on the Russian River. Some of them talked with us calmly as they entered the shelter, informing us of the continuing worsening of conditions outside. Others raised their voices in frustration or panic amongst themselves, and we couldn't help but hear what they said.

These new arrivals reported that this flood was somehow different from all the past deluges. For one thing, they said, the intensity and duration of the rain was beyond belief. The river looked wrathful, furious, and if the rain didn't cease very soon, or if the water level didn't stop rising, they figured this one would be the worst flood in thirty years.

Another dope fiend joined our troupe around that time. His name was Nick. Nick was very tall and lanky. Like Doug, he wore his hair long, but unlike Doug, he smiled a lot. While Doug tended toward a somber, almost patriarchal air, Nick assumed a goofier, more lighthearted attitude. Nick's long leather coat dripped water as he approached our row of folding chairs.

"Anybody got a cigarette?" Nick grinned at each of us in turn. "C'mon! Anybody??"

"Yeah, we got 'em, we just don' wanna go outside and smoke 'em right now. It's rainin' out there, y'know." Doug rested both hands on his lock box as he said this. I kept my eye on that lock box. Sooner or later I planned to exact payment from Doug for my daring rescue of him and his loved ones. I didn't want to hit him up in front of all the other druggies, though. That'd be rude.

"Here you go," I said as I pulled a pack of Marlboros from my purse. I extracted one, passed it to Nick. He thanked me and headed for the door with long strides.

By the time Nick returned from his smoke break, all hell started to break loose. A guy in a rain slicker, rain hat, and hip wader boots burst through the front doors and hollered, "The water's come up again! This shelter's about to flood, people! Stay calm!!" Then, against his own advice, he ran toward Brenda's desk, anything but calmly, and started jabbering at her, gesticulating wildly.

Confusion and cacophony ripped through the Vets Hall. Amidst the chaos, Brenda scowled, spun around, cupped her hands on either side of her cocksucker-red-lipsticked mouth and shouted, "Sandbags! Where's that bitch from Texas that knows how to do sandbags?!! Fuck!!"

Brenda seemed to be losing it. Moments later, she climbed up on her desk and screamed, "People!! We're evacuating this flood shelter immediately...we're moving to higher ground!" Chaos and hysteria ruled the crowd at that point. No one appeared to feel much confidence in the rescue shelter. People seemed to be taking off in all directions.

At that moment, we junkies made split-second decisions. I volunteered to drive Deanna to Santa Rosa—to the hospital. We'd all been told the roads of egress to the east were closed, but the route west, from Monte Rio to Occidental, and on through Sebastopol to Santa Rosa, was high ground; it never flooded, my companions assured me.

"We can make it!" I jumped up. "There's room in my car for four people besides me. Who's comin' along?"

Doug hoisted his stash box up onto his head. "I'm in."

Jane stood close to Doug, grasped Deanna's hand, and said, "So are we, right, Sis?" Deanna nodded, looking worried.

"I'll pass," Mary said. Whispering Linda made a sweeping hand gesture that suggested refusal.

Just then we heard Brenda's raspy shout echoing over the panicky crowd. "The National Guard convoy's here! Let's move, people. Only those with clearance, now." She looked calmer, now, self-confident. I could see she had leadership qualities after all.

Deanna turned to me. "Thanks, but I gotta go with the trucks. I'll have a better chance, I think." She turned and started walking toward Brenda. Jane gave Doug a peck on the cheek, then turned to follow her sister.

"It's for the best," Doug said, to no one in particular. "I'll take the outlaw exit strategy, though. I'm goin' with Marti."

Nick raised a hand. "Count me in."

Whispering Linda spoke, barely audible over the din of the Vets Hall. "Wait—I changed my mind."

Mary looked irritated. "Okay, then, can I come, too?"

I nodded. "That does it. Let's get outta here." I gestured for everyone to follow me. We barreled out into the pounding rain and ran for my car.

Once inside, we took our places. I drove, Doug rode shotgun once more, while Nick, Mary, and Whispering Linda piled into the back. Doug and I resumed replacing the windshield wipers with our sleeves as we sped west down Highway 116—back toward Monte Rio, a distance of around five miles.

I cranked up the car stereo. "You guys like Stevie Ray Vaughn?" We zipped toward the village of Monte Rio at breakneck speed, rain and wind battering my little car. The roads in west Sonoma County are narrow, hilly, and winding—treacherous in this weather. But my trusty Datsun Sentra prevailed. Then we caught the wave, so to speak.

At Monte Rio, Highway 116 takes you across the Monte Rio Bridge, which spans the Russian River just before the diminutive downtown area. When we approached the bridge, the rain pounded us blindingly. I never saw how high the water had risen and had no idea that night was quickly approaching. I pulled the car over to the side of the road just before the bridge. "What the fuck are y'doin'?" Doug sounded irate.

"This'll only take a minute. I wanna look at the river, see how high it's getting—maybe it's not safe to cross!" Heedless of my fellow junkies' protests, I hopped out and trotted up to the bridge in the blinding rain. Fighting the wind, I made my way to the railing, looked over. What I saw took my breath away. Brown, viscous, roiling fluid swept under the bridge beneath me, nearly cresting the concrete I stood on. The liquid in the River hardly seemed to resemble water in the slightest way, it was so dense with mud and debris. And borne on the torrent, to my amazement—a house! Not a little tin-roofed shack either, but the upper story, complete with gabled roof, of a sizeable dwelling.

I turned and ran back to the car, started the engine. "Fuck! You guys, somebody's house is floatin' by! On its way out to sea! I'm turning around!" Everyone agreed it was a good idea. We headed back toward Guerneville. Everything seemed okay at first. I had no idea what time it was. I'd noticed the fading light as I stood on the bridge, but only on a subconscious level. The storm created a night-like atmosphere. But then, somewhere beyond those boundless storm clouds, out over the Pacific the sun set and night arrived.

Darkness fell on us suddenly, almost like a curtain. Doug and I continued to wipe away rain from the windshield, and although we strained our eyes, we saw nothing but a black void. At that moment, I realized we were in water. My car felt like it was floating. *Fuck, it WAS floating!* "Hey Doug," I shouted over the stereo, "It feels like we're in water. What happens when a car's in water? Isn't it...like, doesn't it kill the engine?" I didn't turn to look at him. I kept staring ahead, over the dashboard into the pitch-blackness, as if the night held the answer.

Doug hollered back. "Not if you keep your foot on the gas! Floor it!"

I floored it. And the car went amphibious, propelling us onward till its spinning tires made contact with dry land. I kept my foot to the accelerator and screamed for joy. "We made it!" I took a look in the rear view mirror at my crew in the back seat.

Nick crouched forward, making sweeping circular motions with both hands, on the floor in the back seat, as if he were fishing around for something. He mumbled something, looked up. "Uum, I dropped a rig back here." Whispering Linda snorted, stared out the window. Mary stirred in her seat, reached down, joined in the search.

*Last thing I need in my car is a damn syringe! What the fuck!* "Keep lookin'—and let me know when you find it, okay?" A part of me felt annoyed, but there was no time for that. I was hurtling down a dark, two lane road in the midst of a disastrous flood! I told myself to stay focused.

I sped on, east, toward Santa Rosa. I looked at Doug. "Any idea where we oughta shoot for?" Doug reached out the window with his right arm and swiped at his side of the windshield with his sleeve while, with his left, he kept his lock box firmly anchored to his head. It occurred to me to suggest he take his stash off his head now, but I thought better of it, considering how moments ago we'd almost been submerged.

"I'm thinkin'. But it'll be a miracle if we get through Guerneville."

Just then I heard a commotion in the back seat. I looked in the rearview. Nick snapped his head up, then sat back. I could see him stuffing something in the pocket of his jacket.

———————

"Y' FOUND THAT RIG?" I ASKED.

"Um...yeah," Nick mumbled.

*Damn. What a crew!* But all in all, I felt good about all the junkies in my car, my newfound comrades. My beat-up face didn't matter here. Not one of these dope fiends had asked me how it happened, or even seemed to notice. And the excitement of this natural disaster freed me to forget my own personal disaster for a while. Here at the Russian River, I'd entered a drug-centric Never-Neverland, where lost boys and pirates are on the same team, and

Captain Hook, the only grown-up in the equation, is the County Sheriff Department.

Guerneville loomed ahead now, silent in the darkness. All the lights were out, but I could discern shapes of buildings—the little shops and cafes that catered to the tourist trade—as my car splashed through. On the outskirts of the tiny town, we hit a very deep puddle—actually, it felt way too big to be a puddle...more like a pond—but I kept my foot on the gas, and my little Datsun plowed through once again.

Up ahead, we saw a school bus off the right side of the road. It looked to be stuck in mud or something. As my car drew closer I realized it was propped up with jacks. A man in a rain slicker and big rubber boots stood beside the bus. In one hand he held a jack, and in the other, one of those flashlights with a red plastic reflector thing over the end of it so the beam comes out red and glowing, like a brake light. As we approached he turned our way and swung the red flash like a Star Wars light saber. I had no clue what this signal could mean.

"What the fuck is goin' on with that guy? Should we stop and help him?" As if a bunch of skinny-ass junkies could change a bus tire. Doug looked out the window at the scene. "Let's just assume that any red light means cops, okay? Keep goin'. I've got a plan."

At this point, Nick, Mary and Linda amazed me by requesting that I pull over and let them out. "I know people on high ground," Nick said. "It's cool."

Strangely, I felt kind of hurt, rejected, I guess, that the back seat contingent didn't want to stick around for the duration. I guess I didn't quite grasp the fact that my windshield-wiperless Datsun wasn't exactly a Leer jet. I failed to repress a sigh as I began looking for a dry spot to pull over. "Okay, then."

I rolled to a halt, kept the engine idling, my foot hovering over the gas pedal. No way could I risk stopping the motor! Doug scooched forward and leaned toward the dash so they could pile out of his side.

"Thanks." Nick turned and walked back toward the big puddle we'd crossed only minutes ago. Mary and Whispering Linda turned, waved, and followed him. I pushed in the clutch, slowly started forward, then picked up speed. I looked back after them in my rearview mirror. In the glow of my tail lights I caught a flash of them wading back toward Guerneville.

"Think they're going to that abandoned mine?" I asked, but Doug only shrugged. We drove on, toward the village of Rio Nido, where the redwoods are so tall and so thick that in some places it's dark even on sunny summer days. Rio Nido always reminded me of fairy tales like Hansel and Gretel, like you'd need a duffle bag full of bread crumbs to find your way out. Oh, hey, wait a minute...that's not how the story goes, is it? Hansel and Gretel only thought that a trail of bread crumbs would work.

Well, Rio Nido was like that for me. I always got lost in there. The street signs say stuff like "Canyon One" or "Canyon Six," and I'd drive up the roads and get lost in these deep, dark redwoods with steep hills on every side. I saw plenty of houses nestled in among the huge trees, so I know people lived there, but in Rio Nido all human life seemed muffled and suppressed by the awesome presence of the forest primeval.

Of course, I must admit that any time I ever visited Rio Nido I'd been high, and my high-ness surely exacerbated my lack of direction. I generally avoided going there at all costs, even though I'd once managed to score some excellent LSD in Canyon Seven.

Doug shifted in his seat, adjusted his stash box, and pointed with his left hand, indicating I should turn left into Rio Nido. I complied. As we entered Rio Nido, Doug indicated an immediate right turn. I turned right up a steep hill, and we climbed for what seemed an eternity to me. The rain still beat down, so I took the entire hill in second gear, slowly, so I could reach out and clear the windshield with my sodden left sleeve. Doug continued to swipe at his side with his right.

We broke through the trees at the summit. I stopped the car this time—we'd obviously reached high ground—engaged the emergency brake, stepped out of the car, and stood there in the rain, looking out east toward the lights of Santa Rosa in the distance. Below me, close in, I saw darkness over the immediate vicinity. Tiny points of light shone in one place or another, but from what I could see, all of the River towns were without power. I listened, and heard the sound of water everywhere. It occurred to me that I'd been hearing the sound of the rain for hours and hours, nonstop, and that behind the sound of the deluge was that all-pervasive rushing noise—the River!

The River had been raging all day, fuming, boiling, and now it sounded more ominous still—threatening to rise out of its banks and kick some ass! No. Not threatening—rampaging! The River sounded now like it was stalking over land, towns, roads, kicking ass all over the place!

I shivered, jumped back in the car. "Doug, this is some serious flooding; I mean I can't see it, it's too dark, but...somethin's goin' on."

"I know. I can hear it."

"Well, what d'you wanna do? Hang out here till it stops raining? If we get wired, we can wait till morning. Maybe the flood'll quit and we can get out to Santa Rosa." I felt restless—I wanted Doug to break out the drugs.

"Fuck that! No, we're going somewhere safe. C'mon." Doug pointed the way once again, and I fired up the engine.

"Okay, but when do we get high, anyway? I think I'm gonna need some triage by way of at least a gram or two." I pushed in the clutch, put my car in gear, and lunged forward into the rain.

The safe place Doug had referred to turned out to be the home of a dedicated speed freak—this, of course, did not surprise me. The guy's name was Stanley, and when we pulled up he was on his roof in rain gear, valiantly trying to repair leaks. As soon as he saw Doug step out of my car, Stan clambered down a rickety ladder and waved us inside his dimly lit living room. Oil lamps and candles provided illumination, of course, and judicious homeowners were sparing with those. The power would be out for days, and experienced River people knew this.

"You're just in time," Stan said to Doug.

Doug the Mug flopped down on the couch and set his lock box on the coffee table. "Let's get high." Stanley doffed his rain gear and hung it on a hook. He stepped toward me and held out his hand.

"Hi. I'm Stan. And you are?"

"Marti." Stan made me feel welcome. I liked that. And he seemed more middle class than most of the dopers I'd met at the River. Stanley was tall and muscular with Nordic good looks. Strangely, I felt safer here at his house, and not merely because I was finally inside out of the rain. I found myself wishing my face had healed up all the way, so I'd feel prettier. I even started considering whether Stan could protect me if Evan got out of jail and came looking for me. Doug was too little and skinny to fight Evan, but Stan looked to be up to the task. *Hey, wait a minute!* A consummate addict by now, I admonished myself to stay isolated, mentally and emotionally. *He's a fellow dope fiend, not a prom date. And why would I want another River boyfriend? I'm not healed up from the last one!* I repeated my favorite mantra to myself: *Fuck this—I just came for the dope and that's it.* I settled down on the couch to do a hit.

After we each did up a load of meth, Doug rolled a joint. He lit it, inhaled earnestly, and passed it around. Stanley ducked into the kitchen and came out with a battery-powered radio. He sat back down and started fooling around with the dials, looking for a news station amidst the sizzling, popping static.

Doug heard the knock first. He lunged, stuffing drugs and paraphernalia back into his trusty stash box, and hiding it under the couch. He motioned for somebody to answer the door. Stan peeked out the window curtains then gestured that everything was okay. "It's my neighbors. They're cool." He stepped to the door and opened it.

A young woman burst in, sheltering two children, a boy and girl. The kids looked to be around seven or eight years old. "Stanley, our house is flooded. Can we stay here till rescue boats start comin' around? My kids're scared."

"Sure, c'mon in, Janet. Where's Matt?"

"We heard on the radio they'd be sending boats out in the morning. He hiked down towards the road to see if everything's clear for us to walk it when the sun comes up. A big redwood branch fell on our car and took out the windshield. And we can't get it started!" Janet started to cry. The kids looked at her in dismay.

I figured it would only be moments before they broke down and started wailing. I knew I wouldn't be able to take that. Kids always reminded me of my now ten-year-old daughter, Annie. The pain of separation, and my guilt, began tearing at me. I gritted my teeth, resisting the tears that lay so close to the surface, no matter how hard I pushed them back.

I spoke up. "Hey, Janet, I'm Marti. I've got a car parked outside. The windshield wipers don't work, but it got me up here, and I'm pretty sure it'll make it down the hill to take you to the rescue boats. Okay?"

"Well, I really want to wait till Matt gets back. He said he might be able to borrow a car."

"Okay, that's cool." No more to be said, then. I knew that most of the time when River people make reference to "borrowing" a car they mean...randomly selecting an unattended vehicle, then picking up a rock, smashing in the window, and hot wiring it. I sat back, determined not to become even theoretically involved in yet another felony in progress.

My thoughts returned to my daughter. I told myself she was safer, better off, living with her father. *After all, I'm a crazy drug addict, aren't I?* The familiar, painful thoughts returned in swarms, buzzing around in my head like they always did. I began to worry about Annie, wondering where she was right then.

Suddenly a huge redwood tree toppled over and crashed to the earth, narrowly missing Stan's house and fraying everyone's already dope-frazzled nerves. The kids threw their heads back and howled in terror.

Stan turned and grabbed his rain slicker. "I'm going around back to check it out." We nodded our recognition of his words. No one moved to assist. I felt like I should offer, but what the fuck did I know about redwood trees? Precious little.

Janet's kids looked awfully scared. Janet reached in the pocket of her coat and pulled out a ziploc bag of crayons. She looked at me. "We forgot to bring coloring books."

"Well, I just got here, but I'm sure Stanley has some paper or something they can color on." I got up and joined Janet in the search. We found some lined notebook paper, sat the kids down at the table. Janet introduced me to her daughter, Tara, and her son, Jason. They hunched over the paper, scribbling anxiously. My heart wrenched in me, aching for Annie. I knew I needed to get really busy or do some more dope to numb the pain, or I'd start crying, unable to stop for hours.

"Um, Janet, I'm going outside, see if I can give Stanley a hand." I turned, reached for my sopping wet wool coat, but spotted a spare yellow rainslicker on one of the hooks by the door. I threw that on and dashed outside into the pelting raindrops and total darkness.

When night falls in the redwood forest, it's as if a heavy black velvet curtain descends suddenly—ponderous darkness. Add a storm sky, heavy rain and a power outage, and you've got darkness so complete it creates a vacuum in your soul. I welcomed the vacuum. It helped me deaden my sense of self. *Look out to that darkness so you don't have to look inward. Now, practice forgetting...*

I stood stock still, listening to the drops of rain striking the surface of my borrowed rainslicker. I heard the rain hitting Stan's roof and the sound of the wind in the towering redwood trees. Further off I heard the River, pounding and roaring, on and on. *It feels like the world is ending. Or maybe it's only my world that's coming to an end.*

"Hey, Stanley." I spoke the words into the pitch-black void, "You okay?" I didn't wait for an answer. I needed to keep moving—or be forced to address my pain center: separation from my beautiful child, all the horrors I'd escaped from in Tokyo, getting beat up only days ago, my drug addiction, all of it. *Yeah, keep busy. Anything to forget.* I stepped out into the night.

---

THE NEXT FOUR DAYS AND NIGHTS RACED BY, PROBABLY BECAUSE I did so much speed, and my brain and metabolism were humming along at ninety miles per. Matt returned at daybreak for Janet and the kids, driving a beat-up, yellow Ford Granada. They made it down the hill in time to go with the search and rescue units.

The deal was, sheriff deputies and firemen were making stops at all of the River communities, in canoes and motorized rubber dinghies. They'd pick people up, then row them out of the redwoods and into open areas where they could be lifted to helicopters and eventual safety.

We'd heard about the rescue operation on Stanley's battery operated radio. Governor Dukmejian declared a state of emergency, and he'd asked President Reagan to declare us a national disaster area. Reagan refused right at first, so all of the rescue efforts were local police, with minimal National Guard participation.

Doug stated he'd be needing to stick it out at Stan's till the waters receded. He had warrants, so getting "rescued" would be the equivalent of getting busted, for him. "Stay here as long as you want to," Stan told him, "kick down plenty of dope and everything's cool."

I knew I was welcome. After all, I'd brought cash. Also, it became apparent I was the proud owner of the only running car in Rio Nido. I guarded my keys jealously—and kept a constant lookout for auto thieves.

Hours later, a couple of guys named Robby and Coyote stopped by Stan's place. Both looked to be about twenty-something, and they wore their hair long and straight. Oddly, they wore hunting gear, giving them the appearance of Elmer Fudd with a mullet.

Robby and Coyote asked Doug if he'd do a trade. They showed him women's jewelry and a couple of hunting knives. Doug turned them down. They headed back out into the wild, returning hours later with more merchandise including a couple of shotguns, and presented them to Doug. This time Doug and Stan got annoyed. In fact, Doug was incensed.

"What the fuck are you guys doin' anyway?" Doug scowled. "This shit is stolen. I'm not a fence! Take this shit back!"

"You're looting!" Stan stood up and pushed Robbie and Coyote out the door. "You're looting my neighbor's houses! Get outta here."

Robbie protested. "It's not stolen stuff! I got it from, uh, my aunt's house! Aunt's or uncle's house, I forget which. Look, Doug, just front us something."

"Damn." Doug reached under the couch for his lockbox. "Okay, just this once. But get that stolen shit outta here, understand? Nothin' brings the heat down faster than burglary and stolen shit. Nothing—except maybe a body."

Stan weighed in. "It's not like you're stealing from rich people, far away in the city! You're stealing from people like me, poor fuckers who barely scrape by, and that sucks. Take your fronted bag and get out."

Oblivious to their scorn, Robbie stood with his hand held out, until Doug slipped a half gram baggie into it. He stuffed it in his pocket, turned, and headed out into the storm.

The disaster escalated over the next few days. The floodwaters rose and crested at around 49.50 feet. Some say it was only 48-something, but who cares? All I know is, the water flooded the entrance to Rio Nido, the low part that gives you access to the highway and the rest of the world. One day I hiked farther than ever before, up one of the canyons to the highest point I could, and from that vantage point, the entire Russian River valley seemed to be visible at a glance. My gaze swept over the Korbel winery and the champagne grape fields, all of it flooded. Water covered highway 116 as far as I could see to the east and west. Only the peaked rooftops of houses poked out of the floodwaters. *Biblical! Fucking biblical proportions....*

Each day we'd hike the canyon to look down on the part of Rio Nido that was under water and take turns watching for cops. We'd heard rumors that Officers Briggs and Plummer had sworn to arrest anyone and everyone who refused to evacuate. We all believed it, of course. Logically, the sheriffs would come looking for holdouts like us! The only living beings opting to stay and weather a flood of such magnitude would be criminals, dope fiends, dope dealers, or weed growers—true River People.

One day I scrambled down the hill to check it out. I saw two deputies, one of them clad in a wetsuit, splashing along in his motorized rubber raft, the other in elaborate rain gear, manning the oars of a rowboat. I figured these guys were the dreaded Briggs and Plummer. I hunkered down behind a redwood stump, cautiously observing from afar.

The wetsuit guy maneuvered his raft into the center of what might have been called downtown Rio Nido. The raincoated one followed suit, pulled his oars out of the water, and handed the wetsuit a megaphone.

With a flourish, wetsuit held the amplifying device to his lips, and began barking angrily into it, his face bright red. His words resounded off the water, the empty Rio Nido Lodge, and drifted upward into the lower canyons. "This is DEPUTY PLUMMER of the Sonoma County Sheriff's Department! I KNOW a LOT of you people can HEAR me! You've got till tomorrow NOON to come down here and give yourselves up! Whoever resists this order is automatically UNDER ARREST!! Remember—TOMORROW NOON!"

I crept slowly back up the hillside, resisting the paroxysms of irrational laughter now bubbling up in me. Something about the whole situation struck me funny. Here I crouched, wired to the tits, soaked to the gills in muddy water, hiding from the cops! *And why bother?? Hell! I'm automatically under arrest!! Fuck, how does that work?*

I returned to the safe house and reported all I'd seen. My fellow stoner/outlaws had heard part of the stern warning and chortled. Even ol' Doug the Mug, whose paranoia tended to make him somber, found it amusing. We roared with laughter, then did some more crystal and passed the bong around.

Still, though, it'd been days without electricity or running water! I toyed with the concept of helicoptering to a government shelter. I felt grungy—hell, I was grungy, even though at one point I'd managed to take a shower of sorts.

I created a kind of Grizzly Adams bath plan for myself. I took a bar of soap from Stan's and walked alone out into the woods, wearing only one of Stanley's spare rainslickers and a pair of rubber rain boots. I carried dry clothes and a towel in a plastic bag in one hand and an umbrella in the other.

Once in the woods, I took off the raincoat and boots, and stood naked, lathering my body, then rinsing in the pouring rain. After that, I held the umbrella over me with one hand and dried off with the other. Then I got dressed as quickly as possible in the dry clothes, threw on the raincoat, jumped into the rubber boots and stomped back to the house. It worked pretty well—however the rain was freezing cold.

The thought of a warm, dry, lighted rescue facility complete with showers beckoned me, but in the end I decided against it. After all, my car was still here, and I knew if I left it wouldn't be when I got back. No, I resolved to stay the course and drive out when the floodwaters receded, not a moment sooner. And, in all honesty, I hated to leave the drugs behind. I needed to stay loaded and crazy, one step ahead of my despair.

Each night we'd huddle in Stan's unheated house, in total darkness, listening to the radio. We learned that the River was expected to crest simultaneously with high tide. Since the Russian River empties into the Pacific ocean at Jenner, only a few miles from Monte Rio and less than twenty miles from Rio Nido, this news sounded ominous. Also, we heard about a levee breaking farther north in Yuba County, in the town of Linda, where people had awakened suddenly in the middle of the night to find their homes inundated by water.

We indulged in as much drug ingestion as humanly possible, so our paranoia ran wild. We discussed climbing out, over Mount Jackson, should the water reach as high as Stanley's. We expected a declaration of martial law, so we figured the cops and the army would round us up and haul us off to jail any minute.

Finally, Reagan declared us a disaster area. Huge helicopters, Viet Nam era troop carriers called Hueys, began swooping and hovering over Rio Nido, attempting reconnaissance and rescue. The blades made a deafening clacking sound. I'd look up through the towering redwood trees and barely see a flash of them. The trees were simply too thick and too high for the choppers to land.

By then, lots of us had reached a point of willing surrender to rescue, and we flocked to the available, drier clearings to attempt to be lifted out. But the forest primeval would have none of it. The Hueys couldn't land, although they tried valiantly. The wind from the chopper blades whipped the treetops around so much that the flight crews themselves were in danger of crashing. We watched them swoop vertically and do a 180 out of there.

After that I abandoned hope of airlifted escape. I resigned myself to waiting out the siege till the river shrank back into its banks. And eventually, it did. The rain stopped falling, the sun came out, and the river receded. As soon as the road became passable, I said goodbye to Doug, Stan, and all the dope fiends I'd met in Rio Nido during the flood.

I stepped out of Stan's doorway and walked to my car. I reached into my now dry tweed coat for my keys. Then I heard Evan's voice behind me. "Well, here you are! Hangin' out at Stanley's, huh?"

I felt annoyed, apprehensive, dejected. I felt tired for the first time since I'd left San Francisco days before. I brushed past Evan, opened the driver's side door, seated myself behind the wheel, shut and locked the door. I held my breath as I turned the key in the ignition. I figured there must be floodwater in the engine or something—a consequence of going amphibious that one time.

But the engine kicked into life. I started driving and didn't look back. I rolled out of Rio Nido, turned on to Highway 116, kept rolling till I made it to the 101 South. I had no idea where I was going—it didn't matter. I was driving away from Evan.

Strangely, I still felt lucky. I'd been through a major cataclysm, a natural disaster, and I was pretty much okay. Knowing that all my worldly possessions were in the trunk of my car lent me a sense of freedom. My bank account still had some funds in it.

I stopped in Santa Rosa at the Motel 6 and rented a room where I could shower for hours and sleep for days. I knew I'd find a laundromat close by where I could finally wash all my clothes. Once all that was done, I promised myself, I would set my life in order. *With a shower, sleep, and clean clothes nothing can stop me. I can do anything! I escaped from Tokyo, survived a beating, weathered a flood, and I'm still standing...Hell, I'm a force of nature...And I'm still lucky.*

And yeah, I was lucky—too bad I didn't quite grasp the concept that, if I'd quit doing dope, my luck would increase exponentially; I'd still be a force of nature. But, like I said, I didn't get it—yet.

———————

THE LURE OF DOPE AND MISADVENTURE BECKONED AND WOULD prove irresistible to me. My drug habit was still driving the car, and the real me, the brains, the will, the heart and soul, were still bound, gagged, and locked in the trunk. And with my addiction at the wheel, we'd now spun out of control, careened off the road, and plunged into the river—a specific river. The Russian River! I didn't know it quite yet, but the metamorphosis was now complete, and I had officially become one of the River People.

# CHAPTER 8

# OUTDOORS

SUMMER OF '86 TO SUMMER OF '87—I REMEMBER IT AS THE YEAR I spent outdoors. I preferred to think of it as "outdoors," rather than homeless. "Outdoors" has a healthy, hearty ring to it—as if I'd been camping and hiking in Yosemite rather than sleeping in abandoned houses and crouching under bridges, hiding from the cops. However, no matter how I labeled it, the living conditions were still the same.

My transformation to full-on homelessness took a while. Dope-driven poverty slid into abject indigence over a period of months. For a while after the flood, I sort of commuted back and forth from the River to San Francisco. I'd paid up the rent on my paltry studio apartment, but I never slept there. I didn't feel safe. One glance at that puke-green carpet, and my memory instantly transported me back to the night Evan beat me up. And that remembrance in turn triggered a flashback of the Japan stuff.

So instead I drifted up and down Highway 101 between River and City. And it didn't take me long to squander all of my money. The flood happened on Valentine's Day, and by May, I'd frittered away everything except four hundred and some change.

One Friday toward the end of May, I scored about a gram on the front, shot about half of it, and trekked down the 101 to San Francisco to close out my bank account. My remaining four hundred-odd dollars lay in repose, deep in the financial district in a small savings and loan. I felt incredibly lucky on two counts: one,

I successfully maneuvered through traffic despite hefty chemical impairment, and two, I slipped into a metered parking space only a few blocks from the bank. Parking is very scarce in San Francisco.

Hell, that's an understatement. Parking spaces are an endangered species. Thrilled at my smooth progress, I pumped a few quarters into the meter, strode to the bank, and got in line for a teller. The exterior wall that faced the street was all glass from floor to ceiling, so I drank in the city scenery while waiting my turn.

The bank's situation afforded me a view of the truncated, narrow, side street that ran perpendicular to the quiet thoroughfare where the bank was tucked away. Looking down this narrow street I could see another avenue beyond that—one that ran parallel to the bank's street. Framed in the opening, I saw a dumpster and the bumpers of cars squeezed in close to it on either side.

As I dallied in line, marveling at the shortage of parking spaces in San Francisco, I idly noticed a garbage truck filling the frame of vision presented there. The huge truck zipped in from the right, attached its hydraulic pincers to the dumpster, hoisted it high in the air, and then, in reverse, zipped out of the picture. Exit stage right.

I continued to watch, and immediately, a subcompact car pulled up to the empty space where the dumpster'd been only moments before. The driver had the windows rolled down, so I could clearly see him smiling broadly, obviously ecstatic at finding room to park. Without hesitation he nimbly slipped his vehicle into place, jumped out of the car, and dashed off. Exit stage left.

"Hey, wait a minute," I said to the man in line next to me. "Hey, we've got to stop that guy, warn him. He might get a ticket."

"Um-hm. He might." Others in line made noises of agreement as well. In the next moment, the garbage truck reappeared, holding the dumpster aloft. *Uh-oh.* One of my fellow customers pointed. Another gasped as the garbage truck set the dumpster down on top of the pitiable subcompact, then slammed into reverse and whipped out of the picture. Exit stage right once again.

"Oh. My. God!" One of the tellers nearly shouted. "I can't believe it—the garbage truck..." Everyone nodded in unison. We understood him perfectly.

In a flash the hapless owner of the subcompact returned, entering stage left, a spring in his step, almost seeming to be whistling cheerfully—until he saw his car, crushed under the dumpster.

The customer next to me muttered under his breath as he stepped toward a teller window. "Unfuckingbelievable."

Another teller glanced my way. "May I help who's next?"

"Yeah. Thanks." I couldn't bring myself to comment on the dumpster debacle. It felt like a portent of doom. Nevertheless, I approached the counter, then proceeded to withdraw all my money and close out my account, ripping away one of the last tenuous shreds of stability from my existence. Sadly, I'd become comfortable with my self-destruction.

I hurried out to my Datsun and jumped in, feeling grateful that I'd found it uncrushed with no dumpster on top of it. I headed for a gas station, filled the tank, then went in the restroom and did up a bag of dope. I was already high—I didn't need it. Still, the urge to consume raged in me, and I never resisted it.

Back in the car, I negotiated through traffic toward the Golden Gate Bridge, feeling extra paranoid. I knew that by closing out my account I'd raised my disaster quotient tenfold. That made me feel agitated, along with the sense of dread I always got when I drove through Marin County. After all, Diane lived there, and since I'd only been back from Japan for five months, I still felt very vulnerable. The recollection of my "POW" experience lurked in my cerebral tissue, fresh, very fresh, and I had a hard time keeping it from springing out, causing random panic and reducing me to a screaming, slobbering ER admission.

Earlier on that particular day in May, before going to the bank, I'd stopped by my hellhole of a studio apartment and snatched up my few remaining possessions. With this I'd officially vacated—an easy move that involved very little packing or lifting. I'd already traded most of my goods for crank.

Long before my bank balance zeroed out, I'd started trading things for dope. I guess I was trying to utilize some sort of latent Scottish thrift instinct from my Highland roots by bartering, reassuring myself that I still had some cash in savings. At the apartment, I'd pack my car with clothes, shoes, jewelry, any item I thought might get me a half gram or more, then skedaddle to the River to trade and get mildly high. My fast-growing tolerance for crank raised the bar on scoring. A quarter gram hit could still give me a taste, if the quality was excellent, but if the shit was really stepped on, I needed more in order to get even a ripple of sensation.

One day earlier in May, I'd decided to trade my Niner jacket, the red and gold San Francisco Forty Niners jacket which held so many memories for me. Memories of bygone days, before I launched my meth-fueled trip into the underworld, days when I'd first arrived in California with luminous hopes and dreams, a middle-class lifestyle, and a bloodstream mostly clean of illegal intoxicants. Still, the craving for my drug of choice had overcome sentiment when I found out that friends of mine, Duke and Carol, had scored some premium quality product. Duke and Carol were a couple, and unique at the River in those days—a black male and a white female raising three children of mixed race. Duke was a fervent Forty Niners fan. I knew he coveted my jacket and figured it might fit him. At least, I reasoned, the jacket would fit Carol. I could sell it on that angle.

My ace in the hole was that my jacket sported the autographs of two San Francisco Forty Niners. I'd gotten the jacket signed when I did standup in San Francisco in '84, the year they won the Super Bowl. On two occasions, one of the beloved athletes was in the audience, and after my sets I'd asked them to sign my jacket. One autograph was from the center, Fred Quinlan, the other belonged to defensive back Ronnie Lott.

The Niner signatures increased the trade value, I figured. The autographs would blow Duke's mind! So I jumped in the car and headed for the River, wearing the Niner gear, my red cashmere sweater dress and red pumps I'd worn the night I auditioned for the Tonight Show. I felt a bit like Scarlet O'Hara, fashioning a frock from Tara's velvet drapes, then setting out to seal a deal with Rhett Butler. I most definitely felt pathetic—but only on a certain level. On another level I felt hopeful, desperate, eager to score one more time. A dope fiend always looks forward to the next hit, and, donkey-like, follows that carrot—into the fires of Hell, if need be.

Okay, I arrived at Duke and Carol's place up in Forestville, feeling optimistic. Duke and Carol had three kids, really cute little preschool and kindergarten-age boys. The eldest of the kids, Charlie, answered the door, smiling beatifically, a tiny toy car nestled in each fist. "My Daddy's upstairs."

I stepped into the house. "Hey, Duke? Carol? Yoo Hoo!"

"Marti," Carol's voice rang out from the second floor. Then Duke's. "C'mon up here. We're hookin' up a Hot Wheels track." I took the stairs two at a time, eager to run my hustle and trade the jacket.

Once on the landing, I saw Duke and Carol crouched on the floor in the boys' bedroom, connecting the plastic road pieces together while their younger sons bounced up and down on their beds, screaming and laughing. I couldn't help but smile. One thing about this couple—they were dopers, but they tried to create a home for their kids.

My thoughts teetered dangerously, toward recollections of my sweet little ten-year-old daughter and the fleeting hours we'd shared at Christmas. What had happened to my life? Summer was coming soon. I choked as I realized I had nowhere to live—I wouldn't be able to have my daughter for summer visitation. This would mark yet another instance in which I'd failed her.

Frantically, I pushed the tender thoughts to the back of my mind, thrust my emotions down into my chest, buried them deep, tamped them down with a shovel. *Gotta maintain. If I start feeling, my heart will explode, right here and now.*

"Hey Duke, can I talk to you for a sec?" *Good. Back to self-medication. That's it.*

"Sure." Duke stood up. "Just a minute, boys."

We walked down the hall and stepped into Duke and Carol's room. Duke paused before accessing his stash. "Whaddaya need?"

"Well, I, uh, I need some speed and I wonder if you'd like to trade me a sixteenth for this Niner jacket. I think it'd fit you."

Duke looked slightly annoyed. "Fuck. I'm not trading you a sixteenth! The most I can give you for that jacket would be a dime bag."

Duke knew as well as I did that a dime wouldn't get me off. He wanted cash, and I couldn't blame him. The situation now posed a challenge to my street instincts. This was a battle of wills and I couldn't back down now. I had my junkie pride!

But the addict in me also felt an immediate need to drown out my conscience, my better self, the mother in me. I'd inadvertently unearthed my heartbreak and I still felt raw. My inner addict screamed for dope.

"A dime??! You've gotta be kiddin'! This jacket's got TWO Niner autographs on it."

"Oh yeah? If it's Joe Montana and Jerry Rice, both, I'll trade you a sixteenth. If not, we'll see. Whose autograph's on there? Show me." Duke folded his arms across his chest and tapped one foot on the floor a couple times. "C'mon. I've got a Hot Wheels track waitin'."

"Okay, it's Ronnie Lott and Fred Quinlan." I removed the jacket, draped it over my arm, paused for emphasis, then passed it to him. "Go ahead. See for yourself."

Duke grabbed the jacket, shook it out, stared at it for a moment. "Where're the fucking autographs? I don't have time for this..."

"Um. They're inside, on the back. Can't you see 'em?"

Duke's annoyance increased. He glanced inside the jacket. "Now you're fuckin' with me. I don't see a thing."

"B-b-but hey...lemme have it." I whipped the jacket from his outstretched hand. "The autographs are here, right he..." *Oh fuck.* My eyes scanned the garment for the precious signatures but found nothing except two grayish smudges. Suddenly I realized—I'd washed the jacket at the laundromat before bringing it to trade! Prior to that, I'd always dropped it off at the dry cleaner, but I hadn't wanted to wait for that, or spend the extra cash. *Idiot!* In my haste to save a little time and money, I'd obliterated the heirloom quality, the collectability, the very selling points that made my jacket an item.

I still tried to save face. Turning the jacket inside out, I moved a step closer to my dealer. "Here, check it out. The autographs are there, they're just a little faded. See? It says, 'Ronnie Lott.' Clear as day! See? See?"

"Dammit. Okay. Kick in twenty cash and I'll give you a half gram—but only because you've been a good customer—up to now."

"Oh, thank you, Duke! Thank you!" I pocketed the half gram and scurried down the hall. My mind was racing. I lunged toward the staircase so I could run down to my car and get high. I set my right hand on the banister, and it's a good thing I did, because at the same moment, I stepped on one of the toy race cars! I stepped down on the tiny formula racer with the shiny red spike heel of my right pump—and started rolling. I pitched forward, teetered for a split second, then plunged down the staircase. When I was a kid,

I often dreamed of flying down the stairs at the house I grew up in, and bizarrely, I recalled those dream sensations as I literally swandived to the bottom. I remember thinking, *This is what it feels like to fly! Amazing!!*

Everything seemed to freeze—I had enough time to calculate where and how I might land—I quickly told myself to relax. I instinctively turned my neck to the left and drew my knees toward my chest as I sailed downward. This way, I took the impact on my left shoulder rather than my neck or head. Still, for a beat or two after crashing into the bottom stair, I wasn't sure if I was dead or not. I didn't try to get up at first. I lay quietly, with eyes squeezed shut, waiting.

Then I heard Duke's voice from the top of the stairs yelling, "Marti! Marti! Speak to me, Marti!" He kept saying that over and over. I heard him draw closer to me. Faintly, I heard Carol draw a sharp breath. I opened my eyes to see Duke's face hovering over me. "Oh, Marti, you're alive! Fuck!! For a minute there I thought you were dead!"

As I looked into Duke's face I felt strangely comforted. This guy actually gave a fuck whether I lived or died. Most of the concern was he would've had a lot of heat on him if he'd had to call 911, what with being a dealer and all, but still I could clearly see a friendly affection. The feeling felt alien in its warmth. I wanted to bask in the luxury of it for a second—the feeling of having...friends.

I pulled myself up on both arms. I checked and adjusted my dress, which, to my relief, still covered my torso and upper thighs. I jumped up as quickly as possible and surveyed the damage. I turned my head this way and that way, scanned my body, found spots of rug burn and bruises already forming around my knees and forearms. "Hey, I'm...I'm okay!"

Carol's voice echoed from the top of the stairs. "Oh my gosh—that was a close one!"

Duke exhaled. "Oh, man..." Then started laughing. "Man, it's a good thing we carpeted those stairs! We just got it done on Tuesday! If you'd come around on Monday youd'a been dead!"

"Yeah! Good thing!" I laughed, too, glad to be okay. "I coulda broken my neck!" Suddenly it occurred to me that now would be an excellent time to ask for some more dope. But I rejected the thought. After all, Duke and Carol, I now realized, were the closest thing to friends I could think of at the moment. Dope, I admonished myself, was not everything. Not to me.

After resting a moment or two on Duke and Carol's sofa, I picked myself up and walked out of the house, feeling markedly better. I'd received a flash of recognition—a glimpse of my own humanity. *Friends. People. Far more important than dope. Yeah.*

That night, after falling down those stairs at Duke and Carol's, and in spite of the meth in my system, I curled up in the back seat of my car and slept. And I dreamed. The dream sky was dark and filled with ominous storm clouds. In this dream, I clung to my daughter while being swept downstream in a river of sewage. As we were propelled along, I held her up as high as I could above the foul water and desperately tried to keep her safe and clean while hanging on tight. This I found to be terribly difficult and I wondered how long we could last.

I scanned the banks and the waters, looking for anything to hang onto. Other people were in the water and I reached out to them as friends, but they couldn't help us since they, too, were drowning. Suddenly the current started going even faster and I felt myself being dragged under the repulsive flow.

I struggled to the surface, only to find my little girl had somehow been wrenched from my hands. And the churning muck prevented me from catching even a glimpse of her! I panicked and floundered, sobbing. I looked ahead and saw the torrent flowing toward an open gate, and beyond it lay a darkness even more profound than the sky. I began to despair.

And then I saw him. A man stood beside the gate holding out his arms to me. My little girl stood safe beside him, beckoning to me. I couldn't see the man's face. I fought the current and reached out toward him. He caught my arms and pulled me out of the mire. The dream ended abruptly and I woke up.

In the dark of night, I sat up in the back seat of my car and pondered the dream. I knew the sewage was the life I was living. I knew I was in the gutter, but my addiction had progressed to the point where I couldn't stop the terrible compulsion to use. I constantly felt an awful emptiness from the loss of my daughter. But the gate and the man? I didn't have any idea.

I knew the man wasn't Evan. In the entire time I'd been with him, he'd never qualified as a deliverer. As long as I remained in his territory, I could never completely escape my ex-boyfriend. He appeared at the most inopportune times, wreaking havoc; in a negative way, he was still a part of my life.

For the umpteenth time, I resolved to start making steps to get my life back together and eventually get my daughter back. I needed to be completely independent of men now. To pin my hopes on the appearance of a hero was a luxury I could not afford myself.

I rolled down my car window, stuck my head out, and looked up. Through the branches of the redwood trees, I could catch glimpses of stars. I selected one very bright star and made a wish, something I hadn't done since I was a little girl. I wished that I would get my daughter back, and that I would do standup comedy again. I didn't even feel foolish doing it. It felt good. I shut my eyes, curled up on the car seat, and returned to a dreamless sleep.

This dream—or nightmare, rather—would return to me every few weeks or so for the next fifteen months, eerily reminiscent of the dream about the serial killer. But this wasn't a true nightmare in that it had sort of a happy ending, so I didn't mind it. Also this dream was the only one I ever remembered when I woke up. The remainder of my dream activity was intensely nightmarish, and I never recalled anything specific when I woke up except for the fact I'd been experiencing night terrors.

Reality mirrored the new dream in one way—the river of sewage. The flood left the entire Russian River area devastated for months and months. The water had reached ceiling level in homes and businesses. Environmental tests soon revealed that a very large amount of the floodwater was sewage—both treated and untreated. Upstream in Santa Rosa, authorities admitted to several sewage spills that had occurred, and apparently there'd been a particularly large "accident" during the Valentine's Day flood.

People waited long stretches for their FEMA money so they could get going with reconstruction, but flood cleanup started immediately, and some of us on the bottom rungs of the community ladder found work doing that disagreeable task.

The flood mud was toxic and carried a number of contagions, including typhus. Local authorities proclaimed it a danger to the elderly, young children, or anyone with a compromised immune system.

I started doing odd jobs, like flood cleanup, shortly after I resolved to get my life back together. I still had my car, which, though thrashed, qualified as reliable transportation by River standards.

My first job started with a desire to help somebody. See, I knew this old guy who had cancer. I'd met him earlier, during the flood, in Rio Nido. His name was Joseph. He lived down the road from Stanley's house.

When I met Joseph, I'd been walking along a sort of "creek" adjacent to the roadway, looking for my car keys. I couldn't find the keys in my purse, and since I'd been impossibly high for days, I figured I'd dropped them somewhere outside. This "creek" was formed by overflow, temporary and very shallow, so it was easy to see if anything was in there. Suddenly I saw a small Skippy peanut butter jar floating toward me. The labels had been removed. I could see something inside. I thought it might be cash, since people sometimes stick cash in jars, so I bent closer to fish it out of the stream.

"Oh, wait!" I heard a voice calling, "Can you grab that jar for me? I've been looking for it all day." I grabbed the jar and turned to see who was calling out. I saw a white-haired man, stepping gingerly down the road through the puddles, moving quickly but painfully. His skin appeared slightly greyish, and when he got closer I could see him wincing, as though each stride hurt him. I smiled and introduced myself. "Hi. I'm Marti. I'm staying at Stanley's till the flood's over. You haven't seen a set of car keys, have you? I lost mine."

He smiled then, visibly relieved, "Nice to meet you. I'm Joseph. I haven't seen any keys, but since you saved my stash jar, I'll help you search."

"Oh, okay, here." I handed him the jar. It felt cold in my hand. I figured it must've been in the creek for a while. "Stash jar?"

"Definitely." He held it up and pointed to a folded envelope inside. "This is my emergency primo hashish supply. I've been saving it—for a rainy day." At that, we both laughed out loud. "And," he added, glancing up momentarily at the raindrops falling relentlessly through the redwood branches above, "looks like this is the day. Do you smoke?"

"I guess so, but I'd better find my car keys first." We began to walk very slowly, up and down the creek bank, staring into the water. I felt very conscious of the fact that Joseph was in pain. "Hey Joe—you okay to be walking around out here like this?"

"Better than inside my place." He laughed softly. "My house flooded a couple of days ago. I'm staying with my upstairs neighbor—well, actually he's my tenant, so how can he refuse? Anyway, he's an okay guy; his name is Ronnie. But he's a Viet Nam vet. So he can be moody."

"Can't blame anybody for being moody in this situation," I said, "I mean, this is a disaster, right? If that doesn't justify moody, well, then what does?" Joseph threw back his head and laughed. I decided I liked the old guy. He definitely had pluck. At that point I heard Stanley calling my name. He'd found my car keys between the couch cushions. "Well, guess my mystery is now solved."

"All right, then, but my offer still stands." He pointed down the road to a two-story bungalow that looked like it'd been built right into the hillside. "That's my property. Stop by some time. Stand outside and yell my name. Or you can go on upstairs and knock on Ronnie's door. Just be prepared. He's moody."

During the next few days I visited Joseph several times. I felt like I needed to check up on him. I met Ronnie from upstairs during this time. He seemed pretty grumpy—but I felt like we got along okay. On one of these visits, we smoked a bowl of hash, the three of us, sitting around Ronnie's kitchen table. Once he got stoned, Joseph began to tell me about how his wife had died only a few years before, and how he'd recently undergone a biopsy for colon cancer. Joseph also told me he worked as a butcher at a deli in Santa Rosa, that he was a rabid Grateful Dead fan, and that he moonlighted as a bookie. He handed me his business card. "If you ever need a tip at the racetrack, give me a call—after they get the phone lines back up and running, of course." At that, we all laughed uproariously. Of course, we were wasted. The hash was excellent.

After the flood, I kept in touch with Joseph. From time to time I'd stop by to see how things were going, and one day in early April he asked me if I knew anybody who'd like to work for him, doing flood cleanup at his place. "It's a big job," he told me, "I haven't set foot in there since the flood, and everything is all moldy. Every time I go in there I start getting dizzy. My doctor advised me not to go inside at all while I'm undergoing chemotherapy. I've been staying at my mother's house in Sebastopol. She's driving me nuts—she's eighty-five years old. I'm sixty-four, but she treats me like I'm in high school. She went through my things last night and found some weed—acted like she was going to ground me! It's surreal! I've got to get my place cleaned so I can move back in." He looked very anxious.

"How about if I do it? I can use the cash, Joe."

"Well, if you don't mind mud and mold. After all, I feel I can trust you."

So we sealed the deal. Joseph agreed to pay me ten bucks an hour, cash, starting that day. I rolled up my sleeves and went to work. Government sources supplied each resident of the area with special flood cleaning supplies, like an industrial strength mildew killer and a super powerful disinfectant. I drove down to the Safeway and bought rubber gloves and cleaning rags. Then I rolled up my sleeves and went to work.

I started in the kitchen. By the end of the first day I'd cleaned out one section of that room. The refrigerator teemed with rotten food, rendered unrecognizable by various species of mold. A cast iron skillet sat atop the stove. A six-inch high growth of white, furry mold puffed up out of that pan like a hideous soufflé. After clearing it away I discovered what nourished such a fungus—a quarter inch of bacon grease lay in the bottom of the pan.

The mud sprawled a couple of inches thick on the counter and stove tops, hardened like concrete, so I soaked it with water to soften it, then scraped it off with one of those things plasterers use when finishing walls. I will never forget the smell of that mud. I worked with doors and windows open to let in air. We strung an extension cord down from Ronnie's place upstairs and attached a drop light so I could see.

And so my career in flood clean up began. Joseph gave me the key to his place, and every other day I'd drive over there, park my car in front, and go to work. I told Joe I couldn't handle doing it every day—the mud and mold gave me asthma. He told me he didn't mind. He also instructed me to check in with Ronnie whenever I showed up. That way, Ronnie wouldn't hear somebody downstairs, think it was a break-in, and flip out. "He's moody, remember?" Joseph looked anxious again.

"Right—the Viet Nam thing. Don't worry, I'll be careful with Ronnie," I assured him. Unfortunately, I didn't have all of the data. One thing I had not factored into the equation was Evan. The whole time I'd been involved with Evan, he'd had a lawsuit going on with a former employer, a construction company, for a back injury sustained on a roofing job. Turns out, the employer'd finally settled out of court and Evan'd been awarded something like sixty grand cash. This windfall had arrived about a month or so after the flood.

Evan ripped through the newly acquired money, spending it all on his dope habit. The only durable goods he purchased with it were a new pair of Nikes and a shiny red Camaro. It was a used one, but the Camaro was very glitzy, much admired in the redneck ghetto that was our post-flood River in those days. The place was a disaster area! Everybody's car was mud-damaged or absolutely destroyed. Houses lay in ruins or had been washed downstream. Ownership of any kind of vehicle at all, be it car, moped, even bicycle, carried with it a definite cachet, especially if said vehicle was operable.

Evan, temporarily endowed with rock star status, could now drive up to dealers' houses in his car, flash some hundred dollar bills, and gain their trust for the first time in his life. The O'Reilly boys were renowned for ripping off connections and burglarizing houses in the area. With the arrival of Evan's settlement money, all past offenses were now forgotten. Evan enjoyed his newfound freedom to wheel and deal.

I succeeded in getting Evan to give me a small amount of money, about two grand, when he'd received the settlement. I knew he owed me much more, since I'd bailed him out of jail on more than one occasion, not to mention supporting him—and his dope habit—for more than a year. I'd recklessly burned through the two grand he paid me, depleting it within a few weeks. Or was it one week? Less? Tell you the truth, I can't remember; I wasn't exactly a financial Einstein. My thirst for dope billowed in my brain like a sail, blowing me far from rational thought, and my self-destructive urge, like a rudder, steered me deeper into my downward spiral.

I think Evan resented paying me back even that small amount. His behavior demonstrated that. Neither one of us actually let go of the relationship easily. He clung to me through antagonism and physical threats—and a part of me felt happy to be getting the attention. He seemed to have an almost preternatural sense of where I was and who I associated with. Any time I established a tenuous strand of friendship with anyone, Evan would appear, trigger some kind of mayhem, and fuck everything up.

I put in some days of really hard work at Joseph's those first couple of weeks. Things seemed to be looking up. I would labor intensely, scraping mud out of his house with shovels, wire brushes, hoes, anything I could find, for around eight hours a day. Then I'd run down to Stanley's place, use the shower, get dressed, and go out to score enough crank for the next day. I worked every other day—four days in a seven day week. I spent my days off driving out to the beach and marveling at Sonoma County's scenic, rugged coastline, or visiting Armstrong Woods State Park in Guerneville. I loved walking around among the gigantic old-growth redwood trees, inhaling the tangy scent of the redwood forest, gazing up at redwood boughs swaying in the wind.

I'd work from, say, eleven a.m. to seven p.m., give or take, and I needed to be high on speed to keep going. I'd be so wired after work that I didn't worry about where I'd spend the night. I seldom slept. I had my car, dope, and a place to shower. I felt like that was enough. Every once in a while I'd travel east to Santa Rosa, get a room at a Motel 6, and crash.

Some nights I'd jump in the car, drive west to the ocean, and park by one of the whale watch overlooks. Then I'd simply sit in the car, with blankets wrapped around me, and listen to the stereo. Some nights thick fog enveloped my car and I felt as if I were in a cocoon. At those times I'd turn off the music so I could hear the waves crashing on the rocks. The sound of the surf mesmerized me. On some of those nights I strove for self-hypnosis—with each booming breaker I promised myself everything would be all right. And, deep down, I believed it.

# CHAPTER 9

# CHECK YOUR WEAPONS AT THE DOOR

Late one afternoon, as my workday drew to a close, I stood at the sink in Joseph's cramped kitchen. After scraping away mud for what seemed like ages, I'd finally arrived at the point where surfaces became visible, so I'd begun scrubbing down walls, countertops, appliances, and floor. I heard the squeal of tires, glanced out the open front door, and caught a glimpse of a red Camaro speeding down the narrow winding street. I figured it was Evan—he must have found out I was working there, even though I'd been careful to park my car a good distance from Joe's place in order to avoid detection. *Oh, fuck...that does it...*

I stood listening for a few minutes, waiting for the sound of Evan's car returning, bracing myself, but when my beau-turned-antagonist failed to reappear I exhaled, turned back to the sink, and resumed cleaning the mud off Joseph's toaster. I'd heard you could refurbish small appliances by washing all the mud off, then drying the wires with a blow dryer, so I figured I'd better give it a chance.

An hour or so later a shadow crossed the open front door. I turned, expecting Evan, but it was Ronnie, Joseph's upstairs tenant, troubled Viet Nam vet. I smiled at him. "Oh, hi Ronnie," I said.

I'd checked in with Ronnie earlier that day when his mood had been positive, bordering on unsettlingly perky. But now? Something was way off, way out of hand about his gait, his demeanor.

He shuffled toward me, blinking his eyes as if he'd been rudely awakened from a Vicodin crash. His mouth was set in a thin line. *No lips at all on this guy! Where'd they go?*

I didn't notice the gun until he raised it and pointed it at me. It looked silvery—chrome color, with a long barrel. *Where've I seen one like it? Oh, yeah. Texas. Nestled in the display case of an all-night, drive-through pawn shop in Austin.* For a moment there, I puzzled over whether Doug's weapon was a .44 or a .357, then decided it must be a .357. Of course it was ridiculous to consider that detail. Caliber might matter if you're getting shot at from a distance, but when your assailant is taking aim at you from less than five paces, a gun is a gun. The detail for me to contemplate in that scenario would be whether or not the thing was loaded.

I didn't feel fear exactly. I felt more numb surprise, not that this was happening to me, but that I was so calm in this situation. I reached for a paper towel to dry my hands off.

Ronnie's pace quickened. He crossed the tiny kitchen in two strides, pushed me up against the kitchen counter, and shoved the gun at my head. I could feel the tip of the barrel digging into the right side of my skull. I exhaled and tried to go limp. "Well, BITCH, I hope you're happy!" With each syllable, he jammed the gun into my scalp.

I closed my eyes and listened to Ronnie's breath coming in sharp rasps. He was practically hyperventilating. I fervently hoped I wouldn't laugh. I always started laughing at the wrong times—some kind of crazy laugh-Tourette's thing I have. It used to get me in trouble at home, at school, like when JFK got assassinated. I was in fourth grade at St. Mary's. I'll never forget it! When Sister Richella told us the news, I had to bite my lower lip to keep that nervous laughter from boiling out of me!

"BITCH!" Ronnie screamed this in my left ear as he ground the gunbarrel into my right temple. He was breathing in gasps and yelling between. "Your fuckin'—boyfriend—just—ripped—ME—OFF—for—ALOTTA—WEEEED!!—FUUCK—THAAT!!"

I kept my eyes shut. Ronnie's breathing slowed a little. Silence. I heard him inhale through his nose before resuming speaking, this time so quietly it was almost a whisper, "Now where is he?"

Suddenly I felt extremely annoyed. "Who?" I murmured, eyes still shut, "Where is who?"

"Goddammit! Your fucking boyfriend, Evan O'Reilly."

I opened my eyes and looked straight at him. "He's not my boyfriend anymore."

"BIIIITCCHH!" Ronnie screamed, spittle flying from his lips. "I went out for a while. You were here. I come home, my weed's gone—two pounds of weed—GONE—and all the neighbors up and down the street are tellin' me they saw YOUR FUCKING BOYFRIEND'S CAR peelin' outta here at just the right time! Just the right time for HIM to do the rip-off and YOU to help him." During this burst of speech, Ronnie took the gun away from my head for a bit, so he could wave it around and gesticulate with it.

I inhaled slowly, exhaled deeply, then concentrated on going limp. I knew I wasn't badass enough to relax with a gun at my head. After all, I was wired to the tits on meth! So I did the best I could do—I went limp. Anyway, it worked. I stood there, limp, silent, sort of passively resisting, while Ronnie barked and hissed away at me.

Miraculously, after yelling at me and brandishing his cannon for about twenty minutes, Ronnie simply stopped talking, dropped his hands, turned, gun pointed at the floor, and walked out. I listened to his footsteps as he ascended the stairs to his place. I heard him slam the door. Finally, silence.

I locked up Joseph's house, walked down to my car, got in, and drove away. No way could I hang out and wait for Ronnie to go through another Rambomorphosis. Next time he might pull the trigger.

181

I stopped in at Stan's, used the shower and changed clothes, reciprocating by splitting my last half gram of dope with him. Quietly, nervously, I related the story of how I'd seen Evan's Camaro, and how Ronnie had gone postal on me—well, halfway postal anyhow—after all, he didn't blow my head off. So far, he'd only teetered on the brink of murder.

Stan listened sympathetically but never commented. He possessed intelligence and River savvy, for that I appreciated him all the more; I felt I truly had a friend in Stanley. True friends are a rarity where dope rules. And dope ruled the River that summer—or so it seemed in my world.

I waved goodbye to Stan, jumped back in the car and sped down Highway 116 to Monte Rio, on a quest for some dope on credit. First I stopped at the Pink Elephant, but I didn't see anybody I knew well enough to ask for a bag or two on the front. I turned and walked back to the car.

I drove around the corner and up toward Bohemian Highway. There, off the road and under some redwoods, an abandoned trailer and a tent clung to the hillside, as if trying to escape being noticed. The tent huddled halfway up the slope, the trailer crouched closer to the roadside. I parked on the shoulder, a respectful distance away, then walked up to the tent first, listening for signs of life within. "Hey. Nick. You home?" I spoke in low tones.

"Just a minute." Moments later, Nick's head appeared, then he waved me in.

I crouched and ducked inside. "Got anything? I need a front, like, a half gram? Or even a quarter if it's good. I get paid tomorrow."

"Man, I can't do any business now. All my money's going into renting a place. I found something in Guernewood Park. I'll be taking possession in a week. Whispering Linda's splitting it with me. But Jim's got something." He jerked his head downhill, in the direction of the dilapidated trailer that served as de facto housing for

Jim Snider, alias "Dirty Jim." I never could figure out why the River People called him that—maybe it was because he was always dirty, that is, intravenously high.

"S'worth a try," I said, trying to be philosophical about everything. I unzipped the tent door and stepped out. "Thanks anyway, Nick."

I meandered down the slope toward the trailer. It was old-style—looked to be 1950s vintage—made of thick aluminum and painted dark green, with a bunch of dents in the sides. I figured the trailer'd been dragged out, during or after the flood, then abandoned near the roadside. Jim had no doubt taken up occupancy in it out of desperation, like so many other dope fiends left homeless after the flood. One of the windows was broken and appeared to have been filled in with part of a cardboard box.

Just as I reached the door, a huge, battered, black Chevy double-cab pickup came roaring down the road and screeched to a halt in front of the trailer. A big burly lumberjack-looking guy jumped out from behind the wheel, hollering, "Snider, get the fuck out here right now! It's Craig the Woodcutter! I want my GODDAM MONEY! NOW!" Two other guys stepped out of the truck, chuckling, and stood watching the Woodcutter guy. One of them reached into the backseat and brought out a Budweiser longneck, prying off the cap on one of the hinges inside the open truck door. He sipped it lazily, eyes glued to the spectacle.

Craig the Woodcutter stomped up to the battered green trailer, planted one steel-toed boot on the door, then drew back and kicked it several times. In the silences between the door-kickings, I thought I heard a faint rustling inside the trailer—I couldn't be sure. But it appeared that the lumberjacks heard nothing.

I spoke up. "Um, excuse me, but...maybe he's not home." At this, Craig and his two buddies turned and stared. I didn't give a fuck. I'd just had a gun smashed up against my head by a raving Viet

Nam vet...I only hoped to discourage these stout rednecks from pounding Jim to a pulp. After all, if they left now, I'd probably get a front for a gram or more.

"Oh yeah?" Craig was incensed. A renewed faint rustling emanated from the trailer. This time, I felt sure that Dirty Jim was trapped inside, desperately seeking to conceal his presence. "So you think he's not home? Huh? Is that what you think?"

I nodded. Part of me felt protective, actually sorry for Dirty Jim, since these rednecks definitely bore him ill will. The dope fiend in me hoped there'd be some product left for me after they wasted him. I smiled tentatively.

Craig the Woodcutter snarled, "Well, since he ain't home, I'll just hafta leave ol' Jimmy a NOTE!!" Craig spun around, rushed to his pickup truck, reached in the back, and pulled out a chainsaw with an enormous bar. He strode back toward Dirty Jim's home, pulling the cord to fire it up. The saw leapt in his hands and screamed to life.

The Woodcutter applied the whirling, roaring chain saw to the exterior of the old green trailer. Sparks flew from the metal surface and the chain squealed and screeched. Craig dictated his message, to no one in particular, loudly and with glee. "DEAR—DIRTY JIM, YOU—OWE ME $30—MOTHERFUCKER!" The trailer now yawned open in one spot. Gouges ran along the entire side in a random pattern. Craig stopped the now smoking chainsaw and stepped back. "There! Looks GOOD!" He turned on his heel, stomped back to the truck, threw the chainsaw in back, jumped into the driver's seat, and roared off into the night.

I sighed to myself. *Gee, Toto, I guess we're not in Kansas anymore.* I knocked on the door. "Uh, Jim? They're gone."

"They might come back, and if they see you standing around... they'll know I'm in here." Dirty Jim's voice sounded shaky.

I decided not to push the dope question. "Okay, I'll come back another time." I headed back to my car.

At least, while I still possessed a running vehicle, I didn't count myself homeless. I was "living in my car." One thing about homelessness, whether you're on the sofa circuit in friends' houses or sleeping under bridges, you're in constant motion. You never rest. You only have time for the bare essentials: food, shelter, a place to wash, a place to relieve yourself. Oh yeah—and sadly, if you're a hard-core addict, a safe place to get high.

Summer of '86 strode in on warm, golden beams of light. Hot midday sun pounded down on sandy beaches. In contrast, the thick redwood canopy cast cool, dark shade, almost chilling the deeply forested areas. Ronnie, the Viet Nam vet, circulated threats toward Evan, and, from what I heard around the River, Ronnie sought revenge on Evan for the rip-off.

Ronnie rode a motorcycle, a Honda, to work every night from Rio Nido to Forestville. And Evan found out about it. One night Evan, in his Camaro, followed Ronnie on his motorcycle commute, driving slowly and keeping way back. Somewhere along a curve on 116, near Korbel Winery, Evan shut off his headlights, accelerated, slammed his car into Ronnie's motorcycle, and forced him off the road. Word got around about it, because Evan laughed and bragged to his friends later. Word travels fast on the River.

They found Ronnie in the morning, alive, but with a broken leg and a broken collarbone. The news shocked me—I simply could not believe that anyone I once cared about could do something so vicious.

Nevertheless, a month later I found myself in my car on the road to Oakland, with Evan as my passenger. We'd joined forces on a quest to get some dope. Despite my best attempts at severing all associations with Evan, here I was! This definitely was no honeymoon voyage, and to say that this venture was ill-fated would be an understatement. We'd joined forces in order to locate a few old associates of ours. The first contact was a chick named Denise who worked as a dominatrix. "I work in psychodrama," she'd say, "It's not bondage." I'd called Denise from Duke and Carol's place, to ask about some Valium—I wanted to get some to trade for meth—and she'd invited me to spend the weekend at her new place of residence in Oakland, adding, "And bring that cute boyfriend of yours!"

The prospect of staying indoors—and getting high—in an urban apartment for a few days beckoned brightly. I couldn't resist! "Uh, yeah, sure!" I hung up, thanked Duke and Carol for the use of their phone, and assured them I'd be back with some flyin' Vs in no time. Then I set out to find Evan, which wasn't too difficult. He was still driving that bright red Camaro, and by now it needed a new muffler. Not only was it flashy and trashy as hell, but you could hear the car for miles as it approached. I found him at the Pink Elephant. He'd walked over to the bar because he already had warrants from driving like an idiot and couldn't afford to get busted. If he did, his beloved Camaro would get impounded.

We progressed south through Sonoma County, into Marin, through Novato, San Rafael, then across the Richmond Bridge to the East Bay. Evan suggested we stop by his cousins' place in Richmond to see about getting some crank. Evan's cousins, the four O'Reilly brothers, lived just off San Pablo Avenue, in a pretty tough neighborhood. According to what Robert, the youngest, told me when I'd first met them, their Mom and Dad had "just split" one day. "But they left us the house and kept the welfare checks coming in." The two older brothers raised the younger on welfare, then went to work. Now they were all in their twenties, working and sharing the house.

---

THE MOST MEMORABLE THING ABOUT THEIR THREE BEDROOM, one story home was its "interior design." The O'Reilly cousins adorned their living room walls with rock concert posters and framed pictures of family and friends. The twist was that all of these cherished photos and posters were hung up either below or above window level—that way they were safe from being shot up by incoming bullets. "We're the only white boys in the neighborhood," Robert explained. On hearing this, I felt certain that the Richmond branch of the O'Reillys had done more to incite nine millimeter reprisals than simply being born Caucasian, but I withheld my opinion. We didn't stay long at Robert's place. I liked Robert, but my sisterly affection for him, as it was, had cooled considerably since Robert had assisted Evan in using my car to rob his grandmother.

Robert scored us some crystal and we drove on to Denise's place in Oakland. We met her current boyfriend and a couple of her dominatrix friends. Denise rented the second floor of a large house. We ordered take out, showered, and got dressed up to go out and party. Denise told us her boyfriend wouldn't be going with us. "He has to work in the morning," she said, then whispered, "He doesn't do much speed."

Oh well. I didn't care. I'd had a shower and a promise of a place to sleep for the night. And more dope for the rest of us! Evan broke out his bag and I broke out mine. Once Denise got high, she changed clothes so many times while deciding what to wear that we didn't even step out of her apartment until one a.m. Then we drove around looking for a nightclub we'd like to go to. Turns out we didn't agree on anything till around last call, when we dropped into the nearest dive and slammed down a couple of rounds moments before they closed their doors. Then we exited into the glow of street lamps to discuss where to go next.

"We can't get high in my car," I declared. "Not unless we have to." I was already looking around for a dark alley to slither into and do a hit. My addiction took first place everywhere and in everything, the same way Evan's did. Was I really any better than he was?

Evan turned to Denise. "How 'bout parties? You know anybody that's havin' a party at their house? That'd be the thing to do."

Denise perked up. "Sure. I know a party house or two! C'mon, let's get in the car. We're going to Steve's! It's in Piedmont." Piedmont is a posh area of Oakland. We bolted for the car and headed out with Denise giving directions to "Steve's." We pulled up to a gracious, well landscaped Victorian nestled in the Oakland hills. As we entered "Steve's" through the back door, I noticed a large placard on the wall. "Absolutely No Guns, Knives, or Drugs," it instructed. *What the fuck? This is a house party, not a biker bar. Right?*

Denise strolled through the doorway without even a glance at the sign. Evan and I halted, looked at each other, shrugged, as if to say, "What kinda party is this? No dope?" We stepped into an alcove and snorted all of the speed we had left—just in case.

Once inside of Steve's, Denise led us into a cavernous room dimly lit by a crystal chandelier. An enormous hot tub the size of a small swimming pool sprawled in the center, devoid of occupants. Wisps of steam rose up from the surface of the water. Denise stripped off her clothes and jumped in. I followed. The hot water felt so good that I shut my eyes and let my mind drift away.

Suddenly I heard a splash. I opened my eyes to see a porky, middle-aged man in obscenely tiny black bikini briefs. He'd jumped into the tub and was lunging toward me. He wore half a dozen cheesy gold chains around his neck and as many equally cheesy gold rings on his fingers. I guessed him to be of Middle Eastern descent—and sloppy drunk. His stubby hands grasped at me eagerly as he pushed me up against the side of the hot tub and ground his fat abdomen against my torso. I pushed him away. "Hey buddy— get off me!" I snapped. *Where was Evan? We might not exactly be an item any more but at least he could help me fend off this beached whale.* I kicked at the would-be rapist and hoisted myself out of the water and onto the granite tile shelf that bordered the hot tub.

To my immense relief, a chubby little blond guy, fully clothed, suddenly appeared and handed me a towel. He wore thick black-rimmed glasses. "Wow! Sorry about him." He jerked his head in the direction of the corpulent offender, who was now being led away by a burly dude with a buzz cut. "Sometimes guys like that get past our screening system."

"Screening?"

"What are you drinking? Let me get you something. I'm Steve, by the way."

"Marti. Got any Johnnie Walker Black? On the rocks."

Steve scurried off, returned with my drink. I sipped it. It tasted funny—nothing I could really identify...still, I guzzled down most of it. Then I mentioned the weird after-taste. "This scotch tastes funky...kinda minty or something...what the fuck is wrong with it?"

"Er," Steve mumbled, "Maybe that's the MDA...I heard some-body was spiking the drinks tonight..."

"MDA?" I jumped up, finished drying off, grabbed my clothes. I wanted to get out of there before the stuff kicked in. I'd heard of MDA—heard it was a psychedelic, popular in the '60s and '70s, earning itself a reputation as the "Love Drug." As far as I knew, it had faded from existence. I'd also heard it was a cousin of meth; a concept attractive to me. But I possessed a healthy fear of going nuts on the "Love Drug" and finding myself lusting after disgusting fat guys in bikini briefs. And something told me that porky predators, like the one I had so narrowly escaped, abounded here at Steve's place! "Hey, I gotta go."

"Er...come on upstairs—there's a room up there where you can kick back and not get harassed. I let my friends hang out there while the parties are going."

According to my usual screamingly bad judgment, I followed Steve upstairs. "Listen, Steve," I took pains to make eye contact.

"I really need to be alone right now. So if you're thinking about pimping me out to another sweaty Lebanese guy, I'll find something to stab you with. And I will stab you." I hoped I was making sense. By now the MDA seemed to be kicking in. And it seemed to me the buzz wasn't too bad. "Oh, and Steve? Who is spiking the drinks? I think I may want some more of that stuff."

Steve came up with a plump bag of MDA, sheepishly revealing himself as the spiker. I snorted some, whirled off to find Denise and Evan and eagerly shared my newfound drugs with them. We made our way back upstairs to Steve's "time out" room, where we hung around with him, talking. Steve laid out more lines and began to confide in us. He related how this party house was his main source of income. He'd bought the mansion with his wife, Sue, in the '70s. The newlywed couple had trouble making mortgage payments until they came up with the idea of holding "swing parties." The business, Steve said, thrived and became a way of life—for him, anyway.

"Everything was going great." Steve sprinkled more MDA on the mirror and stared wistfully into some distant, inner horizon. "And then all of a sudden Sue filed for divorce and split. She packed up and moved back to her mother in Nebraska." At that point, Steve elaborated, "Steve and Sue's" became just plain old "Steve's."

"It's a living." Steve mumbled. He sighed. "Gotta go back to work. Hang out as long as you need to." He shuffled out, shutting the door behind him.

I turned to Denise. "So, this is what you meant by, 'party house?'"

Denise glared back. "You're partying, aren't you? Pass me that mirror."

"It's cool," murmured Evan as he hunkered down for a line. "Wish we had a rig so we could bang some o' this. Bet it'd be a rush." Vintage O'Reilly attitude.

Within ten minutes, half a dozen stragglers and party casualties joined us up in the "time out" room. Every one of us was tripping hard, dosed with ol' Steve's MDA—with or without prior consent. I soon found myself questioning the purity, or at least the intensity, of Steve's product, due to my observations of self and other dosees.

After all, I'd tripped numerous times on acid, 'shrooms, peyote, synthetic mescaline, ecstasy, you name it, and I'd never felt so helplessly Freudian until that night. Apparently everybody else felt the same; we all ended up naked or nearly naked, huddled pitifully in a heap on a behemoth slab of furniture which I earnestly believed to be a waterbed. I remember leaning into Denise, who alternately wept and slobbered. I blubbered in her ear, "My mother never loved meeeee..."

Denise nodded in agreement, "Me too, me tooooo," continuing with a mumbled description of childhood trauma rendered unintelligible by her sobs. All around us, swingers and party people, brought low by Steve's brew of MDA, keened and moaned from the depths of their suddenly haunted psyches. Only Evan, the sociopath, seemed impervious to the vibe. He lay on his back, silent, looking slightly annoyed. The waterbed dipped and swayed gently with each tortured confession and confidence, never sloshing, and seemed to buoy up our little conclave—buoying at least our bodies—as spirits sank ever deeper into brooding despair.

WHAT A BUMMER! These were good-looking people, most of them fetchingly nude, and all high on what I'd always been told was the "Love Drug!" Strangely, no drug-fueled orgy ensued. Not one of us appeared to be turned on sexually. All anyone wanted to do was sloppily emote all over everyone else!

I couldn't figure it out. I felt overheated and sweaty. I spoke up. "Er, hey, it's really hot in here. I think the heater on this waterbed is turned up too high!"

Suddenly everyone stared at me astonished, replying in unison, "It's not a WATERBED!" I sat slack-jawed for a moment or two. I'd been convinced it was a waterbed.

"But we're floating. Can't you feel it?" Others returned my gaze, as if to say, "This may be a bum trip, but we ARE still tripping."

I nodded acknowledgement. "Okay, then. Can somebody crack a window?" One of the bummed-out rolled off the waterbed and attempted to open one. He grunted and struggled to lift it with no success. Another downed partygoer joined in the effort.

"It's nailed shut. They're all nailed shut."

"Hmmm. Why? To keep us from jumping?"

Another pathetic reveler chimed in. "Steve manufactures this MDA here in the house. Must be to keep the fumes from escaping when he's cooking a batch."

Evan spoke up. "Dude needs to get a new fuckin' recipe. THIS batch SUCKS!" He jumped up and grabbled his Levis out of a pile on the floor. "I need a beer. Anybody wanna beer? I'll go get it." Every able individual fumbled around and found his or her respective wallet or purse and contributed cash to the fund. Evan wadded the beer money in his right fist. I foolishly offered him my car keys. Oh, yes—yet under the influence of this weird trip it seemed sensible.

"Good luck," I murmured.

Evan looked me in the eye. "I'll be right back."

Time crept glacially along while we awaited the promised beer. Eons seemed to pass. Evan didn't show. Finally someone knocked on the door. A guy stuck his head in and queried, "Is anybody here named, 'Martha?'"

All of my fellow bummer victims shook their heads in unison. I started to do the same, then my drug-addled brain managed to recall that my name was indeed, "Martha," but how would anybody know that? My baptismal name appeared on my driver's license, yet everyone knew me as Marti. I spoke up. "Who wants to know?"

"Well, the cops are here and they're looking for somebody named 'Martha.' The cops want to talk to you about your car. It's been stolen."

I sighed, sat up, looked around for my clothes, and jumped into them. "Okay, send in the cops. I'll talk to 'em."

Moments later two Oakland cops entered the room, much to the chagrin of my fellow tripmates, who skulked in corners or huddled fearfully together on what I will always remember as a waterbed. One cop was African-American, the other Caucasian. Both cops struck me as tall, handsome, and superbly fit. Suddenly the notion entered my head that these weren't cops, but were police impersonators. They were too hot to be real cops! Suddenly it all seemed so funny! I decided to play along. The bum trip seemed to be lightening up after all!

The black "cop" brandished his baton and scowled. "Which one of you is Martha?"

"I am. At least I think so." I stepped forward, grinning up at him. I held out my wrists. "Wanna cuff me now?" I chuckled. "Hey, are you guys strippers or police impersonators?"

"We are Oakland police officers and we are trying to determine if the suspect we now have in custody is the individual who stole your car and took it for a joyride down MacArthur Boulevard, Ma'am! Now I can ignore your snotty attitude and assist you in regaining possession of your vehicle, or I can charge you with refusal to cooperate with an ongoing police investigation."

Now the white cop stepped up and spoke. "We found your car on MacArthur Boulevard. Your clothing and luggage was strewn up and down the road. We gathered it up for you." He paused, then looked around the room. "I've heard they have some pretty wild parties here, if you know what I mean."

Oops. It dawned on me... they were truly cops, and maybe playing good cop/bad cop as well. I attempted to demonstrate cooperativeness. "Hey, thank you so much for helping me get my car back! And I'm awful sorry, didn't mean...uh, it's just that, uh, I figured it was a practical joke or something, I mean, cops asking for me and all, here at the um, party...uh. Really, I am very sorry."

"Right. So let's see some ID."

I fumbled in my purse, produced my license, which miraculously was a valid California one and not yet expired. The officers looked it over. The black cop relaxed slightly. He handed me my license. "Now, as I said before, we've got a suspect in custody. Our dispatcher received a call from one of the residents on this street. The caller reported seeing a Caucasian male, early to mid-twenties, around six feet tall, wearing a ball cap, jeans and a denim jacket, breaking into cars parked in the area. Our suspect matches the description. We caught him lurking around the vehicles on this street. He insists he knows you and that you can verify that. Suspect's identified as Evan O'Reilly."

"Yeah, I know him." I felt way too paranoid to say any more to those cops. They led me downstairs and out to a patrol car. I saw Evan in the backseat. Turns out he had warrants in Alameda County—no big surprise there—and the cops were taking him to the Oakland jail.

"Get in back with your boyfriend," the white cop smirked, "We'll drop you off at your car. It's on MacArthur. Window's broken but you can drive it."

So the "party house" adventure wound to a close. I pulled myself together enough to drive, gave Denise a ride back to her place. She fronted me money and I scored her some Valium from my cousin in Vallejo. In this way I provided myself with some cash for the road. Eventually I headed back to the River.

# CHAPTER 10

# THE ABANDONED HOUSE WITH A TROPICAL GETAWAY

SUMMER BURST INTO FULL BLOOM. THE LAND AND THE TOWNS around the River began to show signs of recovery from the ravages of the Valentine's Day Flood. The community rebounded fiscally. Even dope fiends received FEMA checks, stimulating underworld economics. No check for me, of course, since I lacked a residence in the area. I found myself washed ashore with no options but to score the next bag.

I surrendered myself to the poisonous spiral of despair. I became horribly, constantly aware that this would be the first summer I'd not been capable of having my visitation with my daughter. I struggled to wrap my head around the fact that, only the previous summer, she'd been with me in my rented house in Monte Rio. Okay, Evan'd been there with us, which to me now screamed evidence of my irresponsibility and unworthiness as a mother. My white trash boyfriend had accompanied us to the San Francisco Zoo, the amusement parks, the beach and the shopping malls.

Shame and fear consumed me—I became convinced that I should not contact my ex or my family. I'd made such a mess of my life and was terrified that if her father knew I'd dropped to this level of destitution, he would make certain I never saw my baby again. At this point I figured, with typical addict self-pity and negativism, that she'd be better off never seeing me again if I couldn't pull

195

myself up out of my circumstances. Yes, that's what I thought of my self-destructive lifestyle! My circumstances! Not my addiction, my recklessness, anger, pride, stubbornness...I preferred to confront only my financial situation. I focused on one symptom, incapable of acknowledging the disease. So I did what I'd done for so many years. I shut down emotionally, rushing to drown my feelings and self-awareness in my current drug of choice.

For years I'd lived in a schizoid, weirdly unbalanced universe as a mother. I'd been terrified of giving birth. I felt sure I'd die in the process, but insisted on having natural childbirth anyway. The delivery proved to be the most exquisite spiritual and emotional experience of my life. When my baby arrived, they handed her to me. I held her in my arms and looked into her eyes. She made eye contact with me, reached out and touched my face. I fell madly in love at that moment. The first several months I lived in paradise. Then post-partum depression set in.

A bad marriage, financial disaster, and an incorrect diagnosis of mental illness caused me to doubt my worthiness to be a mom. I lost all confidence in myself. A few months before her third birthday, lost in depression, I signed over custody to my husband, at his family's urging.

I ran away to Texas and got a job working in the oil field. A few years later I found an attorney, fought for visitation rights, and won. The courts granted me summers with my daughter, provided I would contact my ex by certified letter, thirty days in advance of the requested visitation date, showing proof of stable and adequate residence.

I'd get her for the summer and try to give her all the love I had within me during that short expanse of time, all the time knowing that I had to give her up again at the end of the summer. When summer was over, I'd return her to her father in accordance with the court order, my heart breaking all over again. After she was gone, I'd allow myself to cry for one full day only. After that I'd pack up all her clothes and toys and close the door to my soul until the next summer. Then I'd steel myself, resuming a routine of sorts. But my heart remained raw with longing and the terrible, nearly physical agony of separation from my child. I sought relief in the wrong ways—in being a badass, in alcohol—anything to numb that awful pain. So this fueled my addiction. By increments, I'd become more and more of a badass, kickass, wild and crazy, heartbroken woman. It had all led to here, this point, summer 1986; traumatized, beat up, doped up, spun out, crazy, and homeless! Once again, I steeled myself and determined to return to a routine. I shut down all the way—tried to forget everything I ever knew—blanked out so there'd be no tears. Weeping is a luxury. So is introspection, I decided. I gave up hope.

I slipped into a kind of routine of living in my car, if you can call that routine. I continued my hard-core, rampant meth use, making the most of any and all contacts and connections in order to procure a steady supply for myself. This sort of thing is a truly tough gig. Nobody works harder than a dope fiend. Dope fiends are up early and working all day to score, and if you sit down and tally up expenses vs. profits, the average dope addict makes less than minimum wage and works 12 to 18 hour shifts.

At least I could drive around that summer. I covered a lot of territory. Since the flood left the entire Russian River area devastated, flood cleanup went on for at least a year. Work in flood cleanup, though toxic and unpleasant, was abundant. I made money that way from time to time, but as I continued to associate with the dregs of the River community, other people trusted me less and less. Work became more difficult for me to get, so I made money on small time dope sales, managing to survive—barely.

Whenever possible, I parked my car at the local Safeway supermarket, on the very edge of the parking lot, and during the graveyard shift I'd gather up my shampoo et al, then head to the women's room to take a sort of Marine shower and wash my hair in the sink. Employees seldom noticed me, or if they did, they looked the other way. Life seemed somewhat bearable.

In early August the clutch went out on my car. Life deteriorated considerably from that point. I now relied on walking or hitchhiking for transportation. I'd never hitchhiked in my life, but I slowly learned some of the nuances. The roads around the River are full of twists and turns, so you need to make sure you're standing where drivers can see you. I learned stuff like that by trial and error.

One aspect of hitchhiking is risk—you're vulnerable in nearly every way humanly possible—so you learn, or think you learn, to judge situations and character. But deep down, every hitchhiker knows it's a gamble; it's all chance whether you survive any given ride. Even if the person who picks you up isn't a rapist or serial killer, they might be a lousy driver.

During those days on the streets I met a guy named Jonesey who hitched a ride with a couple of guys who'd been drinking after work—they'd just gotten paid, in fact. It was a Friday, and they spun out on a curve, wrapping the old Bonneville they were driving around a giant redwood tree. Jonesey survived the crash. He crawled out of the wreckage with a broken leg and a pocket full of cash from the dead guy's wallet. He told us the other guys in the car were unconscious but still breathing, so he didn't steal from them, only the dead guy since he wouldn't be needing the money.

For obvious reasons, hitchhiking is especially scary if you're female, but it's amazing how a person adapts. I used to carry something in the pocket of my jacket for protection; for instance a screwdriver or any heavy, blunt object I happened to find lying around, provided it was an appropriate size for my hand and my pocket.

I never carried knives, since that could lead to concealed weapon charges, which would enhance any possession beef if I got busted. I felt confident carrying a full can of Pepsi, sometimes in a sock—it's an amazingly effective weapon. In the days before I'd become homeless, I once knocked a guy out cold with a full can of Budweiser. One whack between the eyes and that's all it took.

Mostly I liked to walk. Walking, I'd experience the fresh air, the wind rustling towering redwoods, the sun breaking through their boughs in shafts of brightness, the sweet smell of the forest. Not so bad.

Homeless shelters, as we know them, hadn't been invented back then, so if you wanted to find a flophouse, such as Salvation Army, you needed to go to a major city like San Francisco. Still, around the River, some perks presented themselves.

After the flood in '86 and '87, when I was outdoors, I never wanted for clothing. The flood disaster precipitated an influx of donated goods from all over. Free boxes were set up in town near the Vets Hall and at some of the churches and schools. The coolest one was in Rio Nido, in a tiny Catholic church there. The little church stayed open all the time, and the clothes and shoes were of highest quality. I'm talkin' Gucci loafers and Dior blouses. Somebody robbed it early on, though, and the church had to start dispensing the donations elsewhere. That's extremely lame, robbing a church free store—the stuff was free! But they ripped off everything. I guess whoever it was must've hit the collection box or the candles or some other church property as well. They ruined it for the rest of us, that's certain.

One good thing I found was that I could sneak into any of several campground resorts late at night and use the communal shower house when no one was in there. I'd play it off like I was one of the campers and slip through the gate, or sneak around the back from the beach.

Even though my car sat immobile I still could resort to it for shelter at night. I couldn't stretch out in the back seat, but I could sleep sitting up with the seat reclined—if I was tired enough. Trouble was, people, particularly Evan, could look through the windshield and see me sleeping inside my car. Evan cracked my windshield one night. Another night I caught him trying to set fire to my car. I guess he felt compelled to intimidate or harass me or both. I never could figure out why he persisted as long as he did.

During the first few months after the flood, loads of stricken vehicles lay strewn everywhere so the presence of my disabled Datsun hardly made a blip on the radar. Eventually, though, my car cadged so many tickets for late registration that it got towed away. I never got it back, of course. Loss of a car seemed trivial at that point. My concerns telescoped down to basics: food, clothing, shelter where you can find it. Avoid attack or arrest. Dope use remained a priority on my list of daily survival needs.

Winter at the River is mild by national standards, but it can get cold outside, especially at night—the average low temperature in winter is around 30-odd degrees, but it drops as low as 20 degrees or less sometimes. Sure, it rarely snows, but it rains—heavily! "Keep moving," became my mantra. If you're moving around, you're warmer, and you look like you have somewhere to go, so the cops don't zero in on you. Each day I needed to have a plan for where I'd shelter at night—and I needed to know before sundown, or else I had to simply walk around till dawn, and that activity required crystal meth.

At one point that winter I heard that Dianne Feinstein, then mayor of San Francisco, had set up cots for the homeless downtown near the Civic Center. I hitchhiked down to the city to check it out. The cots were already full by the time I arrived, so I ended up spending the night huddled up under the shelter of what would be the Moscone Center—it was a big construction site. I left the city pretty quickly, deciding to take my chances out in the trees, since I still felt paranoid about Japan. The city brought back too many memories for me.

Up at the river, sometimes I'd sit in the bus stop shelters at night, to stay out of the rain. I slept under a bridge, which is not easy, and I gradually learned to sleep "with one eye open," so to speak, to watch out for psychos and rapists and stuff. This was no mean feat considering I still experienced night terrors from what happened in Japan. I often woke up disoriented and uneasy. But once I got going I regained my composure...well, whatever passes for composure when you're suffering from post-traumatic stress disorder and doing meth every day.

In December the weather got really cold and rainy. Thick blankets of fog drifted in and hunkered down tight. I'd been managing to stay alive by working on and off for a guy named Woodcutter Al. That's what they called him, even though "Bagchaser Al" would have been a more apt moniker. He seldom got around to cutting wood, since he had to get tweaked before he could even consider labor, and he owed so many connections that his credit sucked. When he did work he harvested firewood from a big expanse of forest in Cazadero. I knew Al through Evan—we'd scored him some dope a couple of times. One day in November, Al picked me up hitchhiking through Guerneville and asked me to help him get a sixteenth from a cook we all called Paco.

Paco wasn't even remotely Latino—he was heavily Anglo Saxon—and rumor had it he'd migrated to the River from Topanga Canyon back in the '60s, after selling the bar he owned there. Paco lived with his wife and five kids in a cabin in town, but every once in a while he'd disappear for about six weeks and cook a batch in a trailer way out in the wilderness.

Word on the street was that Paco was currently out of commission due to an unfortunate incident, that incident being he'd gotten startled while zipping up his pants after taking a leak and had caught some of his penis in his fly apparatus. He managed to get the zipper open again and release the tender tissue. However, he hadn't been wearing gloves, and traces of meth ingredients transferred from his fingertips to his dick. He'd not sought medical attention at the time, but had resumed work on that particular meth load, laboring furiously till completion. By the time he returned home he'd developed gangrene of the johnson and needed a stint in a hospital. Whether the gangrene story was true or not, I didn't know or care. What I did know was that Paco was absent from home and that his wife denied having any stash for sale.

I'd managed to get Al and his tweaker crew a gram of product from a dude they called Jumpin' Jason. Jason's dope was always stepped on but it was better than nothing. Before handing over the bag, I asked Al for a job on his crew and to my mild surprise he acquiesced. So I'd been sort of employed from that point on.

Working for Al wasn't too bad. He bought us lunch and beverages. The pay sucked—I got twenty dollars a day on average—but at the time it seemed like a good deal. The work wasn't steady unless the dope was. I did my best to provide sources of crystal and in so doing augmented my meager pay with a percentage of the score.

One guy on the crew, Filipino Trey, was a stoner, yet he managed to adapt to the erratic rhythms of the workday by staying baked beyond recognition. Another member of the crew, Mad Jack, drank himself into oblivion each afternoon on the way home.

Another guy I heard about but never met, who worked only occasionally for Al, was known as "Axe Man." One might think a guy called Axe Man would be a nimble-fingered lead guitar player who delivered blistering blues riffs—but this wasn't Chicago. No, this was the River. He acquired his nickname after being caught by his cousin in the act of banging said cousin's wife. The furious cheated husband had picked up a double-headed axe and pinned his offending cousin's right hand to the wall. Hence the name Axe Man. Apparently Axe Man's hand had mended, but not well enough to warrant him full time labor.

I never felled any trees. I'd had no idea how to do tree work but learned how to cut up the tree after it hit the ground, trimmed branches, pulled brush away, and cut the logs into "rounds," or lengths for splitting. Although I had some experience with chainsaws back when I worked in the oil field in Texas, I had never even seen one of the long-bladed Stihl chainsaws they used to cut down redwoods, and I lacked enthusiasm for the risk involved in learning to operate one.

I felt content to work with the small saw. I had nothing to prove. I just wanted to make some cash every day so I wouldn't be driven to steal food. In the testosterone-laden world of Russian River dope fiends/firewood cutters, I was lucky to be working on the crew at all. My crew members seemed to harbor doubts about my abilities, based on gender bias. They gave me a wide berth when I cranked up my saw. The day I picked up a splitting maul to learn how to split rounds into firewood, everybody ran in all directions. But slowly they accepted me. I also learned how to stack firewood, and how to hold each split piece for maximum accuracy and efficiency when tossing it up onto the delivery truck.

I never let Al or the others know I had nowhere to live. No one asked me anything personal, and I liked it that way. Our crew met each day in the parking lot of the Safeway in Guerneville, and we'd drive out to Caz or Jenner or wherever Al'd found a landowner who was interested in thinning out some of his forest. How he ever got any landowner to allow us access for tree work is a mystery. Perhaps we were trespassing every single time, and Al created the myth of having permission. I'll never know.

Through Filipino Trey, I acquired another employment contact. Trey also worked for a sort of hippie landscaper name Mike. Mike lived up on a very high hill in Sebastopol, off Blucher Valley Road. Mike was from upstate New York. He loved the Grateful Dead, was a big fan, but didn't have the rabid zeal and appetite for psychedelics that would qualify him as a true Deadhead, which is a plus in an employer. Who wants to have to worry that their boss may be peaking on acid when payday rolls around? No, compared to Al the Bagchaser/Woodcutter, Mike was comfortingly middle class. He eschewed chemicals and only indulged in marijuana smoking, and that was after work only. No exceptions.

In December I began working occasionally on Mike's crew. Work wasn't plentiful in the winter—we mostly cleared brush and pulled up scotch broom and other dead stuff from out of people's gardens and patios in preparation for the spring planting. Mike paid five bucks an hour, which only amounted to about twenty-five bucks a day, since we usually worked a five hour day. Mike didn't pay for time driving to and from the job, and since a lot of his clients were in Marin County, we lost a couple of hours right from the gate. And he didn't buy lunch like Al did. But I didn't have to score dope for the boss before work could commence. All told, the pay day was about five hours max with either employer, since one didn't pay for time driving and the other excluded pay for time chasing dope.

Throughout November and December, I'd been sleeping in two different abandoned houses. One was located up on top of the hill above Old Monte Rio Road—a three story house, built halfway down the steep side. It'd obviously started to slide down the hill during or after the flood—it'd been "red tagged" by the county inspector; "declared unfit for human habitation," as placards nailed to the door clearly stated. A number of such houses stood among the hills and canyons of the Russian River, and some were remotely situated enough to provide housing opportunities for some of us homeless.

This particular house was one such shelter for at least six people a night—sometimes more. You had to sneak up there after dark and feel your way into the place, which was dicey, since parts of the first floor had given way. The safest rooms for sleeping lay on the second floor, but to get to them you needed to memorize the layout during the daylight hours. This involved hiking up there and avoiding detection by any of the neighboring homeowners, who immediately called the cops at the sight of anyone suspicious in the area.

I came upon the other of the two abandoned houses by simple good luck. You might say it was an inside deal. One day, after Al dropped the crew, including me, off at Safeway parking lot, Evan stepped up, seemingly out of nowhere, and started harassing me.

I couldn't believe it. I hadn't seen him since my car got towed, since without the vehicle, he had no way of guessing my whereabouts. However, he still drove that white trash Camaro, so I gained the advantage of being able to avoid him wherever I saw it parked.

I fixed my gaze straight ahead and tried to ignore Evan. He walked alongside me. "Hey Baby," he jeered, pulling a bag out of his jacket pocket, "Check it out—want some, doncha?" I stopped walking. I'd felt tired and pissed off already. Now this.

Evan sidled in closer, started chanting in my ear, "Free fix for a fuck! Free fix for a fuck! Free fix for a fuck!" I pushed away, started walking as fast as I could, anything to get away from him. He didn't follow, apparently satisfied that he'd been able to elicit enough of a reaction. I never looked back, just kept walking till I got to the Cinnabar coffeehouse. I stepped inside and got in line, deciding to part with some of my precious twenty bucks pay so I could be sheltered from the street for awhile. I felt all shaky and weird. Tears started to come up from deep within—tears of rage and pain—I knew I wouldn't be able to swallow them this time. I split the line all of a sudden and rushed out the door.

I ran up a hill to a cluster of redwoods with a gigantic old stump in the middle of it. This little hiding place was one of my faves—it lay directly behind and above the coffeehouse, and if I crouched down on the ground behind the old stump, the surrounding trees camouflaged me. When you're homeless, either in a huge metropolis or a tiny burg, you can be invisible to the citizens anytime, if you want to, thanks to your low status. They simply prefer not to see you. If you're one of the street smart, you can melt into the background at will. At the River, in the little resort towns, you have the added advantage of the trees, which are ever present, providing picturesque charm and beauty to the tourists.

I sat down on the layer of needles blanketing the ground in the little grove of redwoods, leaned back against the old stump, and started crying. Tears came splashing down. I sobbed so hard I could feel my ab muscles straining. "Fuck this!" I exhorted myself through gritted teeth. "And fuck that punk!" I looked back over the past few years, incredulous that I'd ever been attracted to Evan and feeling a certain self-loathing that I'd actually loved him at one point. I figured I'd been looking to fill the void of unrequited motherhood that I'd been struggling with all those years. I'd needed, or thought I needed, a man to love—as if that would help to mask the pain of separation from my little girl. That was how Evan had crept in. He'd zeroed in on me like a mark. I'd supported him till it broke me in half. And now that I had nothing left, he hated me, and that's why he couldn't leave me alone.

Finally I stopped crying. I stood up and braced myself. I began delivering a pep talk, to myself, under my breath. "Well...now... today—I don't need a man! And I don't need love either! I need to stay warm and I need something to eat and I need a cigarette and I need a hit of dope and I need a cup of fucking coffee...no—I NEED A FUCKING GRANDE MOCHACCINO!" I exited the shelter of the grove of trees and stalked back down to the Cinnabar, determined not to feel, not to cry, not to let'em find a chink in my armor.

"Um, uh...hey..." I heard a voice behind me. I jerked my head around to see a smiling face, weathered and craggy, surrounded by long dreadlocks, at eye level with mine. "I'm Santi." He smiled again revealing surprisingly nice teeth. He waved a hand in the direction of the somewhat shorter guy on crutches, with a buzzcut, standing next to him. "This is Danny."

"Yeah, uh, hi. I'm..."

"Marti. I know. You used to hang out with Evan O'Reilly."

"That's my name. And I used to, but not anymore." The pain—the rage—started coming back up. I couldn't manage any more words to describe my present relationship to, and torment by, my former boyfriend. I gulped in a breath.

Santi flashed me that ingenuous smile again. "Look, Evan's an asshole. Everybody knows that. Wanna have coffee with us? I'll buy."

"Well, I was gonna get a mochaccino..."

"No problem!" Santi gleamed, and Danny nodded, smiling shyly.

We got our coffees and sat at a table outside, in spite of the chill weather. "I'm much more comfortable outside," Santi told me.

"Whatever blows your hair back." I cracked the lid on my mochaccino, took a tentative sip.

We sat in comfortable silence for a while, Santi looking at the sky every so often, Danny appearing lost in thought as he absently twiddled with his crutches. Finally Santi spoke up. "Hey, Marti, we've got a place to stay; it's up the hill behind us." He jerked his thumb in the direction of my secret redwood-clump-hideout. "We were just coming from there when we saw you—I saw you—crying. I know it's not easy for you. I can tell you've got nowhere to stay."

"But—it's not like that..." I realized that denial was useless with these guys. Why try to keep up pretenses? *What did I have to prove, anyway?* "Ooookay, you're right. I'm outdoors and it sucks."

"Well, good news here. Our pad is top secret, and we have room for a couple more roommates! You can crash there too!" Santi smiled again, with childlike enthusiasm, and jumped up. "C'mon with us, we're going to get some sandwiches and some drinks, and then we're going home. You come check it out." Danny began a slightly labored rise from his chair, balancing himself on his crutches, and Santi stood by his pal like a spotter in a gym.

I went with them. Sure, these guys were a little weird, but hey, here at the River? Who wasn't? I felt drained from working and from the encounter with Evan. The way I felt tonight, the hike up to the place off Old Monte Rio would be a long and exhausting one. Why not check out the house they'd found? *No harm in scoping it out.*

Danny and Santi bought big sandwiches and sodas at a deli. I took out my twenty from work and waved it around, stating that I had my part covered, but they insisted on paying for mine. "See," Santi said conspiratorially, "Danny and I get money every month—checks from the government; it's no problem. You can help us out another time." We started walking. Danny passed me a Pepsi.

"Okay." *Hmmm.* I willed a smile, wrapped my hand around the frosty soft drink can, and stuck it in the pocket of my peacoat—just in case. *If they turn out to be psychos or serial killers, I can always smack 'em between the eyes with this...my favorite weapon. It's worked before...*

The house that Santi and Dan stayed in boasted an expansive sundeck. On one side of the deck stood a three story house with five bedrooms. A one story cottage occupied the other side. A young hippie couple named Ron and Sharon lived in the cottage off and on. I met them that first night. Santi and Dan claimed the big house, along with three teenagers they called "The Lost Boys."

I also met the "Lost Boys" that first night. I don't know if they were runaways or simply kids whose parents fell far short of the family ideal. I didn't ask, of course, and I seldom saw the boys after that. They came and went, as did all the "tenants."

The Lost Boys'd chosen the two bedrooms on the ground floor. The basement couldn't be accessed. Parts of the living room floor and one of its walls had caved into the basement, so nobody dared set foot in the living room. We all regarded the kitchen as the most stable room in the place, and Danny, by unanimous vote, received occupancy there. After all, the guy already walked on crutches; he needed to minimize risk!

"I'll wait here," Danny said, "Santi'll give you the tour."

We climbed, and Santi showed me the four bedrooms upstairs. "Take any one you want," he grinned, "Except you don't want this one." With a sweeping gesture, he pointed out a huge hole in the doorway of one the largest bedrooms. "It's too hard to miss doing a Wile E. Coyote..." He chuckled. "You know the Roadrunner cartoons? You'd be like the Coyote? He always falls..."

"Yeah, heh. Heh. I get it." I looked around. "So, where are you staying?" I needed to select a room that would be far enough from Santi and would provide an escape route if he decided I owed him some kind of conjugal favor in exchange for shelter, even though he seemed like a big kid.

"Cool. Here's my room, it's my tropical getaway." Santi'd covered his tiny room's walls in collage, with what appeared to be pictures taken from travel magazines. He wanted to go to Jamaica, he told me, and he'd pasted the walls with his vision. He confided that if he looked at the photos enough he felt warmer, and that he was "actually visualizing" his Jamaica trip into existence. *Whatever floats your boat, I guess...*

I selected a room. It was on the second floor, but was sort of sunken: you had to step down three stairs from the second floor to enter it. Or up three from the ground floor. It lent me a sense of separation from the men. And unlike a lot of the rooms in the house, the door really worked—it shut all the way. The window still had glass in it. Best of all was its shape—it was a hexagonal room! Awesome.

I hiked back down to Guerneville, to the bridge near the Safeway, to retrieve my sleeping bag. I carried anything that was near and dear in my backpack at all times, but I kept my sleeping bag wrapped up in a black plastic trash bag, in the brush under the bridge during the day. I'd learned how to conceal things and how to slip in and out of places unnoticed. I hauled the sleeping bag up to my new "residence."

That first night I didn't sleep at all. No more than fifteen minutes after darkness fell (and it fell abruptly, as it always does in Redwood country) intermittent screams emanated from the kitchen. I flipped on my cigarette lighter and groped my way down to the kitchen. There I found Dan sitting up in a straight-backed wooden chair, one crutch braced across his bandaged leg, the other crutch gripped in his right fist, as if poised for combat. He held a flashlight in his left hand, the beam aimed into a dark opening in one of the corners of the dilapidated old kitchen cabinets.

"It's the rats, man, they keep coming for me!" Dan twisted in his chair and cocked the flashlight beam in my direction for only a second. Wide-eyed, he whipped back around to face the broken down cabinetry.

"Shit." I couldn't think anything more to say. Rats were part of my life already, had been since the first time I took shelter under a bridge. I'd encountered them a few times in the abandoned house off Old Monte Rio Road, but only fleetingly. Now that I thought about it, they'd probably skittered over me in my sleep and never awakened me. I always slept scrunched down, curled up in a fetal position, with as much of the sleeping bag closed over my head as possible.

"It's my foot. I cut it real bad a while back, and it got infected. I had to take the bus into Santa Rosa to the emergency room. They said it was almost gangrene, but not quite, so I'm lucky. I gotta change the dressings twice a day and I do that downtown in the park so I can throw away the old bandages in the trash cans there. I think the rats can smell my foot and they wanna bite it. That's why I'm sittin' up. Every time a rat comes outta the corner there I scream and whack at it with my crutch. I keep watch till dawn. Then I can sleep a little after the rats go away. Santi comes down then; goes out for coffee and stuff, brings it back to me. He's good people. It's his turn to sleep now. That's why he didn't come down here when you did."

"Oh. Well, hey, uh..." I fumbled around for some words of encouragement to say to the guy but finally judged it futile. "Well, I'll hang out with you a while. I can't sleep anyway. Want a cigarette?" I lit one of my Marlboros and passed it to him. I still had about a half a bag of speed in the watch pocket of my Levis. I figured I'd do it up in the morning. I only worked a few days a week, four if I was lucky, and this week wasn't one of my lucky ones. "Hey Danny? Got another flashlight?"

Turns out he did. I borrowed it to look around for a rock or a piece of wood to hit rats with. I found a brick. We only saw two or three rats, in that many hours, so I ended up going back to my room. I heard one more episode of screaming from the kitchen, followed by a protracted silence. The dawn broke. And it started raining.

Rain fell steadily all day. I went out for coffee with Santi and Dan. "We like to do acid when it's raining," Santi beamed. "There's plenty. Wanna do some too?"

"Okay." I figured it'd help pass the time.

211

We waited till around six p.m., then popped the tiny little blotters onto our tongues. The stuff kicked in quickly. I listened to the rhythm and melody of the rain. I found it surreally comforting—a symphony. Good thing I liked it, because it was the only sound in that old house besides the occasional creak of timbers or the whoosh of the wind through the redwood branches outside.

Santi and I helped Danny to clamber upstairs on his crutches. The three of us sat in Santi's tropical visualization room and talked, sharing a flashlight among us. We also had a couple of candles going but the draftiness of the room made their flames fleeting—sporadic at best. I told them about how I'd worked in the oil field in Texas and how, not long before, I'd been a working standup comic with some success. Then I changed the subject so I wouldn't flip out and start crying about my daughter.

I asked the guys to tell me about themselves. Danny told me he was from Arkansas, divorced, with two kids. He'd been in the Marines—in Viet Nam. Santi told me his parents, he thought, must be in North Dakota.

"North Dakota. Is that where you're from?" I asked.

"Sort of. I came here from North Dakota a long time ago. I was in a mental hospital there. They told me my parents put me in there, but I don't remember exactly. Anyway, one day they came in and told me they were letting me go. I came to California and I've been here ever since."

"Oh, that's good. California is a lot more fun that North Dakota, I'm sure! Heh." *Uh-oh. Damn. Danny's a Rambo flashback waiting to happen, and Santi's certifiable...These guys are psychos, albeit friendly psychos so far, and I drank my Pepsi! What am I gonna smack 'em with if they go off on me?* I made a supreme effort to conceal my disquiet. "This acid is really good. Heh. Thanks, you guys." I smiled at each in turn, eager for a brisk gallop to new conversational pastures.

"I'm God." Santi smiled beatifically. "Wanna go for coffee?"

*Oh, boy. Here we go on a full-blown, acid-induced psychotic break!* "Coffee? On acid? I mean, I feel like I'm peaking here. I don't feel quite divine yet, but I'm pretty high. How about you, Santi—you sure you wanna go to town now? Speaking for myself, by the time the trip hits the God level, it's a lot better to avoid public outings."

"I don't need acid to know I'm God. I saw that long ago, when I got my dreads. One day I just woke up with them. They're a gift." Santi cocked his head to one side as if listening to someone whisper in his ear. He stood up, helped Dan onto his crutches, turned off the flashlight. "Let's go. Coffee'd be great right now. C'mon."

We went for coffee. I didn't want to go around people, but I didn't want to stay at the house alone in the rain either. The idea gave me the creeps. On the way, Santi and Danny told me they were both supposed to be on psych meds, but they'd let their prescriptions lapse back in the summer, and they preferred acid to meds, anyway. I nodded encouragingly, feeling skittish about my companions, hoping to be counted as a friend, not an adversary. LSD, they assured me, made them "more normal."

I had a nice trip with Santi and Dan. Santi and I talked about lots of things, and Dan mostly listened, and I know this may sound absurd, but I learned a lot from Santi that night. His thing about visualization made sense. It renewed my hope. I decided I'd visualize myself with a car, and a place to live, and doing comedy again, and united with my daughter. Since I always carried a couple of pictures of her in my wallet, I took them out and gazed at them, trying to visualize good things for her.

While coming down off the LSD, I fumbled around trying to meditate, and sort of prayed, even though I told myself God would never hear the prayers of a fuck-up like me. When I fell asleep I dreamed that dream I often had—my daughter and I, swept down a river of sewage, me trying to hold her above the noxious tide, losing my grip on her, slipping beneath the sewage, then seeing a man standing up, catching me, saving my daughter too. When I woke up, the sun was shining and I felt almost good.

The next day I went up to Nick's to see about a front for a half gram. He turned me down, but on the way out I ran into a friend of mine, an unemployed construction worker named Jay. "I've got an eightball of kickass dope here," he whispered, glancing furtively over his shoulder as we exited Nick's neighborhood, "I'll front you some, or better still, if you wanna come with me and help me work on my house, I'll give you all the dope you want for free."

He'd made me an offer I couldn't refuse. "Sure, but I have no construction skills, you know that, Jay!"

"Yeah, but you're a dope fiend, and you're an honest one. I know I can trust you not to tell anybody about this. Anyway it's unskilled labor I need. C'mon. I'll get you high."

Turns out the dope was more than kickass—it was amazing. A quarter gram of this sparkly smooth crystal delivered a rush that flung me onto the shores of transcendence. We fired up that first bag in the woods along the banks of the river. Jay led me to a spot where a huge Douglas fir had fallen, forming a bridge across the water. "We gotta cross here, man, it's the only way to get into Mills Resort without being seen. That's where my house is gonna be."

"How can you have a house there and not be seen?"

"Look, it's cool; I'm building it right on the riverbank, right in the corner of the property where it's not officially owned by the resort. I've got clearance from the people that are buying it; they're gonna look the other way till I've established squatter's rights...anyway, let's go, I'll show you. C'mon, I'll cross first. I do it all the time. Just go slow."

We made our way across the fallen tree, then crouched down, snaking our way through the brush to a tiny hut about eight feet square. Jay opened the door and we ducked inside. The room was warm! A tiny pot-bellied stove sat in the middle of the hut radiating heat from still-glowing embers. "Wow!" That's all I could say.

"Take your coat off."

"That's okay." I figured he wanted some kind of payment for the dope, and I didn't want to act like I was into it. I took a fierce pride in the fact that, although I might be homeless, I wouldn't trade my body for a warm shelter and a high. *Better to keep my peacoat on, thank the guy for the dope, and come up with an excuse to get going right now.*

"Hey, look, you're safe with me. I'm a major dope fiend, but I do have some standards! I don't pressure chicks. I'm not gonna rape you or try to have sex with you or anything like that—especially not in this motherfucking hut! I wanna build a fucking house right here, and I've got access to materials. I'm salvaging them out of the river just a few yards away. That's what I need your help for. There's all kindsa lumber washed down the river from the flood that's ended up right here. It's a low point or something, so all kindsa stuff is in there. We gotta pull it outta the river and clean all the mud off it. So are you in? You can have all the dope you want. Work as long as it lasts."

"I'm in." *Man, I am such a dope fiend.*

Jay and I worked for days, nonstop. We'd wade into the frigid muddy river, retrieving two-by-tens, or whatever pieces he needed for his house plan. We'd scrape the icy mud off each piece of wood with our bare hands and lay it out on the ground to dry. I hoped the water was somewhat less toxic by now, since it'd been almost a year since the flood. Jay said he thought it was pretty safe, and that we had access to a hose with clear water for rinsing our hands off. By "access to," I mean once or twice a day we'd borrow the hose from the people up the riverbank, a couple named Hugh and Suzy.

Hugh and Suzy claimed to be in the process of purchasing the old rundown resort. They'd told Jay that the owner lived in Nevada, and they were currently in negotiations. I doubted this but didn't care. I had work, dope, and shelter in steady supply. This was December, and the hut with the stove was a lot warmer than Santi's house. Hugh and Suzy grudgingly gave us parts off the dilapidated cabins around the property, in exchange for meth.

After working furiously for about five days straight, Jay and I began to develop strange symptoms. We first noticed it on our feet. After wading in the river during the day, we'd take off our boots and dry them by the stove overnight. Our socks'd be so far gone after one work shift that we'd simply throw them away. We'd boil water on the wood stove and fill a basin, taking turns washing our hands and feet very carefully. After all, we knew there'd been sewage spills in the river at flood level, so we took what we considered to be the utmost care of our health, under the circumstances.

It went like this: first our feet looked puffy and red, then dark blue spots with inky black centers appeared all over our feet— anywhere below the ankles. The night we saw our feet like that for the first time, we freaked out thinking we had AIDS. Then we panicked, each accusing the other of being a carrier. Then we reminded ourselves that we hadn't shared a syringe or had sex, which made us feel better. After that we slipped into denial. We told ourselves we'd stop wading in the water and get a rake to drag the lumber out. We told ourselves we'd go to the doctor and get help if the symptoms persisted. Then we did some more dope, waited till morning, and went back to work washing mud off some wood siding.

Around four p.m. our hands presented the same symptoms as our feet did. The spots looked terrifying and hideous, yet we felt no pain or even irritation. We decided to take a day off from the river. The house had begun to take shape. Jay ventured up the banks to negotiate with Hugh for some copper tubing and PVC pipe. He quickly returned, eyes big as saucers, and motioned me to follow him. We climbed the steep rise up the riverbank and crossed the stubbly dead grass to a ramshackle garage on the Mills Resort property. Hugh stood just behind the garage, holding the hose and rinsing something off. We drew closer, and finally I saw what he was hosing down. We stood on the edge of a pit about six feet deep and large enough to hold eight 50 gallon drums. To my dismay, I noticed that each drum was emblazoned with a skull-and-crossbones. Several of the drums were rusted and appeared to be leaking.

"She's cool, Hugh," Jay said. "She's no snitch."

"Better not be." Hugh glared in my direction. He turned to Jay. "So what do you think? Is it P2P?" Hugh was hoping that he had found the coveted super meth ingredient, phenyl-2-propanone.

"Where the fuck did you find this shit?" Jay looked outraged. If he hadn't been so skinny and scrawny from rabid dope use, he would have kicked Hugh's ass on the spot.

"Here and there," Hugh replied guardedly. "The point is they gotta be worth something." He raised his chin defiantly. "I know a biker cook down South in the desert—Salton Sea—that'll pay big money for chemicals. And these are definitely chemicals."

"Yep," I said, feeling queasy, "They're chemicals."

Jay and I took our leave of Hugh and scuttled down the bank to Jay's hut.

"Lemme give you the bad news now," Jay said. "That pit was s'posed to house a septic tank. I helped him dig it. Damn! Whatever's been fuckin' up our hands and feet has got something to do with those barrels...Now the good news—at least it's better than AIDS or bubonic plague...doncha think?"

Jay and I reconsidered going to the clinic and getting examined. We feared that if a doctor discovered evidence of poisoning or exposure to toxic waste, the authorities might start an investigation at Mills resort and find the barrels, which would lead to our being labeled as snitches, which in turn would cause us to become victims of outlaw justice...etc., etc.

At that point I decided to terminate my involvement in Jay's homesteading project. We parted on good terms. Jay even gave me a bag for the road. I wore gloves to keep my mind off the spots, redness, and puffiness, which disappeared entirely during the next two days.

On the way back to my room at Santi's refuge, I stopped at Cinnabar Coffeehouse, where I found Santi and Dan sitting outside drinking espressos. "We lost the house," Santi stated. "Two nights ago. The cops came up and raided us...but they let me take one of my Jamaica pictures." He grinned. "So I can keep on visualizing." He gave a thumbs up gesture. A year later Santi achieved his island goal. He made it to Hawaii and lived there for months—a testimony to the power of visualization.

I went back to work on Al's firewood crew and on Mike's landscaping crew. I'd realized with a jolt of pain that my daughter's birthday was coming up in a couple of days. I never knew exactly what the date was on any given day during that year—I seldom looked at a calendar. My life consisted of pathetic struggles for survival—and dope—so that I hardly kept track of the months passing, let alone individual days.

I used my pay from two days of woodcutting to slap together twenty-five bucks, then I bought the prettiest birthday card I could find. I signed it, "Love, Mommy,"—I couldn't see any use in writing more than that—and slipped the cash inside, sealing the envelope. I addressed the card, but left the return address blank.

*I have no address! I have ceased to exist...maybe I shouldn't send this...maybe she'd be better off thinking I'm dead.* In spite of the self-hatred I felt and my self-pitying thoughts, I walked down to the Guerneville post office, bought a stamp, and dropped the card into the outgoing mail slot. I bolted out of the post office and broke into a run. I ran until I reached the bridge.

I stooped down, slipped under the bridge and crouched there, arms around my knees, trying not to think about anything, which proved impossible. I thought about my little girl, and how my life had fallen apart around me. Darkness fell. Rain pounded down on the bridge above me. I couldn't stand the cold anymore so I got up and started walking really fast to get warm. I marched around all night in the rain to drive the cold out of my body. Every once in a while I'd walk into the Safeway and act like I was shopping so I could warm up in there. I'd spent all my pay, so if I wanted coffee or something, I'd have to steal it, and tonight I simply lacked the nerve.

I was coming out of the Safeway after one of those warm-up sessions when I saw Evan. He leaned against the brick wall, smoking a Marlboro. When he saw me, he pushed off the wall and started to follow. The menace which he'd displayed toward me the last time we'd encountered each other had disappeared. He offered me a cigarette and I accepted, happy to save my remaining few for later. As we walked in the rain, he told me he'd wrecked his car, and was passing time till the day after Christmas, then he'd be doing some jail time. "I'm turnin' myself in," he told me, "I got so many outstanding warrants, here and in Marin." He walked with his head down and his hands in his pockets. "My mom kicked me outta her house, so I'm kinda outdoors...listen, I found this place up on a hill and I been crashin' there—it's been burglarized, more like vandalized, by some high school kids an' the owners so far haven't made it down from the city to lock it up or nothin'. An' the electricity is still on in there, so if you're real cool you can sneak in there an' turn on the space heater in this one room. That's what I been doin'. I'm sleepin' till I go to jail. Haven't done any dope in weeks. That way I won't be jonesin' when I get to county."

"Why are you telling me this?"

"I'm not gonna need the place when I go, so I'm letting you in on this. C'mon, I'll show you where it is."

He showed me the house. It was surrounded by fluorescent orange tape. Printed on the tape were the words "police line—do not cross." Evan indicated we should duck under the tape, leaving it intact. We crouched and skittered along the front walk and into the broken front door. Inside, pitch black greeted us. I followed my former tormentor into a tiny windowless bedroom at the back of the house. Once inside, he shut the door and turned on a table lamp which'd been set on the floor. A space heater in the corner radiated warmth.

"We could have sex now and you could stay here till morning. How about it? It's up to you." As he spoke those words, he produced what he obviously thought was an irresistible smile. I squirmed inwardly as I felt a remnant of care for him stirring. Or was I just lonely and sad and cold? Well, the entire situation was laughably pathetic. *Fuck this. Fuck it!*

"Look, Evan, you know I can't do this. Not anymore." I couldn't think of anything else to say. For months now my heart seemed to be frozen deep inside of me. Words couldn't break through to the surface anymore. Even if I wanted them to.

He managed to look affronted. "Well, you can use the place anyway. I'm not gonna tell anybody else. And I'm almost over you. I got a real cute girl now. I was with her today—only thing is, when I'm havin' sex with her I still see your face. I have to think about you to get off. But I know that won't last forever. One of these days, I'll shut my eyes and I'll see some other chick's face, and I won't even remember your name." He turned and looked at the wall. He made a shooing motion with his right hand. "Go on back out there in the rain if that's what you want. You always were a fuckin' crazy freak anyway. But I meant what I said. You can have this place. I promise."

I left him there and headed outside; crawling through the door and under the police tape, I felt glad to be out of there and moving again. The rain let up a little by the time I got to the bottom of the hill. I trudged down Highway 116 till I got to Monte Rio—over four miles—then walked across the Monte Rio Bridge to the Monte Rio Post Office where I stepped inside and sat on the floor. By now, dawn was breaking; I recognized its thin gray light through the fog. The redwoods still dripped water from the storm, the drops sounding on the roof. I shivered and waited for my clothes to dry off a little. Then I got the hell out of there before the post office opened for the day.

# CHAPTER 11

# CHANCE ENCOUNTER

It was Christmas Eve, and I didn't even notice until I hitched a ride into Santa Rosa to score some meth. I knew of a connection in South Park—a consummate junkie couple—who had really decent product. I carried a hundred bucks of somebody else's money and twenty of my own. I never managed to accumulate more than twenty bucks at a time on my woodcutter/hippie landscaper wages...

---

I scored a sixteenth, no small feat, considering I had to wait for hours in line behind a dozen other buyers, each of us struggling to be patient while the stuff got weighed at a glacial pace. Joey, the dude, kept nodding off over the triple beam and spilling crystal all over the place. Georgie, the chick, was in the kitchen eating Christmas cookies with her two young kids. That's when I noticed it was Christmas Eve. I heard her talking about Santa coming. After sticking it out in line I achieved my goal. I now had the dope—and it was excellent. I stuck the teener in my half-empty cigarette pack and shoved it down into my boot.

I headed down Aston Street toward the Pic n' Pay store, taking the longest strides I am capable of. Night had fallen, but for some reason the streetlights refused to blink on. I tried to act very cool, but South Park can be a pretty tough neighborhood, even though it's only Santa Rosa. I mean, it's not Oakland, but you can still get shot or stabbed pretty easily. Also, I was holding, and that always made me feel a little jumpy, probably from the adrenaline rush of anticipation. But I had a long way to go—all the way to Monte Rio, around twenty miles.

A shiny black Trans-Am drove by slowly, its windows darkened, muted bass lines audible from the stereo. The back window rolled down halfway and somebody flipped a cigarette out at me. Sparks showered in an arc near my face. Laughter erupted from somewhere inside the vehicle as I heard the engine rev, and the car accelerated past me. A guy jerked his head out the window and barked, "Dumbass Bitch!" I felt lucky—they didn't stop. *Merry Christmas to me.*

My shoulders stiffened as I heard another car. I turned to see a battered '70s Toyota Corolla approaching, its engine wheezing and sputtering as it pulled up alongside of me. "Um, you need a ride?" I guess it was the friendly tone of voice that drew me to approach the old car and look inside. Two smiling young Thai men sat in the front seat. Neither one could have been more than twenty years old.

I said, "Yes, thank you," and jumped in the back seat, relieved to be off the street. I told them I was going to the Russian River, and they said they could give me a ride all the way. "Thanks! I'm Marti," I said.

The driver looked back at me through the rear view mirror. "I'm Tran, this is Bobby. Hey—where you live at the River? You like it out there?"

"Um, yeah, I like it okay I guess. I need to get to Monte Rio tonight, but anywhere at the River will do."

We rode a while in silence, then Bobby spoke. "What are you doing walking around Santa Rosa all alone? You're a long way from Monte Rio."

Alarm bells went off in my head. My heart pounded in my chest. *They must think I'm a streetwalker and they're gonna to try to get free blowjobs or something. Or just as bad—they've figured out I've got dope and they're gonna try to rip me off.* "I'm homeless!" I blurted it out, "I lost my car and everything, and I know somebody in Monte Rio who is gonna let me stay there tonight." I abruptly stopped talking. I sat there trying to look defiant. I felt really lame.

Turns out Tran and Bobby were pretty cool. "You don't have to go all the way to the River. It's Christmas, right? You can stay with our family tonight. Our grandmother will love it!"

"Y-your grandmother? You live with your grandmother?"

They laughed. "Yeah, and our little sister and our mom, but she's working right now. She'll be home at eleven, and we'll order a pizza."

"Oh, that's really nice of you, but I don't think your grandmother and mom would want to have a street person in their house. I'm homeless."

Tran and Bobby laughed even harder. Bobby slapped his knee. "Well, it's cool, Marti! WE'RE BOAT PEOPLE!" They roared with laughter. I joined in. It was awfully funny.

I started to feel warm inside. I'd been invited into the home of a family on Christmas Eve! And certainly they'd been through something far worse than I'd experienced. For a second I felt like there actually could be a meaning to life, an order, but I couldn't quite grasp what it was. I felt gratitude. For a moment I felt a sort of joy. But I was an addict. My urge to get to Monte Rio, split up that sixteenth, and get high trumped any other inclination. I couldn't accept their kindness. I lied of course—told them I needed to go to my friend's or she would worry about me, and she didn't have a phone, so I couldn't call.

"That's cool," they assured me, "We'll still take you all the way to your friend's place."

I offered Tran and Bobby my last five dollars for gas, but they refused to take it.

––––––––

A FEW DAYS AFTER CHRISTMAS, I HIKED UP TO THE ABANDONED house Evan showed me. The police tape was still there. I sneaked in through the broken front door and made my way to that little windowless room at the back. It felt chilly and smelled a bit mildewy, but once I turned on the space heater it eventually dried out. I slept with my clothes on under the blankets and kept my coat and backpack close at hand. I felt like any moment the owners or the cops might show up, and I'd have to make a run for it.

January turned out to be a pretty decent month for me. The weather was very cold and it rained a lot. But each night I retreated to my little room with the heater and the lamp. I didn't need to use as much dope since I had the option of sleeping warmly on a regular basis. I knew it couldn't last, but that made me savor it even more.

One day I hitched to Forestville to meet Mike for work. We went on a job in Mill Valley. Nobody else on the crew showed up that day so I figured I'd make more money. Mike left me at the job to pull scotch broom and weeds while he did bids on some upcoming projects. When he returned we pulled brush until dark. At the end of the day I felt completely exhausted. Mike paid me a crummy twenty-five dollars for five hours, repeating his mantra that hours spent commuting didn't count. *Cheapskate!* I felt ripped off, but had to take whatever money I could. We'd spent three hours of driving and eight hours working! I was sure of it! The return commute sucked.

Once we got to Sebastopol, Mike started driving straight up to his house at the top of Blucher Valley Road. "Mike. I need to get to Guerneville. I'm working firewood tomorrow."

225

He didn't even register having heard my words, just drove faster. "I reeeally need to smoke a joint," he whined. *Fucking pothead! Now I'm pissed.*

"Let me outta this truck, then. I'll walk."

"No!"—whining again—"I mean, I'll give you a ride to Guerneville immediately after I get high. Just hang out, okay?"

Turns out Mike's roommate Steve turned him on to some dank hydro bud. The weed blew him away. Within three hits, my erstwhile employer was practically slobbering all over himself and his raggedy-ass couch. I stood up and crossed the room, suppressing the urge to bitch-slap him a couple of times. "Hey, uh—Mike. I need to get going now. Remember your promise? To take me to Guerneville immediately after you got high? Well I think you're high now."

My sarcasm was lost on him—sucked away into his THC-soaked cerebral tissues, possibly being stored away in his fat cells. Mike stared back at me, glassy-eyed, uncomprehending. "Uh...uh. I can't drive, 'm too stoned." He managed to communicate this in a whine! Amazing!

My hopes of a ride shriveled up—poof!—gone! I slammed the door on my way out, but I was pretty sure nobody heard me over the Grateful Dead music blasting from Mike's stereo speakers. Nothing bored and annoyed me more than the Dead.

I trudged along the gravel road which wound its way downhill from Mike's house. The night was foggy, cold, profoundly dark, and there were no streetlights on those country roads. I used the glow from Mike's residence to make my way at first, but as I descended, it disappeared over my shoulder. I had a lighter, so I used that sparingly, but in the fog it was a feeble gesture, nothing more.

I made it down to Highway 116 and headed north. I put my thumb out. Miraculously, a guy stopped and gave me a ride to the center of Sebastopol. "I'm stopping at Don's Restaurant," he said.

I got out and started walking again. I couldn't believe how thick the fog was. I literally could not see more than a yard ahead. Light drizzle began, amplifying the dismalness of my surroundings. I walked and strained my eyes for headlights. No cars! The town was completely deserted! I continued to trudge along, hoping to see headlights. Nothing. Finally I stopped and stood still, waiting, unsure of where I was exactly.

Eery silence enveloped me. I waited for what seemed like an eternity, trying not to think of all the serial killers who'd claimed victims in California: Zodiac, Ted Bundy, Night Stalker, Hillside Strangler. *They never caught the Zodiac killer! He could be sneaking up on me right now! Oh hell no.* I felt panic, wrestled it down, lit a smoke. I reassured myself. The Zodiac killer'd be old by now. *I could take him.*

Just then I saw headlights break through the fog. Visibility was so bad, the vehicle was almost on me before I saw the lights. I determined not to let this car pass me up. It might be my only chance! I stepped out into the road, waving both arms.

The vehicle stopped. I could barely distinguish the features of a blue Toyota truck. I stepped up to the driver's side but couldn't see into the cab for the gloom. The window rolled down, releasing a cumulous cloud of pot smoke. Good. I had an angle I could use. Without even looking closely at the guy I started my appeal. "Hey, I need a ride to Guerneville really bad! I'll score you some weed in payment as soon as we get there. Please!" I wasn't lying. I could get weed fronted to me from a number of sources. My credit was good.

The driver hesitated a moment. "Well...I'm going to Occidental. But if you can tell me how to get back to there after Guerneville, then I'll give you a ride."

"Oh, thank you! Thank you!" I leapt into the vehicle. I took a closer look at him after I got in. I saw tousled, sandy blond hair, good looks, and a nice smile. A black, white, and brown spotted dog sat on the front seat beside him. The dog immediately jumped into my lap and curled up.

"What a nice dog." I meant it.

"His name is Pancho."

"I'm Marti."

"Hi Marti. I'm Chris."

"I meant it about the weed. You won't regret this."

He waved a hand dismissively. "Forget the weed. I don't need it. It's fine."

We talked on the way to Guerneville—about music, mostly, but also just a little about standup comedy. Chris told me he worked with a lot of musicians, since the company he represented did silk screening for T-shirts. He said they did a lot of jobs for rock concerts. I listened, nodded, smiled, tried to think of funny stuff to say. I told Chris about a queen named Raymond, a gift shop owner in Guerneville that I sometimes scored weed for who might need some T-shirts done. Good thing the fog was so thick that night. He had to drive slowly, a lucky thing for me since I wanted this trip to last. I felt so comfortable with this guy! And—I liked his dog.

Inside my head I wrestled with my low self-esteem. *Too bad I can't become better acquainted with this man—I mean, I'm homeless! How could I ever date a guy when I'm homeless?* But going out with him wasn't beyond the realm of possibility, was it? After all, I'd lost everything, but somehow I'd managed to hang onto a pair of expensive black high heels. I carried them around in my backpack as a reminder that once I'd been sophisticated and sexy, and that I might be able to rise up out of my current destitution. I could maybe find a decent dress at a thrift store. *Oh, get a grip, girl! Not now. Maybe someday.*

We arrived in Guerneville. I asked him to let me out at the bottom of the hill where my abandoned house headquarters stood. "I can walk from here," I told him, "It's no problem."

His face registered disappointment. "Hey, wait. I'll take you to your door. C'mon."

"Uh—nnooo, that's okay. I've gotta go score some weed. It's business, see, and...um, the connection is real paranoid. They've got guns and everything and...and the place is hot, too. I have to walk up there. I wouldn't want you to be compromised." I felt nervous. I would have died if he'd found out I was such a loser that I slept in an abandoned house.

He looked at me. Then he smiled. "Okay, then. But, here's my card if you ever want to get hold of me." He handed me his business card. I slipped it in my coat pocket without looking at it.

"Thanks!" I flashed a big smile. "Okay, well, I gotta hurry now."

He reached out and touched my arm. "Can I have your number?"

*Uh-oh.* "Sure!" I chirped, feeling really nervous and silly. "Do you have something to write with?" I made up a phone number, scribbled it down and passed it to him. "And thank you again. It was really nice talking with you, Chris."

"Goodnight." He smiled again.

I surged up the hill, willing myself not to look back. When I was halfway up the dark street I heard his truck begin driving away toward Occidental. I felt elated and sorrowful at the same time. Urgently I jammed my hand into the pocket of my peacoat to reassure myself his card was still there. I fondled it between my thumb and forefinger. *Someday. Someday I'll get myself together, and I'll call him.*

I reached my abandoned house hideaway and dropped to a crouch so I could enter unnoticed. Once inside my sanctuary room, I turned on the space heater and the lamp and took a long look at Chris' business card. "Public relations," was his title. *This guy has a business card. And a legitimate phone and address. I have got to get myself together!* Carefully, with great deliberation, I put the card into my wallet, behind the pictures of my daughter. *Someday.*

I left my little hideaway around three weeks later, having found another place even farther up the hill. I'd done some checking around and I heard that no one had been there in at least three years. Of course this one lacked the luxury of electricity, but I didn't feel as paranoid about staying in it. I knew better than to trespass on any property for long, and felt I'd already outrun my luck at the one with the space heater! I also felt uncomfortable with tapping some innocent citizen's electricity.

The house was a tiny A-frame—no doubt built by the owner as a summer cottage. That was the story with most of the houses around the River. In the '50s, residents of San Francisco built places like that, oblivious to building codes, and then forgot about them. Then in the '60s, hippies, freaks, and Deadheads migrated to get away from the city and ended up renting the places or just plain squatting on the land. The A-frame's windows, as well as the door that faced the deserted narrow road, had been boarded up. Still, I found a way to get inside the A-frame. The tiny house had a deck which hung out over the hill. I jumped onto the little sundeck and then opened one of the windows in back, which of course hadn't had boards nailed over it. I used that place for a month or so. I always felt scared walking up that road to the place at night. The whole hill had a vibe that creeped me out. I always felt like somebody might be following me or lurking in the trees, waiting for a victim.

I'm sure the vibe could have been real. Upon release from San Quentin, more than a few murderers, rapists, child molesters, and robbers—as well as dozens of harmless dope fiends—found their way up to the River. Guerneville is only an hour or two, by bus, from the penitentiary. Ex-cons spend their gate money on drugs and try to find chicks they can have sex with. Criminals often attempt to set up shop and stay long term in the area. Most fumble around carelessly and get sent right back up on a parole violation. Some actually manage to stay at large for years.

I knew one guy, Frank, who escaped from a prison in Oregon and lived at the River for around eight years before getting hunted down. According to many accounts, he even robbed a few banks during that time and manufactured crystal meth with impunity before his cover got blown. When a friend warned Frank that some punk had given him up, he took some cops hostage in the back room of the Pink Elephant. Toward the end of the standoff, he released the cops without harming them, but it won him no favor—instead, the sheriffs stormed into the bar and beat him senseless. I heard the story several times from locals. Finally, years later, Frank himself told me his story. After release from his final stint in prison, he returned to the River in order to rejoin his family—a young son. Frank eventually became a friend of mine. He finished his parole.

During that spring, I stayed several weeks indoors at a house full of tweakers. I enjoyed some status in that crowd since the owner of the house, a middle-aged woman from the Midwest, loved to do meth intravenously but couldn't shoot herself up. I'm not really proud of this, but I possessed some skill in that area and quickly became her "nurse." She gave me a room to myself, but it ended badly. I scored a gram of cocaine one afternoon—payment for a delivery to one of the crazy coke freaks I knew—and although coke was not my number one favorite drug at the time, I refused to share it with all the other dopers. My refusal to kick down resulted in my expulsion from the house. I didn't mind. I'd grown weary of puncturing my landlady's veins in exchange for shelter.

Summer of '87 found me "camping out," so to speak—I slept on the ground in my sleeping bag, with a couple of plastic trash bags underneath me to ward off the damp. In spite of my regular midnight showers at campgrounds and the fact that I frequently washed my clothes at the local laundromat, I'd finally lost the battle to conceal my homelessness. A group of self-described local winos approached me and offered me a stake in their daily can and bottle collection. They told me they'd noticed I was all alone. Their leader, a tall, bearded man who looked around forty, informed me they could offer me some protection. Needless to say, this disturbed me. I smiled, thanked them, and told them I didn't need any help. I walked away stiffly. They'd rattled my cage!

I tried to figure out how they knew, because I always made a point of standing tall, with shoulders squared. I tried to walk around as if I had somewhere to go and something to do. Whenever possible, I wore a big smile, and tried to act as if my life was perfect. I did this consciously, for two reasons. One was safety; you never let anybody see you distressed or needing. On the street, that sends a signal out that you're vulnerable, and, like a pack of wolves sensing the weakest or the sick ones in a flock of sheep, the bullies and predators close in. My other reason was visualization; I knew I had to send out a happy wavelength into the ether. I know that sounds terribly "new agey," but I believed in "acting as if," until my hopes materialized. I'd used the same method in Japan, and I'd gotten out of there. I believed it would work again.

But the winos had seen my homelessness. Cold panic shivered through me. *My time is up—next thing I'll be attacked!* I felt I had no escape route. I knew I couldn't go home to my family. I'd called my parents a few times during the past year, telling them my predicament but leaving out the key piece of the puzzle: my drug habit. I always made an appeal for money, but each time my mother'd tell me she wouldn't help me unless I returned to Indiana and got into rehab. At that point I'd sigh, say, "G'bye, Mom," and hang up the phone.

On impulse I decided to hitchhike to Texas. I still had some friends there, and a cousin who might help me. My address book had been stolen long ago, so I wouldn't be able to call anybody. But Austin was a relatively small, friendly city, and I thought if I could get there, I could find my cousin at the hair salon she owned. It seemed like a good idea. I knew it would be risky and that I might not survive the trip, but I convinced myself it was worth the gamble.

On the Fourth of July I stood in the crowds and watched the fireworks displays. I got high and hung out with the dope fiends I knew. I told several of them my plans to hitch to Texas. They all shrugged or murmured, "Cool." They weren't friends of mine—they were merely dope fiends I happened to know.

A guy named Roger overheard me talking to one of these dopers at a connection's place, and introduced himself to me. He explained that he also wanted a way out of the River and that his father lived in Killeen, Texas, near Austin. He told me he'd travel with me—that although he'd lost his car, he had a few bucks saved. Roger seemed clean cut and well spoken. He was young and not bad looking. I was desperate, and I could do worse, I decided. If he turned out to be another Ted Bundy...well, I couldn't let myself think about that. Tunnel vision set in.

Roger and I made plans to leave the following weekend. When the day arrived, Roger told me to meet him down by the River Club, one of the straight bars in Guerneville. I agreed to show up at eight o'clock that night, packed and ready to go. He handed me a semi-precious stone called a tiger's eye. "This stone will watch over you," he said, trying to act all new agey and shaman-esque. I began to harbor doubts about my trip with Roger. But I couldn't see any alternative escape route from the seamy side of life on the River.

At around eight-thirty or nine that night, I walked down to the Safeway with a friend of mine, a drag queen named Diva Marie. His real name was Barry. I knew I was late to meet Roger at the River Club but didn't care. He would simply have to wait.

I'd stashed my backpack and sleeping bag under Diva/Barry's screened-in porch. We intended to shoplift. I declared I absolutely could not think of departing for the Lone Star State without cigarettes. Diva swore she could not live another moment without a fresh pack of Lee Press On Nails. We split up as we entered the store. Hoping to deflect any suspicion, I took a circuitous route, passing through the dog food aisle first. Halfway down, I found myself eye to eye with a friendly, handsome face—a guy with blue eyes, sandy blond hair, and a brilliant smile. He wore a long-sleeved, black Harley-Davidson T-shirt, faded Levis, and black biker boots. I knew I'd seen him before, but couldn't remember when. "Don't I know you from somewhere?" I asked, immediately feeling sheepish for saying something so trite.

Those bright blue eyes registered a flash of recognition. "Yeah! Hey, I remember you! I gave you a ride home back in January. I tried calling you at that number, but they said they don't know you. They got pretty rude after the third or fourth time." He shot me an amused glance. "But anyway, I owe you a commission! That contact you gave me—the gift shop guy? He ordered a lot of T-shirts." He smiled.

"Cool! I'm so glad I could help!" I smiled back at him.

"Hey, are you busy tonight? I mean, I'd like to spend some time with you if it's okay. Would you like to go to dinner with me?"

"Er, yes! But," I lowered my voice to a murmur, "but first I need to finish what I'm doing here. I need a pack of Marlboros, and since I'm a little light on cash right now I'm gonna have to, well...try and steal 'em. Listen, just go on outside and wait for me—I don't want you to be implicated."

"Oh, man." Chris grabbed a bag of dog food off the shelf, turned, and gently took my arm in his. We started walking toward the checkout line. "Oh...C'mon, I'll buy 'em! I can't stand by and let you do something like that! You gotta have standards! If you're going to commit a crime, make it something worthwhile!"

Outside the Safeway store, Barry awaited me. "C'mon, dear," he huffed, glancing sidelong at Chris. "You're going to be late!"

"My plans have changed," I gave Diva Marie/Barry a very meaningful stare. "But we'll talk soon."

"Okay," he sniffed. "Be careful, girlfriend." He turned and waltzed off across the parking lot.

Chris walked me to his new truck, a tan Toyota four-wheel drive. He opened the door for me. He jumped in and began to drive, glancing over at me and smiling his friendly smile. "Where would you like to eat? I'll take you anywhere you want to go."

"Oh, uh, can we make it someplace casual? And how about something outside of this town? Would that be okay?" I asked, suddenly feeling terribly self-conscious. I wanted to tell him that I hadn't really sat at a table in a restaurant in over a year. I wanted to let him know that I felt nervous and scared that local restauranteurs would turn us away once they recognized me as a local street person, one of the River People. I didn't want to ruin this, so I hastily added, "Anywhere will be just fine."

The sun had set by now and the stars started to make their entrances. We drove the pastoral back roads of Sonoma County, talking, for a bit. We talked about everything except personal stuff, which was a great relief to me. Chris smoked a joint. I took a hit to be polite. I hoped he couldn't tell I was mildly high on crystal meth. Like all addicts, I never wanted anyone to know about my habit.

Chris bought me a steak dinner that night. We had coffee and talked some more. As we exited the restaurant, he said, "Now I want to show you where I live. That way, you can find me any time. Okay?"

"Okay."

His house sat on a hillside about a half mile outside of the tiny hamlet of Occidental, nestled among majestic redwoods and fragrant bay trees. One glance around the place told me a lot about Chris. He walked me through the living room, which was a bit cluttered, but with objects I found reassuring: ski equipment, a piano, a tapestry, lots of books. "Alright," he said, "I showed you my place. Now I'll take you home. Hey, you show me your place, will you? I don't want to lose track of you this time!" He laughed.

"Well..." I took a deep breath. "There's a funny thing about my place. Right now all I can call my home is a sleeping bag and a backpack! Today they're stored under a friend's screened-in porch." *There. I've said it.*

He stared at me. "Was it like that when I met you?" I nodded. "Oh man, why didn't you tell me? I would never stand by and let a woman suffer something like that! I live by a code! Listen, I've got an apartment downstairs we can fix up. You can live there, and I'll treat you like a sister!" *Is he my knight in shining armor, riding to the rescue? Guess I need a hero after all.*

I took a breath. I could have told him all I'd been through in the last two years, and how I'd sworn never to get involved in any relationship until I had pulled myself up out of homelessness, but that in this moment, things had changed. But I knew I didn't need to say anything. On some level he understood me—I felt certain of this.

I accepted his offer, but couldn't resist the urge to try and be funny. I looked him in the eye. "Okay, I'll move in downstairs—and thank you! But forget about treatin' me like a sister...or there's gonna be some incest in the family!"

On impulse, I put my arms around his neck and kissed him. He held me in his arms and kissed me back. I felt an electric thrill pulse through me. I'd never in my life been kissed like that. I'd finally come in from the cold.

# CHAPTER 12

# INDOORS

IN ONE NIGHT MY LIFE CHANGED RADICALLY. THE FIRST WEEK was a kind of outlaw honeymoon—a Harleymoon, I guess. Some days we'd jump on the Harley Davidson and roar out into the world. Other days we'd take the pickup truck. I have to admit I loved riding fast on the back of that motorcycle—a fact which surprised me. For years I'd harbored an aversion to biker types and an opinion of bikers as bullies with a hateful attitude toward women. Now I lived with a biker. Or did I? Well, Christopher owned and rode a Harley Davidson. He wore motorcycle boots all the time and a black leather jacket most of the time. I hoped that was the extent of the lifestyle for him. Chris didn't exhibit a hateful attitude toward women. He treated me really well. We went out to a lot of restaurants on the bike. He always opened doors for me.

The night I met Chris, I dreamed my recurrent dream; the one where I was drowning in a river of sewage, trying to hold my daughter up above the rank, poisonous flood. When it came to the part where the man stands at the gate and pulls me and my daughter up to safety, I saw the man's face. It was Christopher. When I woke up, I recognized him as the hero in my premonitory dream. That night was the last time I had the dream. He'd pulled me up above the River.

I still had my beautiful painted shells—the gift Saito had given me in Tokyo. I had carried them in my backpack through all my time of homelessness. I'd slept with them beside me every night. I'd never forgotten what Saito'd told me when he gave them to me—that they'd been blessed by a Zen Buddhist priest, and that they would "...guard over my love life." Now it seemed that the ol' Zen Buddhist mojo had, in fact, accomplished that very thing.

Chris gave me money to shop, so I bought a couple of new pairs of jeans. He bought me new shoes, then his dog immediately chewed up the pair I liked most. But I didn't mind. The dog, named Black Jack Daniels, was a Black Lab/Husky mix. I loved that dog—well, Jack wasn't a dog then, only a puppy. His other dog, Pancho, the one I held on my lap when I first met Chris, died in the spring, of old age. Jack was Pancho's successor. I found it easy to like my new boyfriend. He loved dogs. He played piano. He laughed a lot. He was very laid back—with or without smoking weed. And best of all, he liked me.

During the first few days, we visited Berkeley, where I met his sister, brother-in-law, and niece; then he took me to Monterey to meet his mother. His family was upper middle class—very nice people. What they thought of me is anybody's guess. I hoped they liked me but didn't really expect them to. I thought Christopher might be the rebel of the family, another thing we'd have in common.

It took me over a week to finally muster the courage to talk to Chris about my daughter; how I'd given up custody of Annie when she was three, something that only a few months after doing, I judged to be an unforgivable crime. The tragedy was irrevocable.

I told him how I'd fought for visitation rights and won them when my daughter was six years old. My rights of visitation stipulated that I could spend summers with her in my own residence, provided I could furnish her father with proof that my home was safe and adequate. I was also required to apply for visitation thirty days ahead, the request made in a formal, certified letter. It was now the third week in July, and I knew it would be too late to appeal for a summer visit, but I hoped I could convince her father and grandparents to let me see my daughter before she went back to school.

I expected Chris to hate me after hearing all of this. Instead he listened. Then he said, "When do you want to go? Let's reserve a plane ticket for you." I called my parents for the first time in many months and told them I had a place to stay. I didn't tell them I'd moved in with a man. The way I figured it, they'd never understand or approve anyway. I guess they'd given me up for dead, because they were astonished to hear from me after so long.

My visit to Indiana proved to be less than comforting for my daughter—or my parents. I felt exhausted all the time. I hadn't brought any dope with me. When I saw my daughter I mostly sat there and cried. Her clear, beautiful eyes scrutinized me. The last time I'd seen her was Christmas of '85—more than eighteen months had passed. I tried to explain myself but kept bursting into tears. What a burden I presented!

I felt like an alien, damaged creature. I felt shame, anger, and mortal fear that my ex or his parents would find out I'd been homeless all that time and a dope fiend. I figured if they knew that, then they'd never let me see my child again. I told myself to go back home, work really hard, and get straightened out, so that I'd be able to spend the upcoming summer with my daughter. I don't remember much more of that visit.

I felt relieved to return to California. And to my new boyfriend. Oh yeah—and most of all, to the dope which I used to bury all my emotions so I wouldn't have to deal with life.

Chris picked me up at the airport. He told me he had to go "up north" on business and that he'd be away for about four or five days. I stayed at the house. He gave me plenty of money for expenses, and apologized for leaving me without a vehicle. "It's cool," I said. Unbeknownst to him, I felt elated at the prospect of spending a lot of the money on meth. So far, I'd kept my proclivities secret from him.

As soon as he left, I called a dealer I knew, a chick named Claire, who lived about a mile or two down the road. I hiked down there, scored a sixteenth, hiked back, and started cleaning Chris' house. I worked for days—the place was pretty messy. Paranoia set in as I got pretty tweaked out, and I felt like I was being watched. I started wondering what sort of business trip my boyfriend took, where he'd gone. I kept cleaning and straightening all the while to stay occupied, even ironing all the drapes and sheets and pillowcases. I ran out of stuff to iron and started rifling around in his bedroom closet when a gallon-sized bag of weed dropped off one of the shelves. *Oops!*

I hastily restored the bud to its rightful resting place and exited the room. On the way out I spotted a large cardboard box sitting to the extreme left side of the closet. *Funny, I've never noticed that box before.* I looked in and saw another, bulkier bag of weed. *Uh-oh.*

I walked out of the house and down the road, feeling a mix of thrill and discomfort at the prospect of sharing a residence with a dealer. I liked the idea that he lived outside society's rules. I feared the heat, though, the liabilities. If he got busted, I lived on scene, and I'd become an accessory. *Without getting a cut of the action!*

*Furthermore, if anything goes wrong, anything at all, biker types always blame the women, don't they? And Chris rides a Harley...*Dope dealers, I thought, were generally sexist, but bikers I judged to be extreme misogynists who treated women like livestock. The idea that my new boyfriend might move in both arenas played havoc with my trust. *This will end badly!* I thought about making a run for it—returning to live outdoors once more, out in the woods and in abandoned houses. *But...Chris is a nice guy! He even opens doors for me, when I let him. And he loves dogs! Kids too! He can't be a bad guy if he's nice to kids and dogs!*

I did an about-face and headed back up the hill to Chris's house. My booted feet crunched in the gravel driveway as I made my way toward the three flights of redwood decking which descended the fern-covered hill to the front door. The place felt eerily quiet all of a sudden. *Damn—why did he have to take the dog?* I entered the house; Harley or no Harley, dealing or no dealing, I knew I had to stop running away. Time to stand my ground and learn how to love and be loved.

Chris arrived home later that night. We slipped into a daily routine of Harley rides, rock n' roll, and dope use. By my standards, I was the only one with a dope habit—Chris only smoked weed. And I jealously guarded my secret—I would rather have died than tell him I needed crystal meth to function day to day.

One morning, while riding the Harley to Guerneville for pancakes at the River Inn, I finally came out of the closet with respects to my meth use. I justified it to Chris by explaining that I needed it to clean house, carefully withholding the facts about how dependent I was on the drug. He took the news in stride; even let me know that he could score me some crystal from his partner, a big biker named Jimmy Dean Ritter, aka Firebird. I told him that wouldn't be necessary—I had my own sources. We exited the River Inn and approached his parked motorcycle. "Just don't do too much crank." My new boyfriend muttered these words as he jumped on his Harley and fired it up. As I climbed on behind him, wrapping my arms around his waist, I took great care not to utter a peep in reply.

On the next trip north, Chris brought me along. He didn't tell me the purpose of the excursion, and I didn't ask. I didn't want to know. I used the trip as an opportunity, an excuse, to score some crystal meth. I secretly hoped that Christopher might want to partake of my favorite drug during the long drive. I guess as an addict, I just couldn't help myself—I compulsively promoted my demons.

The breathtakingly scenic route took us through Mendocino County and coastal Humboldt County. I drank in the luscious scenery as we passed through—rolling hills graced with live oaks, towering redwood trees, lonely rugged beaches.

Traveling north on Highway 101, we heard on the radio that the harmonic convergence was happening that weekend. The harmonic convergence is a term used to describe a cosmic event in which all the planets supposedly align themselves with each other. Hippie types really get excited about this, marking the occasion by "converging." Throngs of tie dye, tofu, and tree-sitting aficionados swarm the various new agey hotspots and frenetically commemorate the occasion with whatever Renaissance Festival, wannabe Woodstock spinoff, or Star Trek convention their alfalfa-soaked consciousness can conjure.

I recalled how Chris had mentioned that the village of our destination was a mecca for Deadheads, Rainbow People, and other holdovers from the '60s. Suddenly nervous, I asked, "Shouldn't we call ahead and make a hotel reservation?"

Chris threw back his head and laughed. "Oh, hell no."

"Well, shouldn't we hedge our bets? I mean, if this place we're headed is a hippie town, then they've probably already formed a drum circle in the town square. Tell you the truth, in the past year, I did a whole lot of sleeping in cars, as well as on the ground. I'm pretty much all caught up on camping out—if you know what I mean."

"Marti." Chris turned to look at me. "No problem." He laughed again. I had to love the guy—his attitude, his readiness to laugh. The way things turned out, the Greenpeace and granola bars crowd commandeered the town long before we arrived. Every hotel, motel, B and B, even roadside rest areas, brimmed with New Age humanity—dreadlocked, tofutti'd flower children of all ages, shapes, and colors.

We were on the outs as far as lodgings were concerned. Chris even tried to get us a room in the surrounding towns. No vacancies. He finally called his friends or business associates or whatever they were and arranged for us to stay on their floor. These people, this couple, were cool; they owned a huge expanse of forested acreage on a river.

Whatever the reason for this visit, it took only about thirty-six hours to accomplish. At dusk, we began our drive home. My paranoia decreased a little when I confirmed we weren't carrying anything back with us in the truck. During the return trek, I unsuccessfully attempted to broach the subject of Chris's business. He didn't feel like talking. I backed off and contented myself with petting Blackjack and listening to music— the radio, and Chris' Robert Cray tapes. In order to stay awake and drive all night, Christopher snorted some lines with me on the way home. I didn't realize it at the time but in sharing my speed with him, I awakened the sleeping Crankenstein monster within my boyfriend.

Chris and I began using together. At the beginning I did most of the dope, but in a roundabout way. We'd score, bring the stuff home, divide it up, and get high, but I'd always use mine up first and then I'd ask him for some of his.

Sometimes Chris took me to his partner Jimmy Dean Ritter's place, a ranch house with a big garage, surrounded by acres of pasture land. My first glance at Firebird's domicile revealed a certain degree of meth involvement. Obvious tweakers, biker wannabes, sycophants, hangers-on, and downright stragglers milled, bustled, or crouched in corners around the garage.

Chris would pull into the garage in his pickup truck. Firebird would step out to greet him with a wave, then a cluster of dudes in black T-shirts emblazoned with slogans like "Got Meth?" or sporting red swastikas overlaid with skull and cross bones—definitely speed freak apparel—would swarm around the vehicle and give it the VIP treatment. The meth heads would wax, buff, rotate tires, anything to make a good impression. As a dope fiend, I figured they were motivated by the tantalizing prospect of being rewarded with an extra hit or a front on a bag.

Although my boyfriend appeared to be involved only in marijuana endeavors, I hoped his partner had diversified. Potheads simply do not perform feats of auto detailing to ingratiate themselves with the source of supply, neither do they wear black T-shirts printed with death head motifs, Nazi insignia, or Megadeth tour itineraries. But who knows? They might have been paid employees. Firebird ran a legitimate business restoring vintage cars.

I couldn't figure it out, but I didn't try very hard. I didn't think about it. I avoided going to Firebird's because the atmosphere might make me crave my drug of choice even more—if that were possible. I feared that Chris would discover how serious my habit was and hate me for it. Even more, I feared direct involvement with a dope dealing operation of any kind. I felt convinced that I just couldn't handle the stress or the heat. After escaping Tokyo, I shrank from any thought of losing my freedom again.

One afternoon, I walked out of the bedroom to find Christopher tiptoeing downstairs to the basement apartment, cradling a triple beam scale in his right arm. At that point I decided it was time to communicate. "Look," I said, "I like to put my cards on the table. I mean, I can tell you've got a little something going on in the business arena, and...and well, I've tried not to notice, but I'm not dumb, and I can't play dumb. I like you a lot and I want to stay with you. So let's agree on some ground rules. I don't want to be a part of the business by association. I don't mind knowing that you're a dope dealer, but I don't need any details either. All I need to know is whether we're running a risk of federal, state, or county incarceration. Also, I'd like you to let all your associates know that I'm not involved. I don't want anybody to try to get to you through me, and I don't want to get blamed if a deal goes bad. Okay?" I finished, took a deep breath and looked in his eyes.

Chris shrugged. His face was impassive. "Okay."

# CHAPTER 13

# DOES THIS MEAN THE HARLEYMOON IS OVER?

MONTHS LATER, CHRIS AND I WERE DRIVING IN HIS PICKUP TRUCK down one of the many back roads at the River, on our way to one of our most egregiously white trash crystal connections, when we caught a glimpse of a muscle car in the rearview mirror. The primer gray Camaro approached at a good clip, then, with a flicker of brake lights, zipped in close behind us, almost kissing the truck's bumper. Chris took another glance back and broke into a smile. "Hey—if it isn't ol' Jimmy Dean Ritter!"

My boyfriend swung right and parked on the crumbling shoulder of this ludicrously narrow back road, which hugged the steep slope of a canyon resplendent with redwoods and ferns. A deafening silence permeated the air once the two internal combustion engines ceased chugging and whirring. We were so far out in the boonies, even by Russian River standards, that I knew this supposedly chance meeting could not be coincidental by any stretch of the imagination.

Firebird stepped out of the Camaro and loped toward us. His girlfriend Dina, a willowy Nordic blonde, popped out of the passenger side, adjusted one of the zippers on her leather jacket, and lit a cigarette. Chris and I slid out of the pickup truck and greeted them.

Firebird instantly made it clear that he needed to talk—to Chris (read: no chicks allowed). He and Chris walked up the hill to confer quietly. Dina lit another cigarette. She looked excited, almost breathless. Maybe chain-smoking seemed to her the natural thing to do under the circumstances. "Want one?" Dina chirped, offering a Marlboro.

"Thanks." We smoked in silence until the guys returned. I knew by Dina's attitude that something big was in the mix, but didn't ask any questions. Besides, whatever it was, I didn't want to know too much.

We said our goodbyes and jumped in our respective vehicles. Instead of progressing to our hopelessly trailer-trash crank connection, Chris turned the truck around and headed into the nearest town for a copy of the Santa Rosa newspaper, The Press Democrat. The article jumped out from the front page, describing an amazing incident—a large quantity of marijuana, confiscated from Mendocino County growers, and a bulky load of Thai weed, which was in storage pending an intended sting operation off the coast, had been stolen from police. Authorities estimated the marijuana to have a street value of $500,000.

From what we read in the newspaper, and what we were able to glean from word on the street, we learned that the cops had kept the weed on property which had formerly been a World War II airfield and storage bunker. Ironically, this site happened to be next door to a county criminal detention facility known as The Honor Farm. The bales of weed had been unloaded from trucks and stacked into Quonset huts for the long term. Thing is, this activity aroused the curiosity of certain perceptive inmates, who were currently doing time at the county facility.

According to word on the street, the jailbirds somehow discerned the exact nature of the commodity hefted into those prefab storage units. After being released from custody, having completed their sentences, some of the inmates had returned to claim the treasure trove. Under cover of darkness, they crept across the airfield to the Quonset huts, then, using cutting torches, they breached the sheet metal and absconded with bale after bale of marijuana.

It didn't matter to me that I never knew the identities of those bold few who liberated the weed. I reveled in the idea of such an outrageous, anti-authoritarian statement. Every dope fiend who heard the tale clamored for some of the infamous stolen pot. Word on the street was that the "Bunker Weed" had flooded the market, and the product carried such cachet that it became the dope du jour, perhaps valued even above China White, due to the glamour surrounding its origins.

Over the next several weeks, large packages began to arrive at our house. Big, square bundles, wrapped in thick black plastic. My boyfriend promptly carried them downstairs. I knew these were bales of Bunker Weed, but I never discussed it with Chris, and I never set foot downstairs. I preferred to avoid any open recognition of the facts. I figured the less I actually knew, the better. In the back of my mind, I reserved an escape route, should the worst occur and the cops come raiding the residence. I planned to simply jump off the deck into the underbrush and escape on foot through the dense forest surrounding the neighborhood. Then I'd return to my former homeless state. Not much of a contingency plan, but of course I hadn't really thought it all the way through. I was too busy getting high.

The storm hit us early; that is, the force of the winds and the rain and hail pounding down from the sky are characteristics of weather severity that occur much later in the season. Earlier that evening I didn't notice anything more than the usual late autumn rain. I remember feeling euphoric due to the fact that I was wired on some good speed. Consequently, I'd finally finished cleaning the entire house for the first time in weeks. I gathered together all our laundry, sorted it, and stuffed it into trash bags. Chris was asleep. He didn't like staying wired all the time like I did, so he'd crashed already.

I prepared to carry the four black Hefty bags of dirty clothes up the redwood deck stairs to the truck. I figured that once I stepped outside into the rain, the black plastic would get wet and really slippery. I'd already burned up my flashlight batteries, and since there were no streetlights on our road, I didn't relish the idea of wrestling an unwieldy, slick blob uphill in the pitch dark.

It struck me that I could slip each bag into a large army duffel bag, which I'd recently found in a dumpster. Since it featured handles and a strap to hitch over your shoulder, the duffel would nicely facilitate carrying the laundry-stuffed trash bags. So I slid the first bag of laundry into my duffel carrier, laid it down beside the front door, donned my peacoat, and stepped back into the kitchen to grab my purse. Suddenly I heard a knock at the door. I crossed to the foyer and opened the door to see Firebird Jimmy standing silent on the threshold. "Hey. C'mon in." I motioned him to enter, turned, and walked back inside the house. He followed me. "Chris is asleep but I can wake him up. You want a Pepsi?" I offered that specific type of soda, knowing Firebird favored Pepsi and adamantly eschewed Coke or any other brand of cola.

His reply came as a non sequitur. "Got a Band-Aid?"

"What? Oh yeah, I've got lots of Band-Aids. In fact, I've even got some glow-in-the-dark ones! They're pretty cool...they really do glow—I've tried 'em..." I chattered on nervously, feeling a strange vibe I didn't know what to do with. I have always reflexively dealt with uncomfortable emotional conditions by talking too much. This pattern predated my dope use by decades so it had nothing to do with being a speed freak, although my current meth high no doubt exacerbated my blabbermouthiness.

Firebird stood silent as stone, then ripped through my hedge of babble by putting a booted foot forward and rolling up one leg of his jeans to reveal a huge, bloody, gaping wound below his knee. He said nothing—simply stared at me.

"Oo-ooops! Looks like we're gonna need a bigger Band-Aid! Hey. I'm gonna go wake Chris. Sit down." I ran into the bedroom and woke up Chris. He sat up smiling cheerfully. Chris was always cool. I returned to Firebird. "I guess that hurts pretty bad. Wanna sit down?" Firebird shook his head, remained standing.

Chris stepped into the room, shrugging on his jacket. He turned to his partner. "So what's going on?"

Firebird quickly filled him in, not caring that I heard every word of it. "Remember Stoney? Mechanic, worked on cars at my place? He showed up tonight, late, driving a Chevy Nova. Had three of his buddies with him. Tried to rip us off. He just drove up, jumped out, popped the trunk and said, 'Fill that motherfucker with Bunker Weed! I know you got it!' I laughed at him—until he reached in the Nova and pulled out a shotgun. He cocked it and pulled the trigger. I had my Colt in the back of my pants an' I drew when I saw the shotgun. Couldn't fuckin' believe it when he fell to the ground. I thought it'd be me. I shot him square in the chest—left a big hole for his buddies to stare at. I grabbed Dina and jumped in the truck. For all I know, the cops are on their way here as we speak."

Chris listened, a faint smile crossing his face, as if he relished the challenge. "Then I guess I'd better start getting everything outta the house." He pulled a key from the pocket of his Levis and strode out the front door, leaving me to care for his wounded partner while he hefted the bales out of their hiding place in the crawl space, then hiked up and down the forested hills immediately surrounding our residence, stuffing the bales one at a time into underbrush and clefts in boulders.

Chris pretty much had to feel his way forward through the darkness all the while, due to the insane weather and the fact that we lacked a working flashlight. But Chris performs well under pressure, and between trips to the underbrush that night, he'd pop his head inside the front door, grinning from ear to ear, and give me the thumbs up sign.

I wanted to ask Jimmy how he'd been shot in the leg, but I figured now was not the time. If Stoney'd done it with his shotgun, the leg would've been blown off. I pushed the question to the back of my mind, deeming it unnecessary trivia at this juncture. "Um, Jimmy, where's Dina?"

"She's up in the truck."

"Well, she'd better come inside now. I'll go get her." I walked up the stairs in the downpour and howling wind to fetch Firebird's girlfriend. She sat at the wheel, smoking a cigarette, understandably shaken. Dina talked about going back to their house for her car and some of her things. We figured the best thing to do would be to stash their big Chevy truck on another street, or in the tiny town of Occidental, which lay only a half mile or so from our place. If we left the vehicle parked in our driveway, it'd scream their location—and that of the Bunker Weed—like a lit neon sign over a cheap motel.

We decided to park the truck up a dirt logging trail that wended its way through the forest bordering one side of our narrow street. We rolled up into dense cover, then fought our way back to the house, scraped by wind-tossed tree limbs and pelted with driving rain.

Firebird sat with his leg propped up on a kitchen chair. I'd folded one of my last clean towels under his leg to cushion it, but that wasn't enough. Even though the biker stoically endured, his grimace told me we needed more cushioning. I found an old pillow in the corner and placed it under the towel.

Dina paced restlessly around the house. She'd made it pretty obvious that she wasn't interested in doing first aid on Jimmy. I figured she was in shock or too stressed to function—and who could blame her? Chris hadn't returned. I needed to take charge of the situation. Firebird appeared to be bleeding profusely, the blood soaking through the towel and onto the pillow within minutes. "Look, Jimmy, we...uh, need to do something about that leg. I know this dude, he's a paramedic. I can call him..."

"NO! NO PHONE CALLS!"

"But this friend of mine lives down in Marin County. He hasn't heard from me in a long time. He can't know where I'm calling from, and he won't ask." Finally Firebird assented. I called, and miraculously, my paramedic friend answered. He gave me instructions: how to stanch bleeding by applying pressure with a cloth, how to fashion a tourniquet if necessary, how to treat a gunshot wound. He explained how to assess the severity and nature of the damage. Since I found no bone fragments in the scarlet mush of calf muscle, I learned that Firebird had received a flesh wound. The bullet had burst right through the leg and out the other side. This, I learned, was a good thing.

The paramedic told me we'd need to pack the wound with alum, in order to help the flesh adhere to itself, close the wound, and begin healing. He also informed me that while I packed in the alum, my patient would need either a hefty painkiller or three stalwart men to hold him down. My friend in Marin asked that I not call him back for at least a century. I promised to honor his request, and hung up.

Some problems presented themselves immediately. Only one clean towel had graced my linen closet when Firebird arrived, and it now lay folded under his leg, absorbing blood. All of our sheets and pillowcases were dirty. After all, I'd been poised to trek to the laundromat to wash everything, when the night exploded in my face. I set some water heating on the stovetop, then rummaged in the laundry to find white towels and pillowcases to boil and sterilize. I would need them to clean the wound. I asked Dina to see to that task while I went out to buy alum and get some dope to kill Firebird's pain.

I drove Chris' truck to the good ol' Safeway in Guerneville (open 24 hours) and purchased the alum, hydrogen peroxide, gauze, flashlight batteries, Marlboros, and a six-pack of Pepsi. The storm raged on, which I found reassuring, since it rendered the night darker than usual. And that darkness just might confound the cops in their search for Firebird, the missing shooter. Equally important, the more impenetrable the darkness was, the more chance Chris had of concealing the bales of weed. At least that way, if the cops swooped in, we'd only face charges of harboring a fugitive or some such thing, which is preferable to possession any day.

On the way back from Guerneville I stopped at the home of a twisted tweaker chick named Angie. Angie never slept—her house was overrun with rats from the nearby riverbanks. She sat up all night, every night, with a slingshot, trying to pick the huge rodents off one by one.

My skin crawled at the thought of visiting this madhouse, but I knew the lunatic woman kept a stash of pain pills around her place. She was the ideal person to seek out as a de facto pharmacist. Besides, Firebird's leg couldn't wait while I shopped around the River for opiates in the wee hours of a stormy night.

I'd brought along some weed to trade, since Angie loved marijuana almost as much as she loved methamphetamines. After a bit of haggling and a promise of some additional weed later on, I walked out of Angie's house of horrors with five Demerol, a Vicodin, and a half gram of crystal. The speed, of course, was for myself and Christopher—as well as Dina—to keep us awake, as if the threat of being nabbed with the Bunker Weed wouldn't sufficiently amp our adrenal glands so we could tweak naturally.

To my immense relief, I found our house as I'd left it—dark, still, and blessedly cop-free. I went in there and dosed Firebird with Demerol. He refused to take more than one because, he insisted, he needed to be alert enough to run if the cops came. We waited till the pill took effect, then I fixed the biker's leg. The guy was tough, never flinched, even though the pain obviously ripped right through the Demerol barrier. After the "procedure," as Firebird recovered, I ventured to ask him how he'd been shot like that, in the back of the leg, during the standoff.

"It all happened so fast—kinda like a wild west shootout. He drew the shotgun, I drew my forty-five, and we fired. I looked around afterwards—feelin' a little shaky, I admit—saw myself standing and Stoney lyin' on his back in the driveway with a hole in his chest. I was like, FUCK! I KILLED HIM! And I went to stick my gun back where I had it, in the back of my pants, and it went off. I guess my hands were shakin' so bad I shot myself."

"Oh. Well, you're quick on the draw, anyway."

"I'm a direct descendant of John Wesley Hardin. On my mother's side." Firebird smiled faintly, his voice dropping to a whisper.

"That's good. Outlaw DNA."

He fell asleep—or passed out from the pain. I walked around the house looking for Dina so we could snort a line before she took responsibility for Firebird's aftercare. I spent the rest of the night poised to flee into the forest. Fortunately, the cops never kicked in our door. Chris succeeded in hiding the seven bales of weed. He told me years later that his paranoia escalated to the point where he'd spent hours crouching in the underbrush, watching for cops or potential witnesses/informants.

However, while it was actually happening, he ducked his head inside the house to tell me one bit of trivia only—that he'd needed to empty our laundry out of the army duffel bag. He needed to use the duffel to transport one of the last two bales, strapped over his shoulder, so he could carry the other under his arm and still grope around with the fading flashlight, avoiding blackberry briars and poison oak.

Personally, I don't see how he accomplished the task of getting rid of the stash, but he hiked all the bales away from the house and into the brush and forest off the fire lane and old logging roads in the area, armed with only a racing, adrenaline-accelerated pulse.

In the wan light of dawn, the rain finally stopped falling. Under cover of heavy fog, Firebird and Dina crept from our residence in search of an even more remote hideout. Chris plunged through the forest, reclaiming the scattered bales and returning them to storage in the basement crawlspace. We'd weathered the storm and eluded the cops, so prospects looked good, except for one complication: despite dogged, repetitive search, three of the bales were still out there, whereabouts unknown.

"Hey, uh, Marti..." Chris flashed me his winning smile. "Three of those bales are unaccounted for. I think I dropped 'em down the hillside just off the logging road, but I'm not sure. Listen, I'm really burnt. I gotta crash for a few hours. Can you take a look around and see what you can see?"

I stopped chopping lines and turned to stare at him. "You gotta crash? But we've still got plenty of speed here. I'm gonna get wired and go to the laundromat. If we're not going to jail we definitely need clean clothes and everything. And I gotta wash these bloody towels—and this pillow."

My exhausted boyfriend returned my stare, scrutinizing the wacko, outlaw, Martha Stewart persona I'd slipped into so readily. "You do the dope. I don't want any. It'll only make me more paranoid." With those words, he turned and stumbled off to bed.

I did a hit of dope, rolled a joint, and sprang into action. I loaded the laundry into the truckbed, cranked up the stereo to maximum volume (Psycho Killer, by the Talking Heads) and rolled toward the logging road. I parked, killed the stereo, and rustled through the rain-soaked brush, briars, and branches. My search yielded two of the black plastic-wrapped bales. I hurled these into the truck-bed alongside my laundry, which was wrapped in black Hefty bags. Nevertheless, the third bale, which was encased in the khaki green army duffel, eluded me.

I drove back to the house, unloaded the two bales onto the living room floor, locked the door, and headed for the laundromat. Chris was out cold, so I figured I'd wake him with a payphone call in a few hours. Then he could stash the goods.

During the days following the incident, we got word that Stoney had survived the shootout. Stoney was tough—a mean ex-con, hardened and heavily muscled. After he fell to the ground, his companions loaded him into the car and peeled out of Firebird's driveway. They drove to the hospital, dropped the unconscious Stoney off by the front entrance, and sped away. Hospital personnel attended to him—Stoney needed open heart surgery—and of course they called the cops. Upon identifying Stoney, the cops began a vigil outside the operating room, since the guy was still on parole from the most recent of three manslaughter convictions: Stoney'd kicked a man to death, later stabbed and killed another man, then, not long ago shot another. (This was several years prior to the three strikes law.) The cops must've questioned him aggressively, but Stoney never gave up the name of the dude who shot him, or any other information. He went to prison after recuperating from the heart surgery. Much later we heard he got stabbed to death in prison—word was that it was a hit by a notorious white supremacist prison gang.

Although we searched every day for weeks, we failed to recover that last bale of the Bunker Weed. Tension escalated between Chris and Firebird. Naturally, Jimmy and Dina suspected Chris and me of stealing the bale for ourselves. I even suspected Jimmy and Dina of possible treachery. I knew Chris would never rip anyone off, least of all a friend. Chris trusted me, too, even though I'd worried he wouldn't.

My boyfriend suspected one of the neighbors of stealing the bale, since he'd seen lights on in their house while he crept through the underbrush that fateful night. He became obsessed with the idea and schemed revenge. On a few occasions he'd even plotted a violent home invasion, complete with hostage-taking, in order to wrest a confession from the hapless neighbor folk. Fortunately for all concerned, by the time Chris' drug-addled thought processes reached a crescendo, the meth would wear off, then he'd take a few Xanax to mellow out, and crash. We remained a household of simple drug offenders.

Needless to say, Chris and Firebird lost a lot of money after the shootout. Their business fell apart. Money dwindled, but our meth use skyrocketed. Firebird and Dina had to move out of their big house and stay on the run for awhile. They ended up moving into our basement with their pit bull. During the time they stayed with us, they couldn't resist making incendiary comments like, "Well, if we had that bale to sell…" or, "Maybe you guys oughta sell some of your secret stash so we can score some decent dope…" Even our dogs got in a fight one night. Christopher stepped in to break it up and got a vicious bite on his hand in the process.

I began to make a calculated effort to stay absent from the house as much as possible. I would take to the road on foot, after dark, and roam for hours. I'd walk to Monte Rio, a distance of just under five miles, and from there I'd walk to one of the dope houses I knew of. I could always get a front of some kind, and I did little deals or deliveries to support my needs. Then I'd simply walk around all night, like I used to when I was homeless. I became a de facto street person—I had a place to live, yet I wandered aimlessly around the river, sometimes for days at a stretch, returning home only when the meth failed to keep me awake any longer.

Eventually, Firebird and Dina went their separate ways. She moved in with Jimmy's connection one night and took the dog with her. Firebird got busted on a parole violation and went to prison.

Every few months, I'd hike along the fire lane and the logging road and look for that lost bale of Bunker Weed. Four years later, a few weeks before Christmas, I found it—a large bundle, wrapped in black plastic. A few little scraps of army duffel bag still clung to it or lay on the ground nearby. Electrified, I picked up the moldy blob and hiked back to the house. When I walked in the house to show it to Chris, I found him talking on the phone to Firebird, who'd called collect from prison. Finally, I'd presented all of us with evidence of an honest mistake, instead of a heinous betrayal and rip-off. We were bungling, but loyal.

After four years, the weed was rotten, except for a small amount—maybe a pound or so—in the very heart of the bale, which I hoped might be salvageable. I contacted a renegade acquaintance of mine—a toothless meth cook known as "Billy the Kid." I requested his help in devising a process of drying the moldering weed without destroying the THC content.

The Kid and I shared a friendly business relationship. I'm a good baker, and I'm especially skilled at pastry and pies. I never let my dope habit completely extinguish my homemaking skills. Maybe it was my Catholic upbringing, I don't know. Anyway, for years I'd been making lemon meringue, vanilla cream, and chocolate cream pies, and trading them to the Kid—one pie for a half gram of freshly-cooked meth. Since Billy the Kid lacked the benefit of even a single tooth, he relished the soft, creamy sweetness and tender buttery crusts of the pies I baked. He could scarf them down without the inconvenience of stopping to put in his dentures.

Billy the Kid paid cash for most of the weed. He put it through an attenuated process, soaking it in different cabernets, for instance—remember the Russian River is in the wine country—and drying it under infrared heat lamps. In the end, the vintage product came out tasting, looking, and smelling terrific. I was told it packed a killer buzz. I'll never know. For some reason, I couldn't get in the mood to smoke even one hit of the legendary Bunker Weed. And of course, neither could Chris.

## CHAPTER 14

# MOTEL HELL

BLIND RANDY REACHED IN HIS POCKET AND PULLED OUT ONE of his stoner silks. That's what I called them, anyway. Every time Randy smoked weed, his fingertips hungered for tactile stimuli, and consequently, he packed several squares of lush fabric—satin, velvet, chiffon, or taffeta, on his person. These hunks of finery served as insurance against him reaching out and stroking some chick's garments—or worse, some dude's. Blind Randy was small-ish, a bit chubby, with long dark hippie hair, freckles, and a distinctive Louisiana accent. Randy hailed from New Orleans, and he'd been at the River for over ten years, but the accent clung stubbornly to his speech patterns.

Twenty years earlier, a disastrous car crash had severed Randy's optic nerves, rendering him irreversibly blind, and earning him the street name, "Blind Randy." Although far from innovative, the moniker stuck, and Randy always told me he liked the handle. "It suits meh. Ah'm a blind mothahfuckah. If I was a bad mothah-fuckah, they'd call me, 'Bad Randy.' An' Ah'm not badass, Ah'm smahtass—too fuckin' smaht to let 'em find out how goddam smaht I am. That's why they don't call me, 'Smahtass Randy.' It's my call, cocksuckahs..." Then he'd reach for his bong, draw a deep hit, pull out a swatch of taffeta, and defiantly fondle it between thumb and forefinger.

Blind Randy had one glass eye, which he considered an asset in certain situations. For instance, in line at the Safeway, if the wait seemed interminable to him, he'd pluck his glass eye out and wave it wildly over his head, hollering, "Ah'm a BLIND man!! How LONG y'gonna make me wait? Ah can't read these NATIONAL EN-QUIRAHS to pass the TAHM like evahbody else heah in lahn. Ah'm BOAHED TO DEATH!! Help a blind man out heah!!" And then, miraculously, a new checker would appear and open an additional register, specifically for Randy. Whenever Blind Randy needed to part the Red Sea, so to speak, he'd whip out that glass eye.

Randy'd recently suffered a broken heart and a divorce—in that order, by his account of events. "M'wahf left me for m' business pahtnah. They were sneakin' around behind mah back...puhty damn easy t' do to a blind man. An' they ripped mah ass off in the process—took m' trailah. Now Ah'm on the sofa circuit. Ah gotta have friends or girlfriends, temps, actually, to go with me on dope deals. Ah've still got plenty o'connections, an' business sense, but ah need somebody with 20/20 vision to keep a lookout, look the dope ovah, an' check the face value o' the bills...evahthang m'wahf, or m'goddam pahtnah—that asshole!—used to do."

Tonight, we'd started out the evening smoking weed. This particular strain crept up on us and seemed to sustain Randy from silk to satin to chiffon to taffeta to velvet and back to silk again. A week earlier, I'd agreed to assist Randy—to temp—accompanying him from Occidental to Santa Rosa and providing visual support in a dope deal. My pay would be a percentage of the stash. In the past, I'd been along with Randy on a very large purchase, a major deal, but tonight's endeavor would yield a much smaller windfall. Still, I considered it well worth the effort.

We'd started out hours past sunset—on foot. Randy didn't drive, obviously. My license was suspended, and besides, we didn't have a vehicle. So we'd walked several miles on Hwy. 116, Randy's striped cane tapping frenetically on the asphalt, then thumbed a ride from Monte Rio to Santa Rosa in the back of a pickup truck. Despite the fact we'd bargained with him to take us further, the driver'd insisted on dropping us off in a parking lot on the west side—the wrong side—of the Old Redwood Highway. The journey'd taken hours; it was now past midnight.

I jumped out of the truckbed and extended a hand to Randy, which he stalwartly refused. My plucky blind friend clambered down independently. "Now, Mahti, we got a challenge heah. We'ah gonna have to run across the 101 Freeway to get theah. Othahwise, it'll take too damn long to hitch anothah rahd, and all the dope'll be sold out from undeh us. You up fah this?"

I glanced at the road. We'd need to cross four lanes, two southbound, two northbound, to get across. Since this was a Sunday night, traffic had thinned out enough that it looked...well, possible...by my skewed speedfreak reckoning, at least. In the back of my mind, way, way back, a tiny voice was screaming, *The blind leading the blind! Not good! Nooot gooood!* Sadly, the warning was instantly swallowed up by the clamor of my addictive urges. "Yeah. I'm up for this."

"Good. Okay. Now, we'll join hands—you take m' raht hand, don't let go of me whatevah you do—an' Ah'll handle mah cane, hell, Ah'll drag it if Ah have to. Watch for a gap in the traffic and say, 'Go.' Then run lahk hell! I'll be raht along with ya." Fortunately, few headlights strafed the pavement at that hour, and by the maniacal luck that runs with drunks, addicts, and fools, we made our way across two lanes during a long pause. Breathless, we scurried toward a ragged hole in the chain-link fence that bordered the median of the road. How Blind Randy found that jagged tear in the barricade, I will never know, but somehow he managed it. We crouched on the median's curb, waited for the next gap in traffic, and hurled ourselves across the remaining lanes.

From there, we approached another chain-link barricade, but Randy swept his cane back and forth until he found a yawning slash in the steel mesh. "Theah! The residents keep this cleah with boltcuttahs!" We scrambled through on hands and knees. I glanced furtively to the right and left, Randy listened cautiously, then, emboldened, we struggled to our feet and crept toward the periphery of Motel Hell, a crumbling brick wall shrouded in darkness and crosshatched with graffiti.

"Evah been heah?" Blind Randy's face tilted up toward mine, as if scanning my visage for truth beyond my verbal response to his question. His posture seemed earnest, alert.

"Uhm, no. No, I...I haven't."

"Well, then, stick close to me, and when we go upstaiahs, watch wheah you step! Pahts of the floor've caved in. It's dangerous. This is an abandoned motel, an' the powah's shut off, but some o' the real up-an'-comin' dopefiends around heah have got genaratahs, so they got electricity. The nickel n' dimahs're confined to flashlahts at naht."

"Uh-huh." *What the fuck?*

Randy's voice dropped to a whisper. "Whole fuckin' place was declaihed unfit for habitation an' eviction was undahway, until one of the tweakuhs fell down staiahs an' broke his leg. Then he sued the propehty ownah an' stalled the process. Theah's no runnin' watuh, but they all keep bottled watuh for drinkin' an' portajohnnies in the pahkin' lot. Y'best bet'd be not to get thuhsty. An'anothah thing... uh, pee in the bushes down the block."

I whispered my reply. "Got it." *Man, the things I do for a bag of dope. I really oughta quit this shit. Someday. But not tonight.*

"Othahwise, it's cool. Ah know people heah, an' Ah already put the money in with some othah buyahs. All we gotta do is pick it up, tuhn some of it f' a little cash, an' split. Piece o' cake."

"Okay." *Oh, boy. Fingers crossed...*

"Okay, we'ah gonna skuht the southwest cornah o' the buildin' an' follah the south wall to an exteriah staiahcase, then go to the fuhst doah to the raht. Ah'll knock."

"I'm ready. Let's get in there and get the fuck out!" I shifted impatiently from one foot to the other. "C'mon..." I grabbed his hand and began walking, slightly crouched, adjusting my longer strides to Randy's, moving quickly through the inky, palpable darkness toward the corner, then slipping down the wall toward an exterior staircase—metal stairs painted black, with a twisted railing. I shot a glance up the stairs, noting that the guardrail on the second floor had been partially dismantled. *Maybe somebody's trying to recycle the raw materials for cash...or to set a trap?*

We scuttled to the door Randy'd indicated. He knocked three times with his fist, then tapped a few times with his cane. Somebody jerked the door open an inch or two but kept the deadbolt chain engaged. A voice rasped, "Blind Randy? Izzat you?"

"Yeah," Randy murmured. "It's me. Lemme in."

The door snapped shut; I heard a metallic scraping as the deadbolt chain dropped, then the door swung wide open, revealing a room illuminated by flashlights and Coleman lanterns. *Oops. Guess we're rollin' with the nickel-and-dimers here at the Four Seasons.*

We stepped inside. Our host, a tall, slender, almost handsome guy who looked to be about twenty-three years old, smiled at me and introduced himself. "Hey. I'm Duayne."

"Marti." I nodded, smiled.

Duayne gestured with his right hand, indicating a petite and pretty redhead, sitting on a dingy white loveseat. "Marti, meet Teresa." Teresa smiled shyly and waved her flashlight back and forth.

"All right, Duayne, lemme see the product. Mahti, look heah." Randy cocked his head, paused, extended his right hand to Duayne. "Well, wheah is it?"

Duayne grimaced. "We got burned, man. All of us—everybody who kicked in on the deal. It's Jimbo, y'know, he lives upstairs, he's up there now with his partner, Manny. They fucked everybody around..."

Blind Randy looked incensed. "An' we'ah supposed to lie down f'that? Not this Blind Man, no suh! Blind Randy don't play that way. We gotta go raise some hell. Who else is in with us?"

"Lots of people around here. At least eight or nine of 'em are home right now. B-b-but Jimbo, he's a real badass, and I heard Manny carries nunchucks, so nobody can mess with 'em." Duayne's brow furrowed. He fidgeted with his hands.

"Well, Ah'm from N'Oahleans, and I ain't big or bad, but Ah'm smaht, an' Ah know that a man can pick up a brick, or a rock, or a piece o' pipe, an' theah's gotta be plenty o' that type o' shit aroun' heah, goddam place is fallin' apaht, just hold out a hand and grab a hunk o' this mothafuckin' abandoned, condemned, raggedyass motel and give a yank, and you got a mothafuckin' weapon. Now if we get ouahselves togethah in a group o' concerned mothafuckin' citizens of Motel Hell, an' we stoahm the place, as a MOB, then we can take 'em by foahce!" By the light of Duayne's flashlight, I saw Blind Randy's face grow redder by degrees. He seemed to be talking himself into an aggressive stance—as well as trying to convince Duayne.

"I-I-I don't know..."

"Duayne, don' be a pussy! Y'wahf is watchin'! Cowboy up, mothafuckah, an' defend youahself an' youah investment. Let's go gathah up the rest of the bunch. C'mon."

Duayne squared his shoulders, appearing to summon a few scraps of desperate courage and junkie pride. "Fuck yeah!" He nodded to Teresa. She rose, snatched up an extra flashlight and offered it to me. I thanked her, switched it on, and prepared myself for another lunge into the dank darkness of Motel Hell. Duayne and Teresa took the lead. Blind Randy and I followed. Randy muttered invective under his breath as we proceeded down the length of the south end, then made a left at the corner. Duayne stopped at the first door, knocked, then motioned the rest of us to follow. We entered a room where six disgruntled dope fiends huddled around a Coleman stove, watching water come to a boil.

When meth heads are reduced to drinking instant coffee from a camp stove in order to stay awake—as these were—they're generally volatile, and easily manipulated. It didn't take Blind Randy long to whip them into a dope-starved frenzy. Once the sparks of Randy's vociferous tirade began to fly, the gasoline of the tweakers' desperation exploded into blind ferocity and naked bloodlust. One of the six, a sinewy, wild-eyed junkie, sprang to his feet, volunteered to carry the torch to the rest of the rip-off victims, then bounded out the door. Within minutes, the scrappy, motley residents of Motel Hell's ground floor rallied to the clarion call of outraged retribution. Our angry mob now numbered a dozen strong.

Harve, a rabid junkie with a haunted aura, two gold teeth, and a surprisingly muscular frame, stepped up and insisted on leading the charge. The rest fell in behind him, clamoring, itching, lusting—for reprisal, cash, dope, or all three. Snarling, Harve flung himself out the door, around the corner, down the south wall and back to the black-painted-metal, twisted-banistered, exterior staircase. Eleven more of us pounded down the concrete not far behind, then stampeded up the shuddering stairway after Harve.

Blind Randy and I ran in the midst of the hoi polloi. Somehow, throughout the chaos Randy kept his cane clutched tightly under his left arm. *Amazing.* When we reached the destination, a room at the top of the stairs on the second floor, Harve, Duayne, and three other dopers began smashing their fists repeatedly on the door and shouting stuff like, "Open the goddam door, Jimbo!" and, "We know you're in there! Open up or we'll break the fuckin' door down!"

The door opened, spilling light—apparently Jimbo's domicile boasted a generator and actual electricity—and revealing a heavily-muscled dude in a wife-beater T-shirt, jeans, and combat boots. "Hi," he smirked. I figured this must be Jimbo. His hair was jet-black, short, and slicked back. His eyes appeared to be jet-black as well, but that was likely the meth high—his eyes were no doubt so dilated that the iris had temporarily disappeared.

Directly behind Jimbo's left shoulder stood a second guy that I took to be his homeboy Manny. Manny wore camo pants and a brown leather jacket. He sneered in our direction. Collectively, we stood our ground, unsure what to do next. Suddenly, some tweaker in the back of our dozen growled, "Motherfucker!" and then pushed forward, hard, and we all began to lunge through the doorway.

"What the hell!" Jimbo's smirk evaporated, he jerked backward, then managed to regain his composure and snorted, "Okay, then, c'mon in, losers!" His eyes widened when he caught his first glimpse of the crude weapons brandished by Harve, Duayne, and the rest of us. Jimbo and Manny seemed somewhat intimidated, a touch off balance. *Good...Bullies caught off-guard.* Contrary to what Duayne had said earlier, Manny's hands were empty—no nunchucks in his fists.

"Oookay." Jimbo laughed softly, turned, sauntered to a battered and duct-taped, caramel-colored, vinyl Lazy-boy recliner, and slowly took a seat. Manny walked to one side of the room, remained standing. "You ain't gettin' your money back, fuckers. So go on home," Jimbo barked. Abruptly, he turned and snapped, "Bitch, get me a beer! Now, goddam it!"

From a corner of the room, out of the shadows, a cowed, dark-haired woman scurried to a refrigerator that stood within reach of Jimbo's recliner. *He could've easily grabbed that beer himself. Dickhead!* Meekly, wordlessly, the timorous woman opened the fridge door, reached for a can of Budweiser, popped the top and offered it up to Jimbo, eyes downcast. Jimbo frowned, snatched the beverage out of her trembling hand, glaring, then backhanded her. She staggered back a few steps. "TOO SLOW, BITCH," Jimbo shouted, "FASTER, NEXT TIME! Y'HEAR ME?" The timid woman nodded, then retreated.

Harve and the rest of the Motel Hellions charged forward a few more steps, holding their bricks and chunks of pipe high in the air. They stopped a few paces from Jimbo's Naugahyde throne, seemingly unsure of what action to take. Suddenly and unexpectedly, the vibe in the room seemed to stir, as if the wind had changed. I felt a tug on my sleeve, looked askance at Blind Randy, and noticed he'd flattened himself up against the wall. He appeared to be paralyzed with terror. "Mahti," Randy whispered urgently, "Heah comes Robinnn!"

Of course I had no idea what he was talking about. I heard scrambling footsteps, saw dope fiends scatter like dried leaves in a brisk autumn wind, apprehension plastered across their faces, dread in their eyes. A fit, powerful man strolled into the room, panicked silence in his wake. I concluded that this macho dude was Robin. The guy looked Native American—he'd pulled his long, thick hair back in a ponytail, and wore a half-smile that looked almost playful. Gracefully, he moved to the refrigerator, opened it, and started rummaging around inside. He selected a can of Pepsi, popped open the top, took a sip, closed the door and stood, leaning languidly against the fridge as he idly watched the goings-on in Jimbo's little fiefdom.

The junkie vanguard, the forefront of our little mob, boiled with enough indignation and fury not to waver and break when Robin arrived. Harve spoke up. "Goddam it Jimbo, we want our dope—or our money! Right fucking now! And we're not leaving!" We were like the angry mob of villagers outside Frankenstein's castle, except instead of torches, we'd come with flashlights. I scanned the troops and wondered what damage any or all of us could do against Jimbo by himself, let alone backed by Manny and Robin. *I think I'd better go home now and get some sleep. This isn't gonna be pretty, and all I've got is a plastic flashlight, a chunk of brick, and skittish reflexes...*

Jimbo grunted and chugged his beer. He crumpled the can in his fist and dropped it on the floor. Then he jerked his head around and screamed, "BIIITCH! BEEER!!!" The frightened woman crept toward the refrigerator. Like clockwork, the domestic violence began to unfold a second time. I winced, repressed a shudder. At that moment, Robin set down his Pepsi, slid behind Jimbo's recliner, and in a move quick as a rattlesnake striking, he pushed a hand down onto one side of the bully's neck. It happened so fast I couldn't make out exactly where he applied the pressure, but instantly Jimbo's entire body went slack, and now the former Mr. McBadass showed signs of extreme duress. His eyes bulged, his face turned scarlet, and a big vein popped out on his forehead with the obvious effort he was making, but try as he might, Jimbo simply could not move! *Amazing!*

Robin chuckled and looked down at Jimbo in amusement. "Okay. NOW do you feel badass? Huh? Y'feel like a man, do ya? Big man, smackin' the women around?"

Jimbo started to say something, but the words seemed to catch in his throat. He hung his head. "N-No."

"No." Robin turned toward Manny. "How 'bout your homeboy over there? He backin' you now?" He jerked his chin at Manny. Jimbo's right hand man, sneer vanished, now merely hung his head and shuffled his feet. Robin exhaled for emphasis. "Hm. Guess not." He turned to the woman, who'd frozen in her tracks moments before. "Y'know...what I did to your old man here is gonna last about a half hour or so. Why not step on up and take a crack at him? Seems like it's payback time to me!" He laughed softly and beckoned. She refused—backed away from Robin to hide in the corner again.

"I'll do it," I mumbled. *What is the matter with me? I should be blending in with the background...*I cleared my throat. "Er, sir, I...I will. Hit him, I mean." I boldly stepped forward, thought I heard Blind Randy whimpering softly.

Robin looked at me. The Motel Hellion mob parted. He broke into a grin. "A warrior spirit. I like that." He threw back his head and laughed.

I felt a little embarrassed. "Mister, uh, sir. We came here to get our money back, see. Um..."

Robin continued to grin. "Yeah, you too? Well, I think we're all here on the same business, then—collections!" He stepped around Jimbo and motioned for Manny, who quickly shuffled over. "Get in your pal's pockets and pull out everything he's got. Hand it all over to me."

Manny dropped to a crouch, shamefaced, and began rooting around in Jimbo's pants pockets. Jimbo's face was now purple with impotent rage. After some effort, Manny's forced search produced a nice yield of cash, crystal, and coke. Robin counted out the bills, pocketed a portion, and distributed the remainder of money and dope among our angry mob of methheads.

After that, Robin gave me a ride home. Randy opted to stay at Motel Hell—for fear of Robin, I supposed. When we got to Occidental, I invited Robin into the house. "I think you'd like to meet my boyfriend," I said, "He's cool."

When I introduced Robin to Chris, they got along really well. He hung out at our house for a while, and told us he was a Pomo Indian who'd trained as a Navy Seal, but had gone AWOL and done some time. The move he did on Jimbo the bully was something he'd picked up in the military.

Later, we heard all kinds of scary stories about Robin—how he did collections for big dope dealers, sometimes seriously fucking people up, like pushing guys out of cars going about sixty miles an hour—but he never did any of those things at our house. He always treated Chris and me with respect. No matter what deeds he did or did not commit in life, he clearly embodied a sort of twisted chivalry, like a knight in tarnished armor on that crazy night at Motel Hell.

# CHAPTER 15

# NEBRASKA

PLEASE LET ME BLAME THIS ON THE EARTHQUAKE! I NEVER, ever, had even the least, miniscule desire to visit the state of Nebraska, even to drive across it. But then the Loma Prieta earthquake rocked the San Francisco Bay area in 1989. That quake was really big—magnitude 7.1—hell, it took out the Bay Bridge and Candlestick Park, royally fucking up the World Series for us, among other things.

When the temblor hit, I was home alone. Lucky for me our house lay north of the city by an hour or so. Chris and I were still a couple, but we'd been having a lot of arguments about the lost bunker weed, etc. At the time, our general plan for domestic harmony was to avoid each other whenever possible. Chris was in Santa Rosa that day. The only reason I'd returned to the house was that I'd been on a big drug run, which forced me to finally shut down after about four days of sleepless methamphetamine-induced madness.

So anyway, I was snuggled up on the sofa, and our dog, Black Jack Daniels, was lying on the rug in the middle of the living room, napping. I'd looked all over the house for a book I hadn't read—I always liked to read when I crashed—and the only thing I came up with was this book about Edgar Cayce, the medium from the thirties or whenever, who would go into trances and all that stuff.

Honestly, I have no idea how the book got into our house. I'm no hippie spiritualistic idiot. I'm not a big fan of Edgar Cayce and I tend not to believe in séances and crap like that, but I was reading, no, more like skimming the paperback anyway, and in this one chapter he's supposed to be channeling some dead guy from the "Lost Continent" who's talking about how cool Atlantis was and how they had nukes and lasers and shit, and how sexually decadent yet highbrow the Atlanteans tended to be. Blah, blah, blah...and I'm reading this flamboyant psychic baloney about how the Earth God of Atlantis roared in anger right before the cataclysm or some shit, and all of a sudden I hear this outrageously loud roar.

Really! It sounded like some angry Earth God. Unbelievable, I figured, that I could imagine such crap to be real. Better lay off the drugs for awhile, I told myself. But then I realized the sofa was rocking, and I looked around and saw all the furniture shaking. Suddenly I realized I was experiencing my first earthquake. Black Jack instantly ran out of the house, and I followed suit. We stood there in the yard looking at each other in wonder for a minute or so, even after the whole thing had stopped. There we were, survivors, just me and the hound.

And the Earth God/destruction of Atlantis shit had me rattled. I took that Edgar Cayce book and threw it in the trash. I was spooked. But of course, I tended to be high and susceptible to paranoia most of the time, okay? But I know I heard that deep growling sound.

The power went out when the earthquake hit, but it came back after a few minutes, so I switched on the radio and tuned to my favorite Santa Rosa station, where I heard the DJ saying San Francisco'd been hit hard but Santa Rosa suffered no damage. When I heard that, I knew Christopher was okay, but I figured I had no reason to hang around and wait for him to come home. I felt charged up, restless.

This natural disaster energized me. I sprang into action. I wanted to get down to San Francisco as soon as possible and check up on some friends of mine who lived there. Well, I called them friends, but mainly they were my best connection for narcotics—so it was even more crucial for me to look after their well-being! Okay, back then I maintained a serious level of dope intake, and my life was still all fucked up. I welcomed a chance to blend into the background where an entire city was fucked up, get it?

This connection...well, it was a guy named Andy and his girl-friend, City Baby. City Baby had a purple mohawk and a leopard-print-tattooed scalp. Besides being crazy in the un-fun sense of the word, City Baby insisted on wearing her six-foot pet Burmese python as a fashion accessory. Andy kept a lower profile, since he had the bag. Andy wore suits and looked like a financial advisor or a bank VP.

Oh, and their inventory! The product they carried was par excellence—a doper's dream. I telephoned their house but got no answer, since the quake took out all the phone lines in the city. My next move, I decided, was to travel to San Francisco and search for them. This presented a bit of a problem, since my driver's license was suspended.

Hey, I'd like to take a moment here to describe some of my driving history. In early 1984, I'd been on the road, doing standup at a comedy club in Oklahoma City, and on the way out of town, I stopped at a punk rock bar near the University of Oklahoma. An audaciously loud band from Texas was playing; I think their name was something like "Tex and the Horseheads," but don't hold me to that, since I was so wasted that night I barely knew my own name.

So, I started drinking B-52s, which I think they now call mud-slides. They tasted like candy and went down smooth! And speaking of candy, the eye candy in the place was stunning. The college boys in Oklahoma are almost as cute as the ones in Texas, and that's saying a lot.

Okay, I'm not very proud of this, but I picked up this hot soccer player—an exchange student from Brazil. I knew of a party at a certain friend's in OKC, so I invited him to come along. He asked if I knew where to get some weed, and I said of course I did, there'd be plenty at the party. I got in my car and he slid into the front seat next to me.

As I headed in the general direction of the interstate on surface streets, he leaned in close and offered me a generous hit of cocaine, contained in one of those little translucent pieces of paper that people used to snort off of. After I sniffed mine, he did a hit, then passed me another. I'd barely taken time to notice that this guy only spoke a little English, and my Portuguese is nada por nunca for sure. But we didn't need to talk. We understood each other perfectly—we were out to paaar-tay!

Unfortunately, with the alcohol from the punk club, I'd been smashed, and now the coke in my system pepped me up and filled me with the ferocity of a berserker. I threw all caution to the winds and accelerated onto the freeway. Somehow I got mixed up and entered the exit ramp of Highway 40—a big mistake. Flashing lights zoomed in behind us, and in seconds a police officer in a crisply pressed uniform stood by my window. He said, "Ma'am, I believe you've been drinking."

Now earlier, in a dark corner of the bar, the soccer player had been sitting beside me, knocking back shots of tequila, and I'd been dipping my nipples in salt—you know, sort of a body shot thing. He'd become a bit too excited by this and accidentally bitten one of my nipples. And you know how it is when salt gets in a wound? So I was irritable when the trooper pulled me over.

Now, even though the nice peace officer had spoken to me quite politely, I got all indignant. "I've had a few...cordials, a few liqueurs after dinner, that's all! Don't you have any real criminals in this town? Why do you insist on picking on decent, law-abiding citizens?" I never got drunk without getting ignorant. I forgot all about my passenger and the coke.

"All right, I'm gonna have to impound your car, ma'am," said the law enforcement officer, "I'm taking you in for a breath test." Then he walked around to the passenger side of my vehicle and scowled at the trembling Brazilian exchange student. For an awful moment I thought the cop intended to search him, but instead he told him, "Get lost."

My cocaine-toting party pal didn't hesitate a nanosecond. He threw open the passenger door and bounded off into the night, letting out a ululating scream and a string of Brazilian words which I'm sure were a mix of expletives and prayers of thanks. And I never even got his name...

The cops charged me with a DUI that night. However, my friend Michael, the host of the party I'd attempted to get to, knew some cops and a corrupt lawyer in Oklahoma City. With good ol' Mikey's help I lucked out—no conviction!

But in California I had the stupidity to let my license expire. I guess when constantly high out of one's skull, one is simply too busy to think about DMV-related renewals! Then, in another genius move, I got stopped with a little weed, driving on an expired, and for that and some other stupid antics, the State of California suspended my driving privileges.

Okay, so now you know full well how highly qualified a driver I was at the time. I tried to borrow a vehicle from each and every person I knew who possessed one, but my repeated appeals fell on deaf ears. After I accepted the reality that no one was fucked up enough to lend me a car, I launched a campaign to hitch a ride into the city with somebody—anybody I could coerce. I toured all the dope houses, extolling the praises of the fine quality drugs available at Andy and City Baby's place, if only we could get to San Francisco.

At long last I found someone who was dope-hungry enough, and stupid enough, to agree to drive toward the epicenter of the Loma Prieta earthquake. His name was Panhead Bob. Well, I doubt that any mother would actually christen her son Panhead Bob, but that's what he insisted on being known as. You see, he was extremely proud of the fact that at one time in his life he had owned a rebuilt Harley-Davidson panhead, and although no one in town had ever witnessed him operating or owning a motorcycle of any kind, the moniker stuck.

Panhead Bob was fond of strutting around sporting the leather jacket, hardware and other accouterments associated with badass bike gang members, and he probably had himself fooled. Sadly though, among the junkies, dope-fiends, and petty thieves he hung out with, Panhead Bob was referred to as Bedpanhead Bob. No one feared him. On many occasions, as he stomped by in his black motorcycle boots, children snickered behind his back.

Panhead Bob drove a big, rusted-out, late-sixties Chrysler Imperial with bald tires and one side of the back bumper held on with baling wire. But, miraculously, he carried proof of insurance and a legal registration. Bingo!

As the catastrophic events unfolded in San Francisco, city authorities closed Highway 101 at the Golden Gate Bridge; and, of course, the Bay Bridge had partially collapsed. Parts of the city were in flames. I told Panhead Bob we'd have to bide our time, but that it would be worth it. I even scored him some codeines on a front, to help him relax for a few days.

Finally the day arrived when cars would be admitted into the city. The codeines, however, had sapped Panhead Bob's will to travel. He hemmed and hawed until I promised him that the first place we'd visit would be the North Beach. That's where all the porn theaters and stripper bars are. Panhead Bob stated flatly that he yearned to see a XXX film in the Mitchell Brothers' tradition...and even more ominously, he hinted that he'd like me to watch it with him. "Sure, sure...oh, yeah Bob," I lied, "Of course we'll check it all out together..."

The old Chrysler limped along through the chaos and traffic snarls along 101, and we didn't make it across the bridge until dusk. By the time we threaded our way into the North Beach, darkness had descended. One thing we had going for us—parking was no problem! That's the only time I've ever driven into San Francisco and instantly found parking spaces to spare.

Panhead Bob giggled to himself as he swung the big old Imperial next to the curb. "I got us a spot right direck'ly in front of my favorite porn place! Damn, and it's open!" Panhead jumped out and sauntered toward the hucksters who stood outside, luring tourists and full-time perverts alike into the show. I had no difficulty giving Bedpanhead the slip. In his codeine-swaddled haze, his slack jaw agape, eyes as big as saucers, he never looked back as he entered.

Shivering, I marched quickly down the battered streets, my hands in the pockets of my jacket. San Francisco nights are positively frigid. I needed to get all the way over to Natoma Street, which is a pretty good hike from the North Beach; it's kind of Bryant-Street-Jail-adjacent. Sadly, this was a time in my life when jails presented not only the threat of incarceration, but also served as landmarks and points of origin when getting my bearings.

As I made my escape from Panhead Bob, I looked down at the ground, a reflex I'd developed over my time as an addict. I kept an eye out for money or bags of dope on the ground. You'd be surprised how many 20 or even 50 dollar bills people accidentally drop on the street.

That night I never saw any money on the pavement. What did I see? Tarot cards. Spilled all over the street, sidewalks, and gutters for two or three city blocks! The scene looked as if some fortune-teller's deck, poised to predict the earthquake, exploded as the fulfillment overtook the prophecy. Or maybe, post-disaster, hoards of hippies, Trekkies, and UFO freaks had run out into the highways and byways, trying to read the Tarot or throw the I-Ching to find explanations or figure out the next move.

I stepped over the "Fool," the "Tower," then the "Nine of Swords" from a tarot deck, then picked up one card, some sort of Chinese tarot or other. Written on the face side, like a fraction, were some Chinese characters, captioned with the translation "crisis/opportunity."

Oddly, after the Tarot cards thinned out I saw regular playing cards all over the ground, as if psychic phenomena had rolled over for poker and gin rummy; or as though some street magician had been standing on a corner, a knot of curious tourists huddled close around him, saying, "Pick a card, any card," to one of the marks, when suddenly the whole world erupted, rocked violently, and fucked up his act for good.

I made my way across town, smoking Marlboros like a fiend, occasionally encountering other nicotine or dope fiends who bummed cigarettes from me. As I neared Andy and City Baby's apartment I saw other speed freaks. I knew them by their hasty gait and furtive glances to the right, left, and behind as they turned down Natoma Street, which is more a narrow alley than a thoroughfare. On the last block before my connection's, every single streetlight had gone all blinky, creating an eery yet cartoonish atmosphere.

A long line of desperate drug seekers stretched out from Andy and City's front door. Most of them appeared to be very down-and-out, because they pushed shopping carts full of broken electronic equipment. I figured they'd brought this shit to trade for a hit or something—very pathetic, but it happens.

One guy in line told me he'd filled up his cart at an electronics store on Market Street that had collapsed in the quake. He looked annoyed and jerked his thumb at the other dopers down the line. "Most of these other assholes got their shit at the same place as me. But I got the best components." He then gestured proudly at the crushed and mangled chunks of stereos and VCRs in his load. I nodded uneasily, stepping back from him. This freak had to be very, very thoroughly impaired, by psychosis or controlled substances, to see that metallic rubble as merchandise.

Just then the front door opened a few inches, and light shot down the line of hopefuls. Dan, an unemployed ironworker who acted as security for Andy, glared out at the first applicant. "I told you!" Dan sounded irate, "Andy don't want no more of this shit! He helps one motherfucker, out of the GOODNESS of 'is HEART, and now the word gets around an' all of you fucks show up here! Well you got nothin' comin', not unless you got CASH!" Dan jerked the door inward now, apparently trying to restrain himself from slamming it on the poor wretch's fingers. The desperate junkie at the front of the line had lunged forward, grabbed the door and now clung to it, body and soul, mewling pitifully.

"Wait! Dan," I called out from my place near the back, "I've got cash. Hey, Dan, it's Marti! Tell Andy it's Texas Marti and I've got cash!" As I spoke I walked very quickly up to the door, hands in pockets, thankful I kept my money in my sock. After all, I'd admitted I had cash in a line of wreckage merchants! The cashless ones gazed at me hungrily, slinking toward me with larceny in their eyes.

I stood my ground and waited. And thank all of the angels that watch over fools like me, Andy heard my voice and shouted to Dan almost instantly, "Hey, D, let 'er in!" At this, the doorman grabbed one of my arms and pulled me up the front steps. I leapt two-legged over the threshold, as if completing a series of high hurdles. The disgruntled dope fiends behind me shuffled forward in unison, pressing toward the door, and I heard them moaning softly.

Just as the door snicked shut, I looked over my shoulder at the unfortunate souls left out in the alley. As I glanced back I saw a scene reminiscent of a live, off-off-off, way off-Broadway rendition of the cult horror classic, "Night of the Living Dead," with those flickery, blinky streetlights as special effects. Eeeooooh...to this day, I think of that sight and shudder, then defensively laugh.

Once I'd gained access to the inside of the house, I could relax. "Hey, thanks for lettin' me in, Andy." Then I grinned at his girl-friend, "Hey, City Baby, where's your snake?"

City pouted. "Sabbatha? She's heavily traumatized by the earth-quake, I'm pretty sure. Slithery bitch still won't come out from under the bed. And fuck you for asking, Marti."

Andy motioned to me. "Don't mind City. She's in one of her moods. Come on in and sit down. What do you need?" I flopped into a sagging red armchair. Andy sat on one arm of the couch.

I got right to the point, grabbing my money from my sock and proffering it. "I need as much speed as I can get for two hundred bucks." Andy took notice now.

"Hey, why don't you put that in with me on my next buy? I can give you a few bags now to hold you till it gets here, and wholesale rates overall." I agreed to this and handed over my cash, leaving myself about eight bucks and change for cigarettes. Andy told me to make myself comfortable until the shipment got in. I'd arrived just in time. Another guy, Dave, was preparing to head out for the East Bay, to Concord, where the very best crystal meth could be found. Of course since the Bay Bridge was down, the journey would be time-consuming, but no problem. I could wait.

Andy jumped up and paced into his private "office" area. I stayed in the waiting room, anticipating the next hit of dope, which I knew would be soon. In minutes, my connect returned and slipped two quarter grams into my hand. I went into the bathroom and did up one of the bags. The stuff always caused a rush and tasted great, although the nose burn tended to be intense.

Now I was wired to the tits and had nowhere to go. Although I felt like going everywhere and doing everything on this high,

I dreaded returning to the street, the outer darkness, where the zombies moaned and shuffled. So I sat there in the dilapidated red armchair, antsy and twitching, drumming my fingers on my knees. Time passed and the night wore on as I waited for Dave to return with the shipment. I stayed amused by listening to music and talking to the other "investors" who accumulated in the waiting area.

Within a few hours, the old couch groaned and creaked under the weight of six very different addicts. Andy carried a greatly diverse line of products, and catered to an equally wide variety of customers. Matt, an unemployed electrician who reeked of marijuana, shared the sofa cushions with a very hyper transsexual, a pilled-up, high-on-X, drag queen, and three garage band musicians who were so high on china white that they never stopped scratching. One of the musicians slumped to the left, and as he did he wobbled and drooled onto the drag queen's fishnet stockings.

Shantelle—that was the drag queen's name. She referred to herself in the third person, which I found a little annoying at first. Drag queens, though flamboyant, are never demure, so when the rocker's drool hit her fishnets, she backhanded him up the side of his head. "Okay, Mr. Keith FUCKING Richards," she hissed, "Miss Shantelle only gives ONE warning..." She immediately punctuated the word "warning," by landing a vicious elbow jab into the troubadour's spleen, "...and then Miss Shantelle goes BUTCH! You hear?" The poor guy inhaled once, very sharply, then slid forward, his upper body folded in half, one side of his face scraping the floor. He coughed, then went limp, a real accomplishment for somebody already floppy on heroin.

Shantelle seemed satisfied with herself, and she threw a blazing stare around the room, forcing each and every one of us to meet her heavily mascara-ed gaze. "Any other questions Miss Shantelle can answer? Anyone?" She purred, tossing her feather boa over one shoulder and adjusting a spaghetti strap on her dress. We answered her question with a collective, meek silence. Nobody wanted to see Shantelle "go butch."

As the hours of waiting ticked on, everybody relaxed a bit. The musician recovered and very gingerly sat upright, seeming to have no recollection of the hit he'd taken from Shantelle. In spite of our differences in drug preference, the seven of us actually bonded emotionally—well, sort of. Strangely, not one of us mentioned the earthquake. I guess we were all so wrapped up in the dope thing that we didn't consider it worthy of discussion.

About an hour or so before dawn, there we still sat, bored to death but not wanting to give up on the promised drug shipment, when a guy walked in, introduced himself as "John," and asked if anybody wanted to drive to Nebraska. Immediately we all burst out laughing. Hell, we hooted in derision! He exited amid our jeers.

And so we hung out till everybody ran low on cigarettes. That's when Carmen, the transgender dope addict, offered to walk down to the corner and get more. I felt like walking, so I went along. By now, the sun had risen and scattered most of the zombies, but a few circled tenaciously around the front door, hoping to score. Smoke still billowed from parts of the skyline, and I saw repair crews working on ruptured water lines. Fortunately, Andy and City's water and electricity still flowed. Carmen and I made the trip to the little corner store without being accosted, and I made sure to stockpile my supply of Marlboros for the long haul—the dope might not arrive till after sunset, and the last thing I wanted to do was brave another "Night of the Living Dead" line!

Good thing I stocked up on nicotine, because all day I continued to wait with the others. We all had a bit of stash to tide us over, including me, and I did some more crystal to make up for having sat awake all night and half the day. Around two p.m., that guy John came back through to make another pitch. He said he really needed a driver, somebody to travel to Lincoln, Nebraska with him. When Matt, the unemployed pothead electrician, asked John the purpose of the journey, he said he planned to sell LSD to eager Nebraskans.

"Hey, I know people there, man! They pay ten dollars a hit there…acid's really in demand in Lincoln!" John sounded almost defiant. He told us the job paid cash and drug of choice. I considered the offer, just for a moment, and almost asked John what kind of vehicle we'd be driving and how much acid was involved, then abruptly righted my thinking. Everything in Nebraska would have to suck! I hardly felt tempted…not at that point, at least. My judgment hadn't rattled off its pinions yet.

Unfortunately, I'd underestimated the dope I'd partaken of. This shit had power and intensity. This crystal possessed an almost psychedelic quality, one I'd seldom experienced on methamphetamine. By the time John came back again, at around eight p.m., I was flying! I needed a purpose, I rationalized, something to do. I felt compelled to action, to help the team, the team being all of us—dope fiends everywhere—even in Nebraska! Thoughts like this entered my head, and I had no inclination to screen them, my cerebral tissue having lost its insanity detection system. My judgment and critical thinking abilities had closed up shop. The crystal meth acted like a lead foot on the accelerator of my brain, revving the engine till my reason threw a rod.

*I gotta get outta this house and keep occupied, and why not make some money at it? After all, this guy John is a business associate of Andy's, this is part of an overall operation…I'll actually be helping Andy if I do this job! By the time I drive to Nebraska and back, I'll have extra cash, and the dope shipment will have arrived here! Perfect plan—and besides, didn't Bruce Springsteen make a song called,*

*"Nebraska"? Yes, that's right, there's a Springsteen album with that title...hey, if the state of Nebraska can inspire a rock star enough to name a recording after it, it can't be all bad...* On and on my thoughts raced, providing me with plenty of dope-psychotic rationalizations for doing this thing.

John swore to himself and prepared to leave again, having been rebuffed one more time by the group of us. Then I jumped up suddenly. "Hey!" I called out, "Hey, John, gimme a percentage of the total profits on the acid, payable when we move it. And I want payment in cash for driving. And you've gotta have plenty of dope to keep me going."

"Sure. We can work that out," my soon-to-be traveling partner assured me. "No problem with the dope, I've just copped. We got plenty of stash! Cash is a little thin on this end of the drive, though. You gotta accept partial pay till I sell some of the shipment. Wha'd you say your name was?"

And so I left the apartment without getting a chance to say good-bye to Andy and City Baby, but I managed to leave word with Dan, the doorman. I told him to tell Andy I'd be back in a few days with more money. "And tell Andy not to worry, the Nebraska thing is taken care of." Dan stared at me quizzically for a moment, then shrugged.

"Okay," Dan told me, "I'll tell 'im." And that's how it started— my ill-fated saga—my pilgrimage to the Corn Belt.

"We gotta go over to Berkeley first, pick up my girlfriend," John mumbled as we walked briskly through a knot of mangled-stereo-component-hustling, shopping cart-pushing zombies.

"Speak up, you're mumbling." I felt annoyed by him already, but tried to keep an open mind.

"Uuum, sorry, I just did a hit of 'H' about twenty minutes ago. Here's the car." John stopped beside a gold Toyota Celica. The vehicle looked really nice—only a couple of years old and in good condition, with no bullet holes, duct tape, or primer spots. "Get in. I'll drive till we get outta the city."

"Are you sure you want to drive on the nod, dude? Isn't that why I'm here?" I ventured this, hoping he'd think better of it. And he did. John handed me the keys, and we took off for the city of Berkeley, or "Berscrkly," as it was known...in some circles.

Chauffeuring a nodding junkie through an earthquake-torn metropolitan area was no picnic. Traffic snarls and police presence abounded. I saw fires in the distance, and heard the roar of rescue and repair equipment. John rode shotgun, of course, because he thought he needed to give me directions. All he really did, though, was drool and scratch, his chin resting on his chest. But every ten minutes or so he'd snap awake, lurch forward, and scream, "LOO-KOOUUT!" Needless to say, John's copiloting style increased my stress a hundred-fold.

Okay, we arrived in Berkeley, where we met John's girlfriend Kelly in a park. John insisted we walk around in the fucking dark, looking under every tree for her. Right when I'd come to believe that this chick of his existed only in John's opiated mind, he waved and shouted, "Kelly!" She existed—barely...Kelly sat on a blanket, her back resting against a tree trunk, head drooping, spittle dripping off her lower lip. *Looks like John's ol' lady's got a monster dope habit. Guess I'll be the only one operating machinery tonight...*

Truth be known, I was glad to do the driving. Andy's superb methamphetamine pounded around my cardiovascular system, and I felt like I'd be wide awake for at least a week. The three of us piled into the car. Funny thing is, not one of us brought a suitcase or anything. Of course, I had nothing to bring except my purse, since I couldn't possibly have anticipated this venture.

But John and Kelly? Well, I figured since they weren't packing anything extra either, then they planned to make this a very quick trip. And that was cool with me. Plus, my crank-soaked brain took misplaced confidence in the fact that the junkie couple seemed to be poor planners—all the more assurance for me that Andy, my connection and friend, was the mastermind of this operation. Good! Andy was very professional. *If anything goes wrong I can call him. But nothing will go wrong, nothing.*

The couple insisted on getting completely destroyed on their drug of choice—and pretty much staying that way. Of course I tried not to be judgmental; after all, I never skimped on my highs. But heroin addicts, when loaded, unwittingly possess incredible power to annoy and irritate me.

Kelly sat in the backseat at first, and ol' Johnboy rode shotgun. What a dickhead! He kept up his charming copilot practices, lurching awake at regular intervals to holler out, "Truck!" or "Hey—Watch it!" Shit like that. What an annoying partner in crime. And her, too, for that matter. Every time I glanced in the rearview, I couldn't save my eyes from the sight of that girl junkie slobbering and nodding. Sometimes she'd fall slowly forward till her head hit the back of my neck! Finally I pulled into a gas station, shook John awake and persuaded him to slide his chick over, you know, out of my way.

This new arrangement seemed to be as good as it was gonna get...barely tolerable. When Kelly sniffed, scratched her face, and tipped toward the front, her forehead landed on the surface of the seat back, directly between John and me. Every forty-five minutes or so, "whump!" and that bitch's forehead would crash down on the upholstery a little to the right of my shoulder. This never bothered her illustrious boyfriend, though, since he was wandering through opiate dreamland. Although John rocked and teetered as if mounted on a fulcrum, his body maintained a strange equilibrium, and his forehead never hit the dash. Of course, I shouldn't give him credit for poise here—most likely, only his seat belt kept him marginally in place.

We got to Reno, "The Biggest Little City in the World," in the wee hours of the morning and rented a motel room, where John and Kelly shifted their vegetative state from car to bed. I took a shower, washed my bra and panties and dried them on the heater. I hate to bathe and then put on the same clothes, but at least I had clean underwear! Bored and very wired, I took a little walk around the area right at dawn.

I reached what looked to be a university campus, and as I wandered around looking at statues and libraries, a man approached me. He seemed pretty harmless, and asked if he could walk with me for a while. "I noticed you're tweaking," he said, "You're so obvious. I used to be a speed freak until I got busted. Lucky for me it was California. If I'd gone down here, I'd still be in the joint."

"Man, that's awful! I'm from California, just passing through. In fact, I gotta go—my friends are waitin' for me. We're on our way to Nebraska for a quick visit." I walked rapidly away from the guy— what was I doing talking to him anyway?

He followed me for a minute or two, calling after me in one of those shout/whispers—you know, when you want to whisper but you know you absolutely must get your message heard, so you increase your volume till it becomes a wheezy-sounding growl. "Hey, Tweaker-Chick! Stay outta Nebraska!! They take one look at you there, and they'll pronounce you a nut case—they'll put you in a mental hospital! It happened to a buddy of mine in the '60s, man. We were selling acid in Omaha and he got caught with two hits. He's still locked away in a prison for the criminally insane! For life! Turn back, girl..."

I started running, but he didn't pursue me. He meant me no ill will. The man was trying to warn me, performing the function of the chorus in one of those ancient Greek tragedies. Or like Cassandra in the Iliad—and I didn't heed him.

*Fuck, that was Omaha.* I tried to reassure myself with this weak-as-dishwater argument, but the paranoia started to grow in me and with it, a floating, slow-simmering rage. I figured I'd have to drive faster, work harder to get this trip over with. My judgment had completely skewed. The dope was that potent.

# CHAPTER 16

# GREYHOUND AND WESTERN UNION

I ARRIVED BACK AT THE MOTEL AND WOKE UP MY ILL-SUITED COM-panions. They bitched and sniveled until they got some heroin into their veins, then returned to the nod state that appeared to be normal for them. These people were unbelievable! "We need our dope," they whined, "we're not like you. You're only doing speed. We're junkies and if we don't stay high, we go into withdrawals—we get sick...for us it's serious!"

Everything they needed, they needed more than anybody else in the world, because they had a heroin habit. John and Kelly ran this theme with everything. We'd stop for cigarettes, and they'd start that shit. "We need our cigarettes," they'd mewl as they lit up. "We really need our nicotine, not like you, Marti. You're a speed freak, but we really have pain. We're junkies, and if we run out of nicotine, it's serious!"

Also, the music they listened to...well, they only brought reggae music along, so when we found ourselves in that vast sonic waste-land where all you can get on the radio is Jesus, country, right-wing hate radio, and the hog report (otherwise known as Utah) we broke out the Bob Marley and friends.

Now, I like reggae okay, but I was on speed then and my inner drummer was doing really frenetic solos. Reggae clashed with my rhythms. Junkies and stoners love to listen to reggae music when they're high. The beat is nice and slow, so they can lurch, tip forward, and bob their heads to it and still feel coherent. Also, in reggae the lyrics say the same couple of phrases—over and over and over again. This is ideal for downed-out listeners; they can sing along, reassuring themselves that they're not brain-dead yet.

I longed to hear some R.E.M. or Metallica. Or better yet, some Ozzy Osbourne. But these pussies listened exclusively to reggae artists and one lousy live album of Stephen fucking Stills, for Pete's sake.

I have no idea how long it took me to get to Wyoming, all I know is it was either very, very late at night or equally early in the morning when we had the...argument, I guess you might call it. The junkies jerked awake as I pulled into a busy truckstop for some gasoline. John and Kelly began to whine. "We're hungry, and we need our food! We're not like you, Marti, you're a speed freak and you don't feel pain like we do...blah, blah, blah, blah...if we don't eat we'll suffer!"

"Okay, cool," I told them, "This is a democracy. Besides, I'm hungry, too. John, pay me what you owe me for driving so far." John stingily peeled off two twenties, a ten, and a five. I saw he had very little cash in his wallet. I took a deep breath and steeled myself to enter "Jimmy Joe's Truck Depot."

John and Kelly were a bust, for sure! The junkie couple staggered out of the Toyota, heavily on the nod. Oh, boy, were they obvious! I contemplated walking two or three paces ahead of them and getting a separate table.

The way I figured it, speed is much more conducive to the world of trucking than heroin is. Most likely I could blend in. But those two! John and Kelly stubbornly—and suicidally!—insisted on wearing their sunglasses the whole fucking time! I glanced around uneasily as we seated ourselves in one of the red vinyl booths. My gaze fell on two massive truckers sitting in the booth opposite. They stared stonily at John, who slumped toward his menu, his jaw resting on the formica tabletop. Kelly made an even more incriminating picture. She had already fallen sideways. Good thing she hadn't chosen to sit on the aisle.

A waitress whose name tag said, "Velma," arrived and glared around our booth. She did not approve. "Well!" I spoke briskly. "I've got to do a little shopping. It'll only take a sec. May I please have a burger, no pickle, and fries? Excuse me." John made his best effort to sit upright, but Kelly never moved a muscle.

I could hear John ordering as I headed for what they called the "gift shop" at Jimmy Joe's Depot. "Uuummm...Uh, I'll have the pork chop dinner, and the lady'll have the chicken-fried steak..." I walked faster, murmuring prayers under my breath.

At the gift shop, I settled for a couple of "Jimmy Joe's" items of apparel. I had to put on some clean clothing! After a moment of hasty deliberation, I selected the least offensive T-shirt I could find—a black long-sleeved one with the slogan, "Old Truckers Never Die, They Just Get a New Peterbilt," printed on the chest. What a nightmare! I bought a pair of ladies' underpants, too, fuchsia colored, with the words "Park It Here" emblazoned across the backside in glittery gold lettering. Disgusting, but it was the best they had in stock, apparently. After paying at the checkout, I went into the ladies room and donned my fresh gear.

When I got back to the diner I couldn't believe my eyes. Velma'd brought our food already. Kelly had collapsed over the tabletop, scattering chicken-fried steak and coleslaw all over the place. I sat down and tried to play it off. Picking up my burger, I took a bite and chewed vigorously. My apprehensions made swallowing difficult, however. "John, hey! John, take off those fuckin' Ray-bans and look at me," I spoke as steadily as I could under the circumstances. John refused to remove his shades, accusing me of speed freak jitters.

"You need to mellow out, man..." he mumbled, putting a forkful of pork chop in his mouth. "Uuummmh...Nobody even notices us. We're in control." Just then his head dropped forward, narrowly missing his plate. Nothing blows a druggie's cover like a face-dive into the mashed potatoes. Time for decisive action.

"Check, please!" I called out. I managed to wake John and Kelly by rapping them sharply several times with the handle of my butter knife. Let's...get...th'fuck...going...now!" I hissed. As the junkies stirred to action, I threw down enough money to cover our meal plus tip. I accidentally looked across at the truckers in the neighboring booth. The bulkiest of them succeeded in making eye contact with me. He signaled in John and Kelly's direction, then looked at me questioningly, as if to say, "You can ride with me, Blondie... and I'll kick the shit out of that skinny-ass hippie for you, to boot. How 'bout it?"

This situation had turned from nightmare to seventh circle of hell! To my great relief, John revived himself, stood, and yanked his old lady from the booth. We headed out to the little gold Toyota, with me in the lead. Several burly truckers stood in a knot beside one of the eighteen-wheelers in the parking lot, staring in our direction. They ominously resembled a lynch mob. Good thing my new T-shirt sported a trucker-ism; maybe they'd go easy on me when they brought out the nooses. I prayed quickly under my breath— a fervent prayer that the redneck posse would never progress far enough to see my trucker-friendly panties.

The driver's side door loomed within my reach, and I took the keys out, fumbling a bit. Junkie John somehow quickened his pace enough to come up alongside me on my right. "Gimme the keys, I gotta check my load." *Oh, right. Good idea. Right now, under the glaring lights of the gigantic, revolving neon "Jimmy Joe's Trucker Depot" sign, that's where he decides to open the fucking trunk.*

"Not now, let's stop around back where it's a little darker, Okay?" As I said this, I jerked my head in the direction of the trucker lynch mob, hoping Johnny boy would get the hint. But no, he lacked the subtlety for anything short of a slap in the face.

"Bitch, gimme those keys! I'm the fuckin' boss around here, and I gotta open up that trunk and CHECK THE LOAD!" He yelled the last three words. I couldn't take anymore. I went off on him, grabbing him by the back of the neck and squeezing as hard as I could.

"Never call me 'bitch,' dickhead," I snarled in his ear, "Okay, now we'll step around here and check your fuckin' load..." I hung onto the keys, of course. My mind started racing. I figured I'd better turn the damn car around and head back to San Francisco. Hell with it, the two of them'd be so fucked up they'd never notice.

But then I popped the trunk, and instantly the glare of the parking lot lights revealed sheet after sheet of LSD. At the labs, they drop the lysergic acid onto little squares of paper, often called blotters, and the entire piece of paper containing all those individual hits is called a sheet. Anyway, the sheets in this load were big—about 8" by 11," and I could discern at a glance that we carried reams of such sheets in the Toyota's cargo. The entire trunk had been jam-packed with box after box full of sheets of LSD. John and Kelly hadn't even bothered to cover them up or anything. *Idiots!*

I slammed the trunk shut, then opened it. "Take off your jacket, John, and cover this shit up, will ya? What are we, on a suicide mission?" Reluctantly, John knocked on Kelly's window. He leaned in and told her to pass him her jacket. What a fucking gentleman!

Soberly, I draped Kelly's jacket over the acid load and snapped the trunk shut. God only knew how many life sentences in prison our cargo represented! I got into the driver's seat and gingerly turned the key in the ignition, then carefully pulled onto the interstate, very careful now to signal well before merging, and observe the speed limit.

Our travel continued till we reached the Nebraska state line. I pulled into a rest area and asked John and Kelly to give me another bag of crystal, preferably a half gram. I needed to refresh my high. But fuck all! They passed me a bag all right, but when I tried a little taste of it, I realized it was heroin! Turns out they'd brought plenty of stash, but to those two, stash meant china white. And they made no apologies to me. "Heroin's so much better for you, girl..." Kelly mumbled, scratching the side of her nose. John simply shot me a peevish look. Tensions had been running high between us since Wyoming and our Jimmy Joe's Depot incident.

They managed to bring a surplus of their drug of choice, but completely fell short on supplying mine! The situation angered me so much that I finished the drive on sheer adrenaline. When we finally rolled into Lincoln, Nebraska, we stopped at a Super 8 Motel. John entered the office and checked us in. He returned with a room key for me and one for them. Our rooms were next to each other, on the second floor, rooms 210 and 211.

On the way up to my room, I took the stairs two at a time. I could hardly wait to get inside, shower, and watch HBO. I planned on sitting up all night and keeping an eye on the Celica and its highly bust-able contents. But the flesh is weak, and I fell asleep.

Next day I woke up suddenly around noon. I jumped up and looked out the motel window's curtains. The car was nowhere in sight. I threw my shirt and jeans on, walked to John and Kelly's room barefoot, and knocked on the door. No answer! They'd left me.

Grasping at straws, I ran down to the front desk and inquired about my "friends" in 211. "They've checked out, hon', but they paid for your room, too. Isn't that great?" The desk clerk, a plump and wholesome Midwesterner, smiled as she gave me the news. No trace of sarcasm tainted her conversation. *At least she's nice.*

"Thank you," was all I could say as I headed back to my room. I checked in my purse and found about fifty bucks and some change—not enough to get back home. Grabbing the telephone, I called Andy and City Baby's—collect. Dan answered and accepted the charges, passed it to Andy. "Hey Andy, it's Marti, and I'm in Lincoln, Nebraska. John and Kelly—we got here last night and they've split. I'm stuck here with no car and only fifty bucks. Have you heard from John? I mean, we made this trip for you, right? Has he called, or do you have a number here in Lincoln for them?"

Andy tried to make sense of all this. "John? Who's John? And I don't know any Kelly..." He stayed on the line with me, though. "And, uh, I don't know anybody in Nebraska. Hey, why'd you leave, anyway?"

"Oh, Andy—this guy John came through your place asking for somebody to drive to Nebraska for a big project, you know... (I couldn't say anything specific over the phone, of course, that's anathema)...this big enterprise, and I took the gig 'cause I thought it was in your interests..." I began to despair. This all sounded, well, nuts.

"Hey!" A note of recognition entered Andy's voice now, "Hey Marti, I think I remember this John guy. Looked like a heroin addict? Kinda scrawny and pale?"

"Yeah. That's him."

"Marti, I don't know that dude. But since the earthquake, I've been letting him come in the house sometimes and use the back bathroom to wash up and shave. I never met any Kelly..."

Stark reality chilled me to the core. I was fucked! "Andy you gotta help me! Can you wire me some money? I mean, you know, against what I left with you?

"Sure I can. Okay, give me your number at the motel and I'll call you in a minute."

The telephone rang five minutes later. Andy was a genuinely good human being.He gave me the address of a bus station near to the Super 8, and instructed me to go down there in a couple of hours. The money would be waiting for me, enough for one-way bus fare to San Francisco. "But give me about three hours, okay Marti? I gotta turn some of this...you know."

Of course I knew. The dope had arrived and he'd need to sell some to get the cash up. No problem. I went down to the front desk and paid for another day. Now I'd decimated my cash supply, so I had to eat stuff from the vending machines for breakfast, but that didn't dampen my spirits. With funds headed my way, the future looked bright.

The next three hours passed quickly, then an hour or so more crawled. Finally the phone rang—such a sweet sound! "Okay, go on down there. I'm heading for the Western Union office now. Good Luck!"

I ran down to the front desk and asked for directions to the bus station. The place turned out to be much farther than walking distance. I started out anyway, then decided to try hitchhiking. I stuck my thumb out and instantly a car pulled over. A young guy in an army uniform sat at the wheel. I got in and told him where I was headed. He agreed to drop me off at the bus station, then delivered a solemn warning.

"Listen, girl, never thumb a ride in Nebraska, especially in Lincoln! I grew up here, so I know...they got all kinds of laws against hitchhiking, loitering, panhandling that can land you in jail for weeks...especially downtown...see, the cops are everywhere in that area, and they circle each block constantly. If they see you stop and stand around for even a minute, like to smoke or hang out, they swoop down and bust ya. I'm serious, here! Don't fuck up...take care, now." G.I. Joe pulled in to the bus station as he finished speaking. I thanked him and jumped out.

I waited alone in the Greyhound station for almost two hours, but no money came across the wires. Only one woman worked behind the counter. Finally she looked at me and cleared her throat.

"S'cuse me, hon,' but you've been waiting awhile now, and I think maybe you need to call your friends, see what happened."

"Well, I'd better hang onto my money," I answered, "I'll keep waiting."

She gazed back at me kindly. "My name's Kathy. Hon', I've been where you are. Look, I'll dial your friends' house for ya, and you talk to 'em." She dialed Andy and City Baby's, then passed it to me. "It's ringing." She smiled gently.

I grabbed the phone like it was a life preserver. Dan answered it. "Dan!" I pleaded, "I gotta talk to Andy. Did he make it to Western Union yet?"

Dan started jabbering wildly. "Hey Marti, the cops are all over the place! They kicked in the door—we're all..." I heard a dull thud, then another man's voice came on the line.

"This is Detective Lewis speaking! WHO is THIS?"

I hung up the phone, shaking. "Uh...My friends had a terrible car accident and they're in the hospital. Guess I can't get that bus ticket after all." Kathy told me her shift ended at five. She offered to give me a ride back to my motel if I'd wait around till then. I waited, glad I didn't need to risk hitching.

Once inside my room, I tried to come up with a plan. First, I placed a collect call to an old friend of mine in San Francisco named Jack Pickering. Mr. Pickering was an elderly, outrageously wealthy gentleman from an old money family. He'd dropped out of society in the 1960s to carouse with Jim Morrison and the Grateful Dead, causing countless scandals. Gossips loved to tell tales of orgies and other lasciviousness in his mansion in the Marina district. Mr. Pickering liked to describe himself to me as, "...one of the crazy, crazy, crazy people...but nevertheless very sophisticated, my dear..." Jack loved to drink, but didn't like drugs around his house. He cherished my friendship, though, so I figured he'd help me out.

When I related my story of woe and gave my pitch for Greyhound fare, Mr. Pickering stayed silent for an entire minute. Finally he answered. "You see Marti, I sense that you're very heavily into the drug scene, and I'm afraid I mustn't send you any money right now, since that would probably only enable you to bury yourself even deeper. Tomorrow's Sunday. Try making the rounds at the churches and asking for help. Local charities often come through in situations such as yours. And, my dear, when you do get your bus ticket, once you arrive in San Francisco, give me a call and I'll send a taxi for you." He hung up. Jack was a classy old patrician. At least he offered me the cab ride.

I seemed to get more and more stranded by the hour. Still, no way would I resort to family, or they'd know how bad I'd fucked up. Same with Chris. I'd never live this down if I called him from Nebraska! How could I explain? What a disaster. No, better to take ol' Mr. Pickering's advice. *I'll come up with a way to get home before Christopher misses me. Yeah. That's it.*

Early the next morning, I got out on the road again and managed to hitch a ride downtown with some fat old redneck in a Winnebago. I visited five different churches, sat in on their services, and spoke with each pastor. All I got for my efforts were disapproving stares, possibly because I still wore that "Old Truckers Never Die, They Just Get a New Peterbilt" T-shirt from Jimmy Joe's. Hell, it was all I had!

In desperation, I walked into one last church. I think it was "First Church of Christ." The pastor took pity on me. He wouldn't give me cash, he said, but he'd take me over to the local Mission, or homeless shelter. I winced at the thought of such a refuge. After all, I'd probably have to sing hymns amid hoary old winos, then stand in line for soup. But I had no more options. I agreed to go.

The Mission staff took me in. They gave me shampoo, soap, a toothbrush, even pajamas, and loaned me some clothes so I could wash mine. That was cool. Afterward the administrators delivered their pitch. At the Mission, see, they kept a timetable. Anyone in need could stay for up to fourteen days, doing chores to earn their keep, but after the deadline, the Mission expelled that same needy individual—permanently. But, they informed me, the dear Lord did provide another path, a way that needy souls might find honest work and more lengthy residence at the Mission.

Nearby, within walking distance of the haven's walls, stood two different pharmaceutical testing facilities, and if I wanted to, they assured me, I might participate in a new medical trial. "All test subjects are paid well," the director named Jerry said enthusiastically, leaning across his desk at me, "And each test subject resides here while undergoing the process. We charge a minimal fee for room and board. See what a blessing for you this is!" Jerry leaned back and beamed at me, which gave me the creeps.

"Uh, I need a few days to think about this, I mean, to decide which of those companies to uh, apply at.. okay?" Okay, I checked into the Mission for awhile. That first day, I talked to all the residents, or should I say, inmates; a motley crew indeed. One guy, Justin, had been a carefree college student only a few months before. He'd gone on a road trip with his roommate, Brian, over the summer. They'd been crossing Nebraska when a pickup truck broadsided their car, totaling it. Brian'd been driving. The guys had open containers in the vehicle. Also, Justin's pal was a little too inebriated, so the Nebraska cops arrested him and took him to jail, where they searched him and found a joint. Oops!

Justin fared better—he swallowed the two joints he had on him right after the wreck, and being a major pot head, he only drank Snapple, so he went free for a few hours. But he quickly got arrested for loitering in downtown Lincoln, jailed for 36 hours, then released to the Mission. "I've been here for three weeks and haven't heard a word from my roommate. Signed up for a ninety-day study, though, and I'll get somethin' like three grand at the end. I'll pay the Mission what I owe 'em, fly back to Wisconsin. Then I'll start school next semester. What sucks is, I gotta do a piss test for marijuana every morning at the job. Man, I'd love to get baked!"

"You people are working as human lab rats here," I whispered. "Don't you realize that? Think of the dangers—the consequences..." I wasn't actually arguing with them, of course. I was arguing with myself. The dangers I imagined were things like having to take a urine test for dope every morning—I'd never stay clean!—and worst of all, being forced to stay in Nebraska for sixty or even ninety days till I could collect my pay. *Fuck that.*

Todd, another guy at the Mission, spoke up. "Hey, these studies are a hunnerd percent scientific..." Todd seemed to have difficulty speaking clearly. "Perf'kly safe. I been doin' 'em fer th' pas' two years...been in all kindsa exper'mnts..'n I'm fuckin' normal! Hey... lookit me. I feel great..."

Sure. He felt great. But there was a strange quality about him that filled me with uneasy feelings. He radiated a freakish vibe, and if I'd had a million bucks, I'd have bet it all that if he lifted up his shirt, we'd see feathers growing out of his hide. Or worse yet, scales. He'd probably sprouted gills or a vestigial tail by now! I shuddered.

No experiments for me. But I stalled for time with the Mission boss, Jerry. For ten days, I faked it, pretending to go over to those pharmaceutical testing companies across the way, but instead I walked downtown with Nate, a tall good-looking guy who'd been released from a federal penitentiary only days before I'd arrived. Nate had been attending the University of Nebraska when he'd been apprehended by the feds. They'd caught him in possession of a quarter ton of weed, he said, but he'd received some leniency because his uncle was the DA in Omaha. Whatever. He was friendly and loaned me money for cigarettes, a generous deed. And Nate still had wit, a sense of humor, since he hadn't begun participating in a drug study yet.

One day, Jerry gave me the ultimatum—become a human guinea pig or get out in 24 hours. All of a sudden, I thought of Billy Castor, a friend of mine in Houston, Texas. I could ask him for help and maybe he wouldn't hang up. Billy'd been incarcerated for auto theft at Huntsville Penitentiary, one of the worst hellholes in the U.S. prison system, when he was only seventeen. There in Ellis unit he'd done three years of hard labor, planting okra and picking cotton, watched over by the "highriders," redneck guards on horseback who brandished shotguns and were never stingy about using up ammo.

After his release from prison, my friend Bill had risen like a phoenix from the ashes, starting up a welding business with his friend Robby, a former pool hustler. Bill and Robby became very successful, developing their small business venture into an international corporation. For a couple of years I'd been ashamed to call Billy and let him know where I was, since I was so fucked up. I'd forgotten his home phone number, but I did remember the name of his company.

I asked Jerry to call 411 for me and get Bill's business number, since none of us residents were allowed to use the phone. I held my breath as he asked to talk to Billy Ray. "I'm calling from a charitable institution," the mission director boomed in his unctuous baritone. "Do you know someone named Marti? She says she knows you and would like to speak with you." For a few terrible moments I thought my friend would disown me.

Then Jerry handed me the telephone. I tried to give Billy a highly sanitized version of what happened. "Billy," I pleaded, "Please help me. I'm at a mission in Lincoln, Nebraska, and I'm broke. I drove out here with a couple of people but they left me stranded. I know it sounds stupid, but that's all I can say."

"Marti, you're on drugs, aren't ya? Some deal or other fucked up?" Billy Ray always could read me like a book. "Look, Marti, I'm gonna send you the money to get back to California, but consider moving back to Texas, why don't ya? Seems like the West Coast is bad for you. And, in the future, don't just call when things are shitty. Call me and keep in touch, even when things are nice, got it?"

"Yeah, okay Billy, I got it. And thank you! But I can't move out of California right now. I gotta go back there."

"Why? Sounds like you're moving right now. You've come as far as Nebraska already...oh, well, find me a Western Union address and I'll send you a couple hundred dollars." That's how I escaped from Nebraska. Billy wired me the money and I rode the Greyhound.

On the long trip back to San Francisco, I thought about how badly I had screwed up, yet how lucky I'd been. After all, I'd survived driving on a suspended license in a possibly stolen car with two junkies who'd perhaps ripped off a huge acid lab after the earthquake. And I'd been fortunate enough to miss the bust at Andy and City's house. Yes, the time had come for me to think about rebuilding my life. I gave myself a nominal scolding en route to California, but it didn't take. I still craved dope.

# CHAPTER 17

# HOMECOMING

WHEN MY BUS ROLLED INTO THE SAN FRANCISCO GREYHOUND station, I could see the city rebuilding after the earthquake damage. The progress astounded me. This would be a perfect backdrop for my life reform! I called Jack Pickering from a phone booth. True to his word, Jack sent a taxi for me. Let me take some time now to tell you a little bit about Mr. Pickering, okay?

I'd been a guest at Jack's place before, long enough to know Mr. Pickering as a fascinating person and a man of substance, as well as the crazy old sot he appeared to be on the surface. I'd carried on enough conversations with Jack to know that he came from an old money family, the American equivalent of landed gentry, and that he and his wife had hobnobbed with west coast socialites, as well as Alfred Kinsey and his wife. I like to think that Mr. Pickering donated money to Kinsey's research. He was always open-minded and open-handed.

Mr. Pickering once told me that, in the early '70s, he'd donated his house to an organization called C.O.Y.O.T.E. (Call Off Your Old Tired Ethics) while they drew up their charter and began their battle to get legal rights, and provide education and assistance for, sex workers. In a drunken stupor, Jack revealed to me that he'd once loaned his house to the Satanist Church, a sort of freedom of religion thing he called it, but his true motivation must have been to annoy his wife. Mrs. Pickering promptly rewarded his efforts by filing for a divorce, and a messier split has likely never been recorded in the San Francisco Chronicle's society pages.

Jack even kept a scrapbook of all the gossip columns that breathlessly recounted tales of the Pickering divorce, and the so-called orgies that he'd been hosting in their once-stolid home. These articles always included photos featuring Mr. Pickering, usually dressed in a Nehru jacket and jeans, wearing beads and carrying on with hippies, acid-trippers, poets, and rock musicians.

He dwelt in eccentric splendor in a four-story Victorian mansion located in a ritzy part of San Francisco. Generations of Pickerings had handed down exotic heirlooms from Katmandu, Burma, and the old kingdom of Siam. These treasures filled Jack's place to bursting. I loved to wander the rooms, delighting my eyes with gorgeous silk temple garments from Thailand, medieval tapestries, and antique weapons of war from all over the world.

Nineteenth century Pickering ancestors, fond of safaris and big game hunting, had bequeathed many a ghastly hunting trophy to their descendants, ending with Jack. Zebra skin rugs and tiger hides lay on the gleaming alabaster flagstone floor in the sunroom, and an umbrella stand made from an elephant's leg accosted visitors as they stepped into the foyer. I found these disturbing yet ghoulishly captivating. Jack even owned a set of bongo drums fashioned from two human skulls, and a grotesque shrunken head from New Guinea.

I'd first made Mr. Pickering's acquaintance through a chick I knew who worked as a dominatrix. She was the ex-girlfriend of one of my former coke connects. Her name was Darragh but she worked under an alias as "Elektra." On the day Elektra introduced me to Mr. Pickering, a porn director had set up shop in the mansion, and auditions were already under way. Mr. Pickering's house, with all its fantastic contents, made an excellent backdrop for a porn flick, I guess, because the wacky old millionaire rented the place out for such productions frequently. The pornographers always richly stocked Jack's bar during shooting, which thrilled him, I'm sure—he loved to party.

I had no interest in trying for a part in the movie, but Elektra wanted to go for it, and she asked me to hang out. I'd never really watched a porn movie so I stuck around out of curiosity. The applicants kept on arriving. I recognized this one porn star chick because she'd been in the news several times for cavorting with politicians and royalty. She wore a very conservative tweed suit and pumps that reminded me of a real estate agent or bank manager. Groupies and hangers-on approached her from the shadows, asking for her autograph, chirping, "I love your work!"

Old Mr. Pickering took a shine to me immediately, and I got a kick out of him, too. The old profligate! What a charmer! "My dear," he whispered, "would you like to join me in a little peep at the goings-on? We can lurk behind this fifteenth century Italian tapestry...there's a slight tear in it where one can get a full view. Let's you and I secretly observe, shall we?" A devilish grin crossed the old boy's face. I know it sounds cartoonish, but the old guy actually did talk exactly like that—he was a real trip!

"I'm game," I laughed, and huddled with Jack directly behind the brocaded antique wall hanging. I couldn't believe my eyes. The director sat in Mr. Pickering's den, behind a massive square desk made of glossy birdseye maple. He swiveled lackadaisically back and forth in the leather upholstered office chair. Pickering had gotten creative with this chair, adorning it with a pair of antique red velvet epaulets, trimmed in gold braid. He'd installed them at either side of the chair's back, comically promoting this piece of furniture to the rank of admiral. (Those epaulets, Jack later told me, had once rested on the shoulders of a nineteenth century Prussian field marshal's uniform.)

The director, a skinny blond man with bloodshot eyes, yawned and motioned to his weary assistant. "Bring in the next guy." Moments later I watched a male porn actor audition for the lead role by doing a kind of, well, trick with his penis—twirling it in circles, using no hands, of course. He twirled clockwise, then counter-clockwise. "Okay, thanks..." the director muttered. "Next!"

The next man to arrive removed his shirt, displaying impressively cut pecs, stepped up to the desk and unzipped his fly, exposing his humungous yet still flaccid johnson. The director looked bored, rolling his eyes. All of a sudden the porn guy took half a step back and slapped his beefy tool on the maple desktop. We heard a resounding "smack," and instantly his penis stood erect, even larger than before. The man maintained this pose, hands on his hips, for an amazingly long time till the director finally said, "Thanks, dude." Having completed his stunt, the actor zipped himself up again, turned, and exited.

I stayed for one more audition, but they were all pretty much the same. Elektra didn't get the part she wanted, but they invited her to be an extra. I guess they were making an epic porn movie or something. Extras—damn!

So, since I'd met Jack under those circumstances, I wasn't surprised when my cab pulled up to the mansion and I saw a couple guys with cameras and tripods. Mr. Pickering had a love affair with film. He once showed me some of his old eight millimeter home movies from the '60s—footage of Jim Morrison and his entourage doing a naked samba line, and Janis Joplin, brandishing a bottle of Southern Comfort and mumbling to herself.

Sure enough, Jack had rented his house to another pornography crew. "Don't mind them, my dear," Mr. Pickering told me at the front door, "They'll only be here for a coupla days...mmm...yes... and how was your trip from...Kansas, was it?" Mr. Pickering looked like he was pretty lit up. The porn guys must've stocked his liquor cabinet early.

"Nebraska." I managed to say it politely but felt the urge to scream. "It was Lincoln, Nebraska. Can I smoke in the house?" I started to light up a Marlboro.

"You've forgotten the rules, Marti?...shame, shame....mmm... absolutely no smoking in my house. I never smoked—I'm a skier, have been all my life. Did I ever tell you about the times...mmm... back before my divorce...mmm...you see, my wife was good on the slopes too, and we used to ski at Sun Valley with the Shah of Iran. They can say anything they like about the Shah, but his wife had a world-class ass! And La-de-da and Da-de-dah...mmmm."

"C'mon, Mr. Pickering," I said, putting the cigarette out and stashing it back in my pack, "Let's step inside and sit down." I knew I needed to maneuver the old guy over to an armchair before he passed out. Whenever he started saying, "...And La-de-dah and Da-de-dah," Jack Pickering wasn't merely tipsy, he was three sheets into the wind. I feared he might fall down and hurt himself. I really did like the guy. I mean, you had to love him. He was such a naughty old rake!

I took Jack by the hand and guided him into his house. The place bustled with activity. Adult film industry people hurried back and forth. One of them grabbed a phone and called out for several pizzas. Another reached into his backpack and brought out a jar of Skippy peanut butter and a plastic spoon. He stood there and ate a few spoonfuls of it, then put the lid back on the jar and returned it to his pack. These people were crazy about pizza and peanut butter, for some strange reason. Perhaps those two foods, in combination, boosted testosterone or libido or something. Who knows?

Jack assigned a room to me, temporarily, on the second floor. I could take the stairs or ride the antique elevator. The elevator creaked and swayed, so it felt a little scary, but it was worth the risk to see the vertical murals. See, the elevator door wasn't solid, but constructed from wrought-iron mesh, so as you rode you'd look at the walls between floors. Some derelict artist friend of Mr. Pickering had decorated those walls with all sorts of art—in a style reminiscent of both Salvador Dali and Hieronymous Bosch, simultaneously. That was a freaky ride. We all loved it. Most of the time though, I took the wide, sweeping staircase. That always made me feel a little like Scarlett O'Hara in Gone with the Wind. Occasionally I slid down the banister, reciting lines from the movie under my breath, like, "The Yankees are comin' !" Or, "...Frankly, Scarlett, I don't give a damn."

I decided to stay at wacky Mr. Pickering's for awhile. I told myself I'd make a new start—re-enter the mainstream, even. Jack wanted to help me out, in his own way. "I can get you a job at mmm...my favorite store, my dear," he proposed, smiling sweetly. "I'm a long time patron of the establishment, so I've got some pull. You'll love it—mmm...it's 'The Liquor Barn' on Lombard Street. They don't pay much to start, but you'll get a handsome discount... And La-de-dah and Da-de-dah!"

"Uhh-huh. Okay, I guess I can check it out." Really, I wasn't feeling enthusiastic about applying. After all, I didn't even have a driver's license, and if they did a background check, they'd see all my outstanding warrants. Still, I promised Jack I'd go down there in the morning.

Even though he was thoroughly marinated, the playful old degenerate still had the verve left to make the rounds, introducing me to all his other guests/tenants. First I met two house painters named Roger and Cool Breeze. These guys worked all around San Francisco, restoring and painting Victorians. In the wake of the earthquake, their business was booming. The partners worked long hours, drinking profusely. I immediately bonded with them on a subconscious level, probably because they reeked of marijuana.

Also their lifestyle amused me. Roger and Breeze were diehard hippies who stubbornly refused to drop the flag. I mean, they still said things like, "...far out," and "...right on," for Pete's sake. To complete the equation, they drove a '60s vintage Volkswagen van, complete with Grateful Dead stickers on the bumpers and rear window.

On that particular evening, Jack and I found the two pothead artisans swilling Yagermeister right out of the bottle. Cool Breeze reluctantly offered us a slug of it, stating mournfully, "We're drinking to forget. See, we lost a contract today...kinda because of what Roger did, right, dickhead?"

Roger jumped to deliver a rebuttal. "Fuck, man, it was an accident! I spaced out for one second, dude, an honest mistake. That crystal chandelier was a heavy motherfucker—I mean, I realize I shoulda used both hands, okay? I'm sorry, Breeze, but we got insurance, right?"

"Right." Cool Breeze sighed despondently. "But our rates shot up when we smashed that piano..."

Mr. Pickering didn't linger with the stoner tradesmen. He indicated I should roll on and meet the rest of his household. I complied. Moments later we stepped into the elevator and descended to the basement to meet Anikka, a petite redhead with porcelain skin who introduced herself as, "...certified dom, former bondage dungeon owner, currently full-time student."

"Mmmm, Annika's making a bold new start since the police raided her place of...mmm...her dungeon in Berkeley," Old Pickering winked, "...an unfortunate turn of events...mmm...perhaps you read about it...coupla three months ago...in the Chronicle?"

I shook my head and glanced around the dimly lit room. In fact I had read the article in the San Francisco paper. The story impressed me. What happened? Well, one Friday night these Berkeley city cops are sitting in their patrol car, eating donuts or whatever they do when they're bored. Suddenly this big shiny Bentley flashes past, right down University Avenue, doing seventy-five in a thirty-five and swerving.

The two patrolmen peel out after the vehicle, flashing lights ablaze, but the suspect only increases speed. They turn on the siren, then run the plates on the Bentley, and see it's registered to a very prominent citizen. Now they figure they've got a car thief in their sights! They call for backup. In minutes, two more squad cars join the chase—until the driver of the Bentley sharply diminishes speed, turns a corner into a narrow alley, parks sideways, hurls himself out and runs down a narrow flight of steps into an unlit doorway. The cops follow, guns drawn, expecting to find a street gang leader holed up in a chop shop or a drug lab. What they do find is a plush and elaborate S&M club and gothic bondage dungeon. The police find the driver of the Bentley, the very prominent citizen himself, huddled and shivering under a sofa in one of the outer rooms.

As the bust progresses, they find all sorts of wealthy and influential clientele, in compromising positions. And of course they arrest the owner of the establishment and her entire staff. What a switch that must've been for those employees, with the leg iron on the other foot, so to speak! The city shut the place down and issued a statement saying that an investigation would follow.

Poor little dominatrix! I bet she took the rap for everything. She was probably on probation or going through a nasty civil suit. But the bondage babe had friends, and one of them introduced her to Mr. Pickering, who, although twisted, was in many ways a gentleman of the old tradition. I guess the wayward old boy couldn't resist a damsel in distress. Annika now rented Jack's basement as her living quarters. The ex-dungeon mistress paid a little extra for storage of equipment she'd salvaged from the bust.

The place looked like the Spanish Inquisition! A quick glance around revealed leg irons, studded and zippered bondage masks, elaborate harnesses, handcuffs of leather and of iron, and a formidable piece of furniture she referred to as a "throne of discipline." That chair sported loads of chains, thick straps, and a wicked spike or two.

*Fucking medieval!* If Torquemada lived today, he'd be listing that chair on eBay! I repressed a shudder. Annika swept her hand over the hoard of torture devices, a dismissive gesture. "I'm through with the punishment business," the slender redhead sighed, then brightened, adding, "Now I'm selling this S&M gear piece by piece so I can go back to school to learn massage—only deep tissue massage! I bet that hurts, if it's done right, huh?" Her green eyes gleamed.

"Uh, I don't know," I muttered nervously, "...uh, nice to meet you anyway." I turned to Jack. He picked up my cue in spite of his blood alcohol content. We headed for the elevator. Annika followed after us several steps. "Come back and visit. You can hang out!" She chuckled fiendishly.

As we reached the ground floor, Mr. Pickering's eyes lit up. "It's Spike! He's a Rhodesian Ridgeback. Mmmm...Here, Spike!" The huge dog lumbered up to us and sat down. "I'm... mmm...acting as Spike's guardian for the next six weeks. He belongs to Yvonne, one of my tenants, but she's in rehab, you know—mmmm...and so is Gretchen. Let's go to the kitchen and get some butter."

"Butter?" I stared at the old hedonist, wondering if he'd had an attack of dementia.

"Hmm, yes. Spike loves butter!" Old Pickering trotted down a hallway and into the kitchen, the dog trailing joyously. Jack opened the refrigerator, pulled out a stick of butter, sliced off a bit, and fed it to Spike.

We sat around the kitchen table with Roger and Cool Breeze, who'd wandered down in search of beer. What a hangover these guys'd have come morning! I pictured falling chandeliers and smashed pianos all over town.

Mr. Pickering showed me promotional photos of the missing two tenants, Yvonne and Gretchen, who worked the female wrestling circuit but presently were undergoing heroin withdrawal. According to him, the two enjoyed a good degree of success in the business. "They were especially...mm...popular in Iowa," Jack assured me. "They did it all—mud...oil, but mostly in the ring. Yvonne billed herself as 'Yolanda the Slave Girl' and Gretchen wrestled as 'Heidi the Farmer's Daughter.' Gretchen says it's the road that got to them...boring...different hick town every night...mm...Yvonne says they needed narcotics for the pain—sports injuries...mmm, getting thrown down on the mat...and La-de-dah." Jack stopped speaking and gazed fondly at Spike. The brindle-coated hound wagged his tail.

I picked up a couple of Yvonne and Gretchen's 8 by 10s. The "Farmer's Daughter" wore a gingham mini dress and pigtails and "The Slave Girl" wore faux fur. Those poor chicks—I had to sympathize with them. Wrestling to support their habit! In fucking Iowa! After my recent taste of the Great Plains, I felt I knew the hell they must've gone through.

"Those chicks were hot, man," Roger mumbled, "...n' strong, real strong."

"They worked out." Cool Breeze added, muttering, "Gretchen was hotter, though..."

"Yeah." I spoke as a reflex only. Thoughts of dope now occupied my mind. The girl wrestler story made me want a hit—real bad! And after my time in Nebraska, I felt entitled. Yet a part of me still held back. I was in with Mr. Pickering—he'd assigned me a nice room—and I had a job to apply for in the morning. *Why fuck that up?* I mustered my feeble resistance and determined to give this new lifestyle a try. *For awhile, anyway.*

The next morning arrived blanketed in chilling fog. No way did I feel like getting out of bed, let alone trying a new lifestyle—fuck that bullshit. I decided to go downstairs, give ol' Pickering an excuse, and buy some time.

In the hallway, I bumped into Roger and Cool Breeze. The booze-guzzling, bong-slinging house painters crept feebly toward the elevator, dragging their hangovers behind them like a block of granite. Breeze nodded painfully in my direction. "Hey, Marti... Wassup?" He muttered this absently.

"Oh, nothin', how 'bout you? You're not going to work, are you?" These guys had grit! As the three of us boarded the elevator, a fetching young woman rounded the corner, waving and shouting.

"Hey! Wait up, you guys!" She bounded down the corridor toward us. We had no choice but to wait. We stood paralyzed in astonishment. This chick wore an outrageous costume, barely anything at all, really. It reminded me of a sort of French maid uniform, infinitely short and skimpy. She wore wickedly high-heeled, black patent leather, over-the-knee boots with cruelly pointed toes. And she carried a backpack.

"Cool!" she squealed as she bounced in. "Hi, I'm April! I'm on my way to work and I can't be even a second late! Not today!!" April sounded breathless with anticipation. "Ooh, I love my job...I'm in the movie they're shooting downstairs, an' it's my first big scene. I never woulda got the part but this one actress came down with the flu, and they're letting me do it."

"Uhh, congratulations, you'll prob'ly be awesome," Roger offered through cracked lips, his voice gravelly. Breeze managed a smile. The sight of April rendered both stoners slack-jawed.

"Thanks!" She smiled broadly, then eagerly reached into her backpack. "Oooh, I'm so psyched." April pulled something from the pack now. My mind strained to identify the contraption. *Something...I'd seen one somewhere...in some store window in the Castro, maybe?* "And..." April continued while donning the apparatus, adjusting buckles as she bubbled on, "...and I'm gonna be featured! I get to do my scene partner—this other chick—with this strap-on!!" The would-be porn starlet turned to Roger and Breeze, waggling her hips, evidently proud of the prop. The dildo bounced around obscenely. "How do I look?" She glanced around at each of us, eyes shining. No one met her gaze.

Mercifully, the elevator stopped, releasing us passengers on the ground floor. The pornographers were hard at work, setting up lights and cameras in Jack Pickering's expansive living room. I strode quickly for the front door and never looked back, anxious now to be away from there—even if I had to get a job, which actually is a fate worse than death for a dedicated dope fiend.

But I didn't apply at the Liquor Barn that day. I didn't have to. Instead, Jack asked me to help him out, promising to pay me for my time. "The IRS is auditing me again," Mr. Pickering confided. "In fact, I have a mandatory appointment with two of their henchmen in only a few days. I need to dress for the occasion. Will you accompany me...shopping, that is? I need you to drive, Marti."

"Cool." I readily agreed, knowing how fun it'd be to drive Jack's vehicle. Mr. Pickering owned a saucy ride—a classic black Lincoln Continental stretch limo, complete with suicide doors. I didn't bother to warn the old guy about my suspended license and all. Better me behind the wheel than Mr. Pickering. I mean, he'd be, "... La-de-dah-and Da-de-dah-ed..." by eleven a.m. at the latest.

Jack directed me to head out for the Haight-Ashbury district. There we found a parking place smack dab in front of a very shabby secondhand clothing store. The wily old guy quickly selected a hideous pair of plaid polyester double-knit trousers. The colors absolutely screamed, too—brick red and lime green plaid over a horrendous saffron-yellow background. In addition to that, the zipper seemed to be stuck halfway up, and the slacks were at least three inches too short.

"Perfect! Exactly what I need for my initial meeting with the auditors! And this shirt completes the ensemble. What do you think?" He grinned and held out a disgusting turquoise velour sweater, circa 1972.

"Are you gonna try to look insane, or penniless? Hey, can you plead insanity in a tax case?" I asked. All sarcasm aside, though, I fervently hoped Jack'd get past the IRS. He'd told me earlier that in former audits they'd frozen his assets and it'd been "highly inconvenient" for him. But Pickering always gave the tax men a fight to the finish. I had to admire Jack's warrior spirit!

According to Pickering, his heirs were out for blood, too. He had a son and daughter, corporate types, real landsharks, I guess. Although they didn't need his money, they constantly filed requests for competency hearings. Jack's son especially disapproved of his father's bacchanalian existence. "You see, Marti," Jack once told me with a chuckle, "I'm the only one in my family that isn't square!"

It seems Mr. Pickering was under the gun, but holding up well. He still possessed that crazy sense of fun. "C'mon, my dear, let's head back to the hacienda. I feel the need for a...mmm...pick-me-up...glass of wine or two...and perhaps you'd like to assist me in some renovating?"

"Sure, Jack." I hopped into the Lincoln and slid behind the wheel. Jack got in the back seat with his pauper's attire.

"I believe my...mmm...subterfuge will succeed. They won't freeze all my assets! Not this time, my dear—I've devised one hell of a plan to thwart them!!" Mr. Pickering sat up straighter against the plush upholstery. His head wobbled slightly, an early sign of inebriation for Jack. He leaned forward eagerly. "Drive faster!"

We returned to Pickering headquarters, where I parked the car in the garage while Jack hurried into his house, probably jonesing for a drink. I walked inside and found the adult film project in full swing. Cast and crew ran amok through the front part of the stately Victorian mansion.

On my way to find ol' Jack, I passed by the great room, where the porn people were shooting a scene with the door wide open. Stalwart, I fixed my gaze straight ahead and damn near sprinted past the area. No way did I want to inadvertently catch a glimpse of April, in French maid outfit and strap-on, doing her thing!

I found Jack in his office. Although he managed to sit up straight at his desk, one glance told me he was, "...in his cups," as he liked to call it. I call it wasted. But Pickering was nothing if not a genial drunk. "Welcome, my dear!" He smiled, waving me in. "Sit down, sit down...and La-de-dah and..."

"Right, Da-de-dah?" I interrupted him. He nodded sweetly at me, almost batting his eyelashes. Jack had an agenda, all right.

"Marti, I need you to assist me in a secret mission." He reached into a drawer in his desk, pulled out a grocery bag, and dumped its contents onto the richly polished maple desktop. Bundles of hundreds, twenties, and fifties thumped softly as they landed.

"Quite a pile of cash there, Jack...uh, what're you doing?"

"My dear, I'm preparing to redecorate!" Jack winked at me, his head wobbling ever so slightly. "You see, I have bolts and bolts of imported silks around the house...mm...and I like to paper the walls with them. From time to time I apply a fresh new color, and La-de-dah and...Da-de-dah..." He stood up, walked a few steps to the corner of the office, and gestured toward the bolts of bright blue, green, and red silk leaning against the wall. "I believe I'll use the cobalt blue this time, Marti...give me a hand, mmm?"

Jack hadn't uttered a word about all those bundles of cash all over his desk. I stepped up to help him with the fabric, averting my eyes from all that available dinero. I mean, I can't say the money didn't tempt me, but I wasn't a thief. An addict, yeah, but I never ripped off a tipsy old man! Hey, I had my personal code of junkie ethics to uphold, after all.

I worked with Jack on the walls of the office. I held the fabric flat to the wall, yard by yard, all the way to the ceiling, with the help of a ladder, of course. We both wielded staple hammers to attach the gorgeous brocaded silk to the building materials. After a few minutes of this, Jack started picking up bundles of money, separating them into thin stacks, and concealing them under the fabric, stapling them in place. "This, my dear, is a wonderful, crazy way to confound the IRS! And La-de-dah...Only you and I are privy to this, Marti...I'm trusting you not to tell anyone else about my technique, mmm?...and...Da-de-dah...." Jack turned and gazed at me affectionately, in a sloppy drunk way.

Now I was in deep. Jack and I shared a secret. He'd handed me a responsibility I never asked for, and one I kind of resented. I couldn't rob him. He was such a sweet old guy. Still, I made careful mental notes of where the highest concentrations of cash lay hidden, in case I might need to borrow a little...*only in an emergency, though. Yeah, that's right...extreme situations only.* I took a deep breath. "Okay, Jacky Boy, let's do this then," I assured him, "and you have my vow of silence on this, you maniac—as long as you pay me for the labor!"

Together, Jack and I quickly completed our redecorating chores. The old eccentric paid me a couple hundred bucks for the day, an adequate wage, which I stuffed into my jeans for safekeeping. Now I knew I could score. I threw off my good resolutions. "I'm going for a walk. I need cigarettes. I'll be back in a few."

Jack waved absently at me. Then, smiling jubilantly, he headed for his newly-stocked bar. The porn chicks still hung around the place, so naturally Jack flirted with several of them as he poured himself a generous snifter of cognac. You had to love the old degenerate. What a wicked old freak. The term "senior citizen" didn't seem to apply to Pickering.

As I stepped out the front door, I bumped into two men in suits. I recognized them, since they'd dropped by the place only the night before, asking to speak to Mr. Pickering. Jack had refused to go to the door. Instead, he'd asked me to stall them off.

"Tell them I'm not home. You see, my dear, they're from the Iranian Embassy...mm...they visit me once a year, and La-de-dah...

They're after this." Jack waved his hand in the direction of an enormous brass vessel. "It's an ancient Persian sacrificial urn," he said, eyes alight with a naughty sparkle. "I bought it from the Shah of Iran, and although I know he was a bit of a despot, he was a friend... mmm...socially, and I can't in good conscience turn it over to the regime that ousted him, you see...mmm, it's more for his wife's memory—and La-de-dah!" The old rogue wobbled his head and looked off into the distance, as if in his mind's eye he still beheld the glory of Mrs. Shah's behind—several decades in the past, of course.

The night before, I'd given the diplomatic liaisons an excuse for Jack, but now they'd returned, and I didn't have time to get involved. I shouldered past them, saying, "He's inside. Good luck." *Fuck it. Let 'em see the film crew and the bar and everything. It's a slice of Americana...*

I skipped down the steps and headed along Pacific Street, fondling the bills in my pocket. I figured I'd call around, find some speed, score, then get back to Jack's before an hour elapsed. After all, I now had cash, since Jack had paid me for my help. In the world of dope, cash is king. In this posh neighborhood, however, I'd never even seen a phone booth.

I headed south toward the seedier districts, where my interests now lay. My lust for dope, awakened by the feel of money in my fingertips, smothered any resolutions, feeble repentance, or desire for the good life in me. I'd returned to full fiend mode.

I stopped into a Korean grocery, bought a fresh pack of Marlboros, lit one up, then lunged onward in my quest. Finding a phone booth, I dropped in quarters, dialed Andy and City Baby's, and listened to it ring eight times. I started to hang up when, miraculously, somebody answered. "Dan!" I recognized his voice. "Dan, it's Marti. Is Andy around?"

"Yeah, he's here," Dan replied in a subdued voice. "We're all here."

"Can I talk to Andy? It's important. No, wait, I'll just come over there in person, okay?"

"Whatever." That was all Dan had to say. He hung up.

I started hiking toward Natoma Street as fast as my long, speed freak legs could carry me, which was pretty snappy. My feet flew. I felt carefree. Since it was early afternoon, I'd arrive at the connection's in bright daylight. No hoards of zombie cranksters queued up in the alley. No broken streetlights. Easy score, I figured.

At least I got part of it right. The zombies had disappeared into the cracks and shadows, no doubt dispersing hurriedly after the bust went down. When I reached Andy and City's door, I knocked twice and it swung open. Dan stood there, stonily silent. I caught a glimpse of City Baby just behind him. Her mohawk, normally so jaunty, looked limp and ragged, and her leopard-print scalp tattoos seemed lackluster at best.

"Hi," I said, nearly breathless with anticipation, "Can I talk to Andy?"

"Yeah, sure." Dan nodded vacantly, ushering me inside. "Sure, he'll be back in a few. Sit down anywhere. The cops tossed the place but we're almost back to normal."

I found a seat on a dilapidated armchair, making an attempt at upbeat conversation. "Hey, City, um...you look great," I lied shamelessly. City Baby returned my bogus compliment with an icy stare, whirled around and stalked off into the bedroom.

Dan bummed a cigarette from me. We both lit up and sat in silence. A few minutes later, City returned. She marched straight up to me with one arm behind her back, thrusting her face toward me till her nose was only a hand's-breadth from mine. I successfully fought the urge to bitch-slap her. Seconds later, she jumped back a step, then pulled her left arm from behind her back and started waving it at me. "See my snakes?" City Baby squeaked, hopping from one foot to the other, displaying four tiny, brightly colored serpents twined around her fingers. The snake-babies writhed frenetically. I figured she'd been dosing them with crystal meth. They were definitely spun.

"UUhh...yeah, they're—um, perky," I ventured. I knew she was trying to freak me out. I'm not afraid of snakes so I wanted to take the fun out of it for her. I leaned forward. "Can I hold one of 'em?"

"Nnnooo!" Damn, that chick had a shrill voice. She began twining one of the unfortunate reptiles into her frayed mohawk. "They're MINE!"

The front door opened. Andy walked in, wearing a backpack. He glanced at City, then looked down, shaking his head slowly back and forth. Without removing the pack, he flopped down on the couch, exhaled loudly.

"Marti. See you got back from Kansas."

"Nebraska. Hey, it sucks that you got busted. It must have been a nightmare."

"Yeah, it sucked, but we're back. I've got you covered. We've gotta take a walk, though...C'mon." Andy looked weary, but he stood, started walking out the door. I followed.

We made our way down Natoma Street, then continued on till we reached a huge pile of rubble and broken slabs of concrete. Andy led the way past all of that, weaving, ducking twisted lengths of rusty rebar that protruded from the concrete chunks. We wended our way through half a city block of wreckage and I got completely disoriented. Somehow we ended up at the edge of a parking lot enclosed with chain link fence. Inside the fence I saw row upon row of junked, crushed, or abandoned vehicles—cars, trucks, delivery vans, school buses.

"This is where I'm doing all my business now. Way too much heat at home. And City Baby's not right...the bitch is losing it—she's sucking up all my stash...It's fucked up." Andy pointed toward the bottom of the chain link, where I could see he'd made an opening with bolt cutters. "C'mon." He lifted up the fencing, held it for me to duck under. I crouched down behind a car, hoping not to be seen. Andy led the way again, zigzagging, bent low, till we reached one of the school buses in the middle of the parking lot. One of its doors was bent. We crawled inside.

Andy opened his backpack, pulled out the dope and a small digital scale, and as he did this I caught a glimpse of a pile of cash, in bundles. *Fuck! I'm on the wrong end of this transaction—why can't I be the dealer??* Of course, the thought raced through my mind, but it didn't provoke me to self-realization at that point. I knew why I couldn't deal! By now, I was way too much of a dope fiend to keep the books balanced, so to speak.

Andy weighed out an eighth-ounce—my investment return. "Sorry it can't be more, but the bust fucked everything up," he murmured, "I'll make it up to you later. Hey, this stuff is really pure— you're gonna love it." He unfolded a small pocketknife and passed it to me.

I took some of the crystal on the tip of the blade and snorted it. It was kickass all right. "Yeah, you can make it up to me. I'm so fucking glad to be out of Nebraska! I'm staying here in the city for a few weeks, so I'll be back in a few days, okay?"

"Yeah, no problem, Marti." Andy waved his arm in a vague gesture. "I'm thinking about fixing up this bus a little bit, moving in. I like it here. It's...quiet." He smiled almost blissfully, locked his fingers behind his head and leaned back. It occurred to me that, in the war on drugs, this particular soldier now suffered acutely from battle fatigue. He continued speaking softly, eyes closed. "So you know where I'll be...and if you ever want to drop by, spend some time..." He sat up suddenly, leaned forward, put his hand on my leg, smiled again.

"Uuhhh...yeah, sure, right..." *What the fuck is this guy thinkin'?* I stood up abruptly. "Gotta go now."

I split, zigzagging through the metal maze of twisted, rusty vehicles. *Poor Andy! He's flipped out from all the stress.* I reached the chain link, crawled under, kept going. Figured I'd better go back to ol' Jack's, kick it for awhile. The only complication with that plan was that I now had a nice crank buzz going, plus a pocket full of the stuff. No way would he approve! I resolved that I'd be very low key, disguise my high...blend in. But the crystal meth high tends to be obvious, especially if it's excellent quality. And Andy's crystal had started pumping its high octane, borderline psychotic juices up and down my central nervous system. So I stopped, ducked into an alley between buildings, and did up some more.

Didn't take me long to get to Pickering's. I climbed the flagstone steps leading up to Jack's front door—took 'em two at a time, feeling peppy and primed to encounter a different kind of crazy—completely different from the brand of insanity down at Andy and City's... But insane is insane. No use sifting through the varying degrees of aberrant behavior, right?

Suddenly Jack flung open the front door. He stood there, surrounded by an assortment of porno people, plus Roger and Cool Breeze, looking outraged. Annika glared at me indignantly, hands on hips. Along the periphery of Pickering's posse, some chick in a fur coat swayed back and forth on extreme spike heels. The chick stared vacantly, and drooled.

One look told me something was not quite right! Pickering seemed way out of control. Hell, he had to be in black-out mode! He wore a crumb-encrusted bib and held a piece of buttered corn on the cob in one hand and a flashlight in the other! The old boy appeared to be exploring a new level of alcohol toxicity...Jack was tripping all right—on a sort Jack Daniels-sponsored Magical Mystery Tour. Mr. Pickering aimed his wild, bloodshot eyes at me and snapped, "There you are! What have you done with my money?!!" Jack was so wasted he'd run out of La-De-Dah's—I'd never seen him this bad.

At first, I thought he was asking me how I spent the cash he'd paid me for helping him drive around, and "redecorate" his office. It took my brain a while to flash on what was really happening— old Jack had been looking for the cash I'd helped him stash only hours earlier. I guess he'd completely forgotten what we'd done, but damn!—I sure hadn't.

Speed-enhanced rage bubbled up within me. The old coot actually thought I'd ripped off his money! My junkie pride felt wounded. *Well, fuck him!* I huffed back at him. "Jack! Remember? The money's in safe keeping...you know, your shelter from the IRS?" I only hinted around, vainly hoping to jog whatever memory lay dormant under the wooly blanket of alcohol swaddling Jack's skull, never taking into consideration the intense paranoia engulfing my own brainpan. My paranoia buzzed away now, whispering ugly rumors to my drug-drenched mind.

I wanted to scream loudly at the top of my lungs, tell Mr. Pickering where the money was hidden, and have done with it. But there they all were—the porn people, Annika, Roger and Cool Breeze, even the drooling skank in the seedy mink—and obviously they all knew the extent of Jack Pickering's incapacitation. This, I figured, would be a perfect opportunity to steal all the cash and pin it on me. If nothing else, I'm a loyal person, and the old fuck didn't deserve to be ripped off. I would never let that happen, I decided. So I stood my ground.

"Jack," I said, "Can we talk? In private, I mean?"

Roger stepped to the forefront, shouting. "No way, man! Me 'n Breeze'r sick of you chicks workin' your way in an' gettin over on Jack—that sucks, big time. Right, Breeze?"

"Right, Roger!" Cool Breeze affirmed his partner's opinion, adding, "We all know what you're up to, Marti. I mean, Nirvana here," Breeze paused and turned, pointed toward the drooling skank, "...she's like...been sexin' Mr. Pickering, workin' her wiles on him, and now we find out you been robbin' him blind! Fuck that, and fuck you, sister!" Breeze took another step forward, shaking one fist, waving his bong at me in a vague gesture.

*Sister? What is he on?* I marveled at how aggressive these stoners had become. Somebody must've slipped some angel dust into their weed stash. Now Annika chimed in. "Yeah, fuck you, bitch!" The porn workers—I counted six in all—began to mutter under their breath, an ominous sound. Suddenly the whole motley lynch mob moved in unison, leaving Jack on the threshold, taking a couple of steps toward me, still muttering. I took one hesitant step backward. Decided to make a last attempt at diplomacy.

"Jack—Mr. Pickering! Listen to me! You made me promise never to reveal the hiding place to anyone ever!! I keep my promises...now, can we just relax and wait for the buzz to wear off, huh? Okay?" I looked into Mr. Pickering's bloodshot brown eyes as I made my appeal. A glazed void seemed to engulf him. No hint of recognition there...so I turned my back on the scene and started walking, careful to keep my gait casual. I didn't want Jack's enraged entourage to think I was scared or anything. After all, the only weapon brandished so far was a lit bong.

Still, I looked back over my shoulder to be certain. No one followed after me. I guess they didn't really give a fuck about anything. I kept on walking. I felt bad about Jack, though. I wanted him to know that I hadn't taken any money, but what could I do except wait for him to come off the alcohol binge? Once the porn crew split, I figured, things would settle down. The porn production at Jack's place was like the circus in town. The excitement, the confusion, all of that. When they pulled up the stakes and rolled on, life at the Pickering house could return to normal. Well, to some semblance of relative normalcy, anyway. Yeah, that'd be the time to call Jack.

The next time I saw Jack, he let me know that, as soon as he'd sobered up, he remembered stashing the cash in the silk wall covering. He then checked and found the cache intact. We remained friends.

In the meantime, I had traveling to think about. I decided to cover the seventy or so miles back to my place by bus. Hitchhiking was illegal in Marin County, and I couldn't take a chance on getting busted with dope on me. I headed down to Lombard Street to catch the Golden Gate transit to Santa Rosa. Once in Santa Rosa, I'd hitchhike the rest of the way home.

As I walked, I began to wonder about Chris, my old man. Boy, would he be pissed! I'd been gone a long time. He'd never believe my story about Nebraska and why I headed off into a disaster-ravaged city to score crank. Even worse, what if he did buy it? That'd suck just as much! Because see, he cared about me. The fact that I had done something so crazy, so stupid, and so lethally moronic—without making any money on the acid deal whatever—well, better not to give him the details. He had a knack for making money on dope deals, and any waste of time or excessive risk really rubbed him the wrong way. I cared about Chris, too; loved him, deep down, although when high I hated to admit it to myself.

I caught the very next bus north, and a few hours later I arrived in Santa Rosa. What a sweet, innocent city it seemed. The sun had not quite finished setting, so in its remaining pinkish-gold glow I clearly saw immaculate streets, with innocent citizens walking to and fro. I beheld the normal world, populated by those who worked during the day and slept at night. Fleetingly, a question rose into my conscious mind: would I ever be a part of this?

But that sane thought drowned pitifully, swept away in the monsoon of dope-sucking, self-destructive urges and tendencies I'd adapted myself to. I trudged onward, down the fuck-up trail, headed for even more misadventure, personal catastrophe, and chronic drug abuse.

When I saw my boyfriend Chris again, he asked where I'd been for three weeks. "I heard somebody stabbed you. I was looking all over the place! You coulda called y'know." I reminded him that we didn't have a phone. He paused in thought, shrugged, started to walk away, then turned back to me, his face earnest. "Marti, I've been thinking. This dope thing is gettin' way too crazy for us. We need to quit this shit—now!"

I snapped back at him, "Whaddya mean WE, Mother FUCKER?!"

# CHAPTER 18

# CLIMBING OUT FROM UNDER THE ROCK

CHRIS MEANT WHAT HE SAID. WE DID NEED TO QUIT DOPE. BUT I was too much of a hard case to entertain even a fleeting thought of getting clean. My denial ran deeper and murkier than the Russian River at flood level, colder and more lethal than a Pacific Coast riptide. My addiction swept me along toward self-destruction, exactly like the river in that recurrent nightmare I kept experiencing during the homeless year. The putrid torrent of sewage which threatened to drown my daughter and me, the one Chris pulled us out of in the same dream, was my own addictive behavior. When I first met Christopher and fell in love with him, the dream ceased, and I thought that the premonition—the prophecy, you might say—had been fulfilled. I know now that the dream foreshadowed his leading the way toward recovery from the disease of chemical dependency.

In early 1990, Chris began working on his recovery, attending support group meetings and associating with others who were like-minded. At first I didn't think he'd stay with it for long, but I had underestimated his personal power and commitment to change. He did change. The tough, biker persona began to peel away. He started to look happy, genuinely smiling and laughing often. He began to reveal more of his true personality, and at first I hated him for it—because I'd lost my partner in "crime," my number one dope-using buddy. After all, I was a humongous dope fiend. I identified myself as a dope fiend and fiercely clung to my addiction as if it were my very sense of self. Perhaps it was. Unrelenting heartache, grief, and rage had ravaged my soul for years. Savage guilt over abandoning my daughter ruled my heart with an iron fist, holding forgiveness and hope just out of my reach. This guilt and shame fueled my addiction.

Chris is a positive thinking, steady human being. He wholeheartedly embraces life. Chris had decided that enough was enough. He progressed steadily, racking up months of clean time. He got a job working for a hippie artist dude, selling handcrafted wind chimes at a roadside stand along the Russian River. After a while he got his truck running, enrolled in the local community college, then began studying at Sonoma State University. He even joined a dojo and studied martial arts.

I ripped in and out of Chris's life like a tornado, but he never stopped loving me. And no matter how hard I tried to, I couldn't deny that Chris's lifestyle had changed radically. Even more than that, I couldn't refute the fact that he truly had changed. Now, he took life even more in stride, and obviously seemed to be enjoying new challenges, which really pissed me off, since I continued on doing the same old things each day, scoring, shooting up, and surging forward at hyperspeed only to find more nothingness within. I reached a point where no matter how much dope I did, it failed to get me off. But I still needed it to function. I felt like a slave, chained to my habit. My life yielded no joy.

I attempted to quit by my own willpower several times—without success. Every summer, when I pulled myself together and went to Indiana to see my parents and visit my daughter, I managed to stay off dope temporarily. My parents would clean me up, even buy me some clothes and take me to a hair salon for a makeover. I'd pose for pictures with my daughter, looking like a nice mom.

However, I always returned to California where, after only a day, I'd see one of my dope fiend buddies on the street, they'd offer to get me high, and I'd fall back into the cycle. When it came to peer pressure I was always weak.

Luckily for me, several things happened which drove a wedge between my true self and the stony sarcophagus of my addiction and denial. I went to jail for ninety days for possession of an ounce marijuana and failure to pay the related $100 fine. Out of negligence and stupidity, I'd been dodging the local cops for years, racking up failures to appear until one day the sheriffs nabbed me on my way to Rio Nido to score crank. Good thing I wasn't holding at the time, or the cops could've tacked a possession charge onto the bench warrant.

I stood in court, trying to look innocent, a feat I proved incapable of accomplishing. The judge, a staunch conservative infamous among the River People, glared down at me from his lofty perch. "So, finally we meet," he said, dripping disdain and sarcasm. "I've reviewed your paperwork many, many times as you failed to appear and demonstrated flagrant contempt for this court. Well, congratulations, Miss! Today is the day. I'm giving you the maximum sentence, which, believe me, is NOT NEARLY ENOUGH: Ninety days in county jail, no early release." He banged his gavel, ruffled his papers, and made a shooing motion with his hand.

I turned and scuffled toward the back of the courtroom, anxious to escape that building, thirsting for a few gulps of sweet freedom before turning myself in. As I pushed open the heavy glass door, a buff young Latino, tattooed like a gangbanger, approached me on my right, whispering, "Pssst! Hey, what did you do, lady? I've never seen the hangin' judge look so pissed!"

"Too many FTAs on a nickel and dime weed beef," I mumbled shamefacedly, "Sorry if I, um, set the mood..."

He chuckled. "S' cool. Good luck at the farm, Chica. Next time pay your fines."

"Right." I shuffled out of the court building, dreading my up-coming jail time. So far I'd never done more than a weekend, but now was guaranteed to spend at least ninety days. I'd seen the Rod-ney King beating on television at one of my dope dealers' houses; it intensified the fear and paranoia with which I regarded the cops. Still, I knew better than to blow it off—no, this time I would have to go through with it.

Chris encouraged me to show cooperation by arriving on time to serve my sentence; he even offered to drive me over there and drop me off. When the appointed day arrived, how-ever, I felt annoyed by the prospect of being so straightforward with authority. The way I saw things, I would need to load up on dope, to ingest as much as possible in preparation for the or-deal—and I felt ashamed to admit that to Chris. Instead I went on the offensive, growling, "I don't wanna ride with you. I'll hitchhike."

"Suit yourself." He gave me a knowing look.

After stopping at a few sympathetic dope houses, I managed to get amped up, but not totally spun—a delicate balance. I kept pro-crastinating so that I arrived at the county facility much later than originally intended, but not past legal deadline. While the cops were screening and admitting me, I saw nearly a dozen dope fiends from the River, filing in and out under the supervision of guards. All of them waved or nodded, registering mock disbelief or friendly enthusiasm at seeing me there, no doubt alerting the cops that I was one of the River People.

*Hey, maybe this won't be so bad. At least I know plenty of dope fiends—but hey—knowing dope fiends inside is both a curse and a blessing! Chris warned me that if I get caught with even a CRUMB of dope while serving a jail sentence, it'll be a felony!* The idea of using in jail or screwing up in any way terrified me. With acquain-tances inside, I would run across more than a few opportunities to get high, but could I muster enough self-control to withstand my urges?

The night I arrived I was so wired and antsy that I acted...a little twitchy, to say the least. My friends, who could tell I'd ingested too much dope, laughed at my self-induced agitation. The guards, however, regarded me much, much differently. They put me in solitary confinement for two weeks, which definitely settled me down, then returned me to general population status. I am so lucky they never tested me for drugs. I guess they thought I was a nut case; I'll never know.

When I got transferred from solitary back to the dorm, they assigned me a single bunk in the front row, directly under the cops' glass observation windows. Three really cool Native American chicks—Miwoks—shared the front row with me. They were tough, fun, and very good laughers. We knew a lot of the same people; so I trusted them.

The Miwok chicks thought I was hysterically funny—even when I wasn't trying. As far as jail goes I lacked experience, and it showed. One day I remarked, "We've got the best seats in the house—it's not even crowded up here in our section! We must be doin' something right, huh?"

Those chicks roared with laughter. Olivia, who occupied the bunk to the left of mine, filled me in. "Marti, we're up here so they can keep an eye on us. The guards consider us security risks." Then she leaned in and whispered, "They're a little scared of us."

"Scared of us? Why? They've got guns and everything."

Olivia erupted into a fresh fit of giggles. "They don't have guns! Haven't you noticed anything? Look at their utility belts. All they've got is, like, handcuffs and flashlights."

"B-But...they're COPS! And they're guarding us. Why don't they have guns?"

Olivia turned to me and smiled meaningfully. "Because if they had guns, WE'D have 'em."

"Oh." I nodded to indicate I was now hip. And I began to relax a little more. After all, the cops are people, too. Realizing that improved my outlook. I felt a touch less oppressed by authority.

I adjusted fairly quickly to the total lack of privacy, metal bunks, paper-thin mattresses, flourescent lights, bad food, and noise. I'd been homeless, which, I believe, is much worse; and I knew I was only doing three months—a piece of cake! Some of the women in there were headed for prison, to serve long stretches on drug charges. Several still awaited sentencing, after having already spent a year in custody. A few were being held in county between prison terms. The majority of us were locked up for drug possession or related charges. I had a lot to think about—and a lot of time to consider how easily I could end up doing major time for drugs.

Since I loved to read, I checked books out of the jail library and read constantly to pass the time. Chris contributed a lot toward making my jail sentence tolerable by sending me a subscription to the L.A. Times, the only newspaper which delivered to correctional institutions. I was jailed during the conclusion of the Rodney King trial and the ensuing riots; and since lots of my fellow inmates hailed from Los Angeles, they offered me candy bars, cigarettes, and instant coffee in exchange for the privilege of being first to read each new issue. That worked out well for me.

Christopher also made sure I got mail every day—a letter or postcard. Some of this mail was from our dog, Black Jack. Chris would ghost write for Jack in a hilariously canine style; the "handwriting" actually suspended disbelief—it looked as though a dog had taken pen in paw and scrawled each letter. Two out of three characters of the alphabet were backward or upside-down, yet not too difficult to decipher. My fellow inmates roared with laughter as I shared each letter from Jack around the dorm. One woman, red-faced and breathless, managed to stop giggling long enough to say, "Your dog writes better than my boyfriend does!"

In jail, while my head was clear of dope, my personality began to emerge, and I actually started to consider myself a part of the human race again. Sure, I screwed up and started doing dope as soon as I got released, but still, I experienced a taste of the chemical-free life, which lies just outside the realm of addiction.

Not long after my release from custody, the older of my two younger brothers called me—we finally had a phone again, thanks to Christopher. "Hey, Sis, I'm having a surprise party for Dad's seventieth birthday. I want you to be there. I'll pay for your airfare and everything."

"Um, I don't know, I...can't take your money, it wouldn't be right."

"Listen, you gotta come! I love you. Mom tells me you're on drugs or something, but I told her I don't care if you're even... shooting up heroin! You're my sister and you belong with our family! Now do it, okay? Or I'll come out there and find you!"

*It's not heroin, it's meth. But you were close, Bro.* I felt ashamed and touched by his goodness. The thought of my clean-cut brother combing the River drug dens in search of me was more than I could take. "Okay, I'll come. But I gotta pay you back for the plane ticket."

The seventieth birthday party totally surprised my dad. I don't know how my mom and my brother kept it secret from him, but they succeeded. I've always adored my father—he's my hero. During the party, I seized an opportunity to speak with him alone. I'm one of five children, so I didn't get many chances for time alone with him, but when I did, he always made me feel exceptional, intelligent, loved and...safe. I longed to communicate to him how much he meant to me, and what a wonderful father he was.

I began recounting the precious moments we'd shared throughout my life—the conversations with him, the things he'd taught me. I told him how, as early as five years old, I could ask him about anything, any issue, and he'd give me the straight stuff, on my level. I didn't mention the talk we'd had in his car on the day he picked me up at the airport after I escaped from Japan. The memory haunted me.

"All of that was so important to me! Dad, I remember all these conversations as though they happened yesterday. I know you probably had the same sort of exchanges with all of your other children, but for me, they stand out as key events in my life. I've always felt as though you were more than a father to me—you've been teacher, mentor, friend, even a kind of comrade-in arms..." I held my breath, wondering if I sounded crazy.

My father's reply came softly. "We're kindred spirits, Martha. I remember every one of our conversations—they are as significant in my life as they are in yours." He dropped his hands in his lap and looked at them. "I worry about the rage I see in you. It's boiling beneath the surface. It reminds me of the way I felt after the war, and I fear for you. Every time you come home, we get you fixed up, you get better...but then I have to let you go back to California. I'm always afraid that one of these times, you'll jump on a plane, and... and I'll never see you again."

"Oh, Dad, I'll be okay. Don't worry." But I knew he was right. Back at the River, I teetered on the brink of total disaster and misery—it'd become a way of life. I longed for an escape, but simply could not see a way out at that point. But our conversation stayed in my mind, and I believe it became a guidepost on my gradual ascent from the abyss. I became more conscious of my awful rage and began to wonder how I might alleviate it.

That summer, I spent several weeks with Mom and Dad, and visited my brother and his wife—successful, middle-class people with three adorable kids. I hadn't seen them in over five years. And they welcomed me! I couldn't believe it. I got to spend a few weeks with Annie at my brother and sister-in-law's place. We baked cookies, did our nails, and watched movies with my brother's kids—blissful experiences.

The younger of my little brothers, who is the coolest guy in the world, got married later that summer. I stayed to attend the ceremony and reception. My brother treated me with kindness and respect, which made a tremendous positive impact on me. Annie and I shopped for dresses to wear to the wedding; my parents picked up the tab, for which I felt simultaneously ashamed and grateful. At the wedding, my family, as well as my brother's bride's family, accepted me and I blended in. I felt like a real, loving mom and a nice, beautiful woman.

Sadly, after that summer, I returned to California and my addiction. I forgot my true self once more, slipping back into the underworld and my own self-pity and rage. I continued in misery, trapped in my disease. I needed to learn a few more lessons.

In early September 1994, I ended up in the emergency room. I'd been experiencing abdominal pain for months, but avoided seeing doctors for fear they'd discover drugs in my system and have me arrested. My protracted neglect finally resulted in sudden illness: extremely high fever, chills, and vomiting.

Chris was gone in Berkeley that day, so I decided to wait it out until he got back. My teeth were chattering...no, slamming together. I wrapped myself up in a big wool blanket. Hours passed as I faded in and out of consciousness. I did some dope to try to stay awake—I dreaded losing all consciousness. After quite a while, a strange sense of quietude and a weird apathy blanketed me. All of a sudden I didn't care what happened—I only wanted to sleep. In the next moment, a javelin of searing pain shot through my midsection. I vaguely noticed my stomach swelling up. But strangely, I didn't care. I felt so very, very calm. I knelt, put my head down on an armchair, and faded away.

When Chris got home he shook me awake, pulled me to my feet, half-dragged me to his truck, and drove to the hospital. The doctors immediately admitted me to intensive care. I'd had a cyst on one of my fallopian tubes, which had abscessed and burst, resulting in peritonitis. I stayed in intensive care for weeks fighting the infection. During this time I determined to quit smoking. After all, I had tubes in my nose and mouth, and IVs and everything! When I got out of the hospital, I successfully continued to abstain from smoking.

Over the next year, I struggled with my conscience regarding using. I felt the compulsion to feed my habit, but every time I got high, I felt sorrow over what I was doing to my daughter, Chris, my parents, and myself. One day in June of 1995, I got high with my ex-con friend Frank, a bank robber and dope fiend who'd spent twenty-three years in San Quentin, Soledad, and a state prison in Oregon from which he'd escaped, then been returned to after running amok for eight years. After release from his second stint in Oregon, Frank came back to the River to spend his remaining years near his young son. I liked Frank, he had a great sense of humor and a lot of heart. Anyway, we did up some dope, and Frank turned to me and said, "Marti, you need to quit dope."

"Screw you!"

"No, Marti, you gotta quit! You spend all your energy chasin' down a bag, then when you do it up, it only makes you sad because you miss your daughter. You oughta quit dope so you can get her back. And your old man, Chris, he's a mensch. He quit. He can help you." He glared viciously at me, his most threatening prison yard stare, no doubt.

I tried to act tough. "What is this, Frank? You got an agenda?" I didn't want to let my guard down, but he had my full attention. And I knew his observations were absolutely correct.

"No. I'm only gonna say this once, so listen. You're a creature of the light, Marti. I can see you, because I've lived in the darkness all my life. If I'm crouched outside a house at midnight, and the lights are on in there, I can see everybody inside, but they can't see me. That's what the light is—it shows things up. I'm a creature of darkness. But you—you need to quit that dope and step all the way into the light. Make yourself happy."

For the first time in years, I couldn't think of a comeback. Frank had blown my mind. And my cover, too.

———

I SKIDDED ALONG IN THE DOPE SCENE FOR SEVERAL WEEKS MORE, only halfheartedly. Finally, like every addict does, I reached the ultimate fork in the road—The Jumping-Off Point. That's where you either find recovery or you die. It's a real place. Despair stalked me every minute of every day. I looked at my life, present and future, and saw a dismal, sepia wash; a never-ending tunnel of misery and nothingness. I saw minutes stretching into eternity—the seventh circle of Hell. I knew I couldn't last much longer before I destroyed myself. I felt heavy with pain and hopelessness. Then suddenly I did something I cannot explain. Call it whatever you want.

I got down on my knees beside my bed and...well, prayed. But this was nothing like the stuff I was brainwashed with in Catholic school. It was more like talking than praying. I kept my eyes open, didn't fold my hands or anything. I remember saying, "God—whoever you are, wherever you are, please help me. I'm so unhappy. I want to be happy. Please help me." After that I stood up, walked into the kitchen, grabbed a phone book and started calling local treatment facilities, asking for immediate help. But I couldn't get into any of them. They all had very long waiting lists or cost thousands of dollars. One county facility told me to try calling back in a month or so. But I got recovery without rehab, as it happened.

That was the first week of August, 1995. My parents called and let me know that my daughter Annie, who'd lived with her father in Florida for the past year, had recently moved to Indiana by herself. My folks offered to buy me a plane ticket to come and visit for a few weeks so that I could make contact with Annie. They scheduled my flight for August 8th.

I resolved to make a radical change in my life, even if that meant staying in Indiana indefinitely. At the time, I mistakenly believed that the reason I couldn't stay off drugs was because of outward circumstances. I did not yet understand that the powerful impulses of addiction crouched in my neural pathways, directing every thought, feeling, and action toward using. I didn't know anything about addiction or recovery yet. All I knew—on a level so deep it was still mostly unconscious—was that I had to get clean or die.

August 8th rolled around and I freaked out. I didn't use that day because I didn't have enough time or money to score. But my addiction still raged within me. I acted like a complete idiot to Chris. I got hysterical and cried all the way to the airport. I even jumped out of the car a couple of times. I've always been a drama queen, but this was ridiculous, even for me. I've got to hand it to Chris. It's a miracle he didn't just back the car over me, toss my suitcase on top of my corpse, and peel out.

# CHAPTER 19

# BREAKTHROUGH

MY DAUGHTER ANNIE STOOD IN MY PARENTS' LIVING ROOM. She'd grown into a graceful, beautiful young woman—with woefully little help from me. Now eighteen years old, Annie regarded me skeptically as I sat on my folks' sofa, trying to come up with excuses for myself and the life I'd led.

Suddenly she interrupted my chain of blames and shames to say, "Mom, I don't know what's been wrong all these years, but whatever it is, you can change it. I decided a long time ago to make my own happiness. I did it. And Mom, I've got my own apartment now—so you can come and stay with me until you get yourself straightened out."

And that galvanized me. My true moment of epiphany arrived in that instant. Annie offered me forgiveness, and I accepted. All of my new life stems from there: At that moment I got my first contact with a power greater than myself—unconditional love from my daughter, which sparked my inner healing force. I know it sounds all new age-y and everything, but that's exactly what happened. In that moment I felt none of the old shame and fear, only love and possibility. I took a deep breath and answered her. "Annie, I've been a drug addict for years. But you're right—I can change it. I'll change my life. I will never do drugs again."

"I don't want to hear promises unless you keep them, Mom."

Over sixteen years have passed since I made that promise, and I've kept it unbroken with help from a power greater than myself. It's amazing how well a daily program of recovery can work, if it is practiced consistently. I maintain my daily program, and I receive connectedness, education, and guidance through support groups.

Today I don't drink, or use, or smoke cigarettes, and I don't miss any of those substances I once craved. I even quit caffeine. I don't need it. When I stay in a state of love and possibility I find the energy I need to accomplish my goals. I've discovered the strength that comes from opening my mind to unconditional love and endless possibility.

Addiction is a primary disease. It affects the brain and the body. But human beings possess a wondrous innate power to heal. It is possible to come back from addiction and reverse the damage. Recovery is a developmental process, and it is not easy, but it is deeply rewarding. I've advanced one step at a time.

Recovery begins with abstinence and continues on the path to self-improvement. With abstinence, the brain can begin healing, and the path opens up into a new superhighway. Abstinence is the key, but recovery is the car, the road, and the destination. After nearly ten years of being trapped in the trunk, blindfolded, bound and gagged, with my addiction driving, I was now in the driver's seat, my drug habit kicked to the curb!

After my moment of clarity, I began to work on my recovery one day at a time. That's the only way an addict can do it. I have to live in the present moment, otherwise it's too easy to be immobilized by regrets about the past, or panicked by fears about the future. I stayed in Indiana for about a month, during which time I began the long, healing journey with Annie and my mother and father, but soon realized that I needed to return to California. After all, I'd left a hell of a lot of wreckage there. I knew I owed it to Christopher to come home to him. With thirty days clean, I'd begun to see how much it cost him to keep on loving me.

When I told my daughter I needed to go back to California, she said, "Okay Mom, but don't you drop out of sight on me again. I can't have you in my life if you're not consistent. Understand?"

I understood. We'd begun to build our relationship. No way would I risk damaging that. When I got back home, I called my daughter every day and wrote to her twice a week, to let her know I was still clean—and to keep in touch. She'd say, "I'm proud of you, Mom," and my heart would swell to breaking point. I'd be inundated with love and gratitude. I still am, every time I think of how my daughter forgave me and allowed me to be a part of her life again. I started learning about positive self-talk and positive thinking. I learned to visualize and believe in the outcome of my goals. I continue to discover the power of trust, love, and forgiveness each day.

Chris was tremendously happy and relieved that I came home and stayed clean this time. He helped me field phone calls from old dope associates. I was afraid to answer the phone for fear I'd get triggered—and relapse—when somebody called and offered to sell me a bag. Chris would pick up and tell them, "Marti doesn't do dope anymore." Then he'd slam down the phone for emphasis. (That was back when we had an old school phone and you could still slam down. Now the only option is to push a button. Not quite as butch.)

It didn't take long for local dope fiends to catch the drift. Meth Monster Marti was out of the market. I owed money—$20 here, $30 there, to a few small-time dealers; not many, since toward the end of my downward spiral, it'd been damn near impossible for me to get anything on credit. Chris and I decided it would be best to immediately pay up the debts wherever possible.

We knew it would be a slippery spot for me to go to a dealer, so Chris went for me. Turned out these dealers, rather than being disappointed at loss of commerce, were palpably relieved, even buoyed in spirit, to hear that I had quit doing drugs. These vendors of contraband no longer had to deal with the possibility that Dope Meister Marti might show up at three a.m., attempting to trade a hubcap for a dime bag. All of these dealers even told Chris to congratulate me on getting clean. "Tell her to keep up the good work," each one of them urged, as they waved him out of their trailers and ramshackle houses.

Christopher and I rebuilt and strengthened our relationship. And we had fun in the process. We laughed a lot. I rented movies from the previous nine years, in order to catch up on some of the pop culture I'd missed as a dope fiend. We started watching a lot of comedy together. I used to look at him every day and say, "Thanks for waiting for me." And he'd say, "No problem, Marti."

I know that recovery is a constant process. I practice it every day. When I first got clean, my thinking, my self-concept, changed drastically for the better. I felt elated to finally be free. And what a relief it is not to have to score each day! Being a dope fiend is a full-time job. You work really hard to get high. In a twisted way, it takes a lot of creativity, tenacity, commitment, and focus to survive as an addict.

When I cleaned up, I discovered I could apply my creativity, commitment, tenacity and focus toward healthy, constructive ends. Although I don't dwell on the past, I never forget where I've come from. I find steely strength in remembering that I've survived drug addiction, slavery, violence, abuse, and all kinds of fallout from my myriad personal fuckups, and can now live exuberantly with a clear conscience. I can look back, laugh, sometimes cry, but I always celebrate the present moment.

When I first got clean, I felt driven to work out—especially cardio. I'd walk, and after I saved enough for a mountain bike, I would ride for miles each day. I began a weightlifting program, too; when you're building your muscles you're building your brain. Exercise is essential to mental and physical health—it's a form of medicine, and I make sure I get a steady supply of it.

The process of recovery involves building new neuronal pathways in the brain. I started doing affirmations. They work. Cognitive behavioral therapy (CBT) is a valuable tool for me also. By taking contrary action against negative thought patterns, I carve out a new way of life. I found a wonderful therapist and have engaged in a form of therapy for post-traumatic stress disorder, which helped me tremendously.

Gratitude and love are the forces which carry me along in this new life path and continue to heal me. There is so much love, and beauty, and power and...well, magic...in this life, and it is available, accessible. All I have to do is open my mind to it. I believe that I get what I expect from life. Whatever I concentrate on increases exponentially. So I focus on what I have now, and what I want to create in my life. When I wake up in the morning, I think of my recovery and I start feeling stoked. If I wake up depressed, I start saying, "Thank you," and I repeat those words with increasing passion until I'm truly feeling it. I want to feel grateful and hopeful and loving every minute of each day.

Eventually I started going to coffee house open mikes and learning to do standup again. After I'd built up a little over five minutes of material, I began driving to San Francisco to do comedy—140 miles round trip—four or five days a week. I performed wherever and whenever I could get on stage. In standup, stage time is everything.

Later, Chris and I rented an apartment in Los Angeles. I practiced and learned whatever I could in the comedy scene there. After a while I started getting some paying gigs. I related these little successes to my daughter. I think she worried about me working in close proximity to alcohol and other temptations. "Mom, can't you do comedy in churches or something? Why does it have to be in clubs?"

When I'd go on the road, Annie always wanted me to call her each night after the show to check in. One time, I'd had a really good set, and some college students invited me to smoke a joint with them. "No thanks," I told them. Then they offered me a line instead. "Thanks again, but no thanks," I said.

Afterward I went up to my room and called my daughter. I told her how well my act'd gone over. Swept up in the moment, I blurted, "I killed, honey! Some kids around your age thought I was so funny they invited me to get high with 'em." (I only told her this in order to describe how cool they must have thought her mother was.)

At this, Annie replied, "Mother, I forbid you to talk to those people! Stay in your hotel room and do not go back down there! Be careful!" And as always I felt crazy with gratitude for my wonderful daughter. Simply hearing her address me as, "Mother," is a thrill. Over time I've shown her how strong my recovery is.

My daughter met the perfect guy and married him. She planned a gorgeous wedding ceremony and reception. They bought a house in Indianapolis. Months later Annie got pregnant. After she told me her due date, I booked some gigs in Illinois, Indiana, and Michigan for a month or so leading up to that date, so I could be in the area to welcome my grandson Drew into the world—and to support my daughter in motherhood. Annie is an example to me. She's such a good mother; so loving and patient. She's intelligent, talented, generous, funny, and gorgeous. She helped me save my life. And she allows me to be a part of her life—a precious gift. Occasionally I find myself longing—wishing to go back in time, to erase the hurt I caused Annie through my failings as a mother during her childhood, but I know I cannot change the past. What I can change is the present. I can be the best mother and grandmother that I can possibly be, one day at a time.

# CHAPTER 20

# STAND YOUR GROUND

COMEDY PLAYED A HUGE ROLE IN MY RECOVERY. I LEARNED HOW to connect with other human beings through laughs. I've played to audiences of over two thousand and under a dozen. I've performed in comedy clubs of course, but also in biker bars, homeless shelters, even a federal penitentiary. And every one of those audiences gave me something valuable above and beyond the laughs—or the lack thereof.

Of all the gigs I've booked, it's the hell gigs that have afforded me some of my biggest life lessons. As I said earlier, when I first returned to standup, I began building my act in redneck bars and hippie poetry coffeehouses in Sonoma County. After about six months, I'd put together ten minutes or so. Of course, my stuff wasn't pounding yet, but on certain nights I killed, and after one of my better sets, a guy in a cowboy hat approached me, asking if I'd like to perform in a fundraiser for a Native American casino. "It'll be a coupla months—July maybe. We can only pay you fifty bucks, but you'll get a lot of exposure, and we got a bigshot headliner comin' in from L.A., so it'll look good on your resume."

*Fifty bucks! My first paying gig—a giant step in my comeback!* "Wow, I'd love to do it! Thanks, Mister..."

"Buck's the name." He handed me a business card. "Gimme a call, kid. I gotta go onstage." I glanced at the card. In the dim barroom lighting, I could barely make out something about a Chevy truck dealership.

At that moment, the open mike emcee called out, "Let's hear it for Buck Wade!" Buck grabbed an acoustic guitar, leapt onto the stage and began strumming away in a country music style. In spite of my punk/hard rock preferences, I had to admit he sang pretty well. The song appeared to be an original. *Not bad...*

Next, Buck belted out a chorus of, "Shoot that dog," and encouraged the audience to sing along. An inkling of a red flag waved feebly in the back of my brain, but I pushed it away. *A paying gig! The first since my downward spiral...*Stalwart, I hung out through five more dog-shoot choruses so I could shake Buck's hand. "Thank you for this opportunity, Mr. Wade. I'll work really hard!"

"Great! I'll keep you posted on the details. Gotta head out now." He grinned, spun around and marched toward the exit.

That was May 1997. The prospect of an upcoming gig raising money for Native American casinos invigorated me. I loved the idea of helping the Miwoks or Pomos. After all, I knew Robin—he was a Pomo—and how about those badass Miwok chicks from jail? They were all still locked up—and that totally sucked—so for that very same reason, I thought I should do my part to help get those casino dollars rolling in to the reservations...

For weeks, I heard nothing from Buck, and I hesitated to call him or I might rock the boat. I really wanted the gig. Finally, in mid-June, he notified me that the event was set for July 11th.

On June 30th, Buck called to let me know the date'd been moved back to July 30th. "Sorry about this, Marti—but we got a real good headliner. He's a Native American comic named Charlie Hill. An' I'm thinkin', this'll be really cool because you lived in Texas, right?"

"Uh, yeah, right."

"Heh. Heh. Yeah, so it'll be kinda like cowboys an' Indians, huh? Get it?"

"Uh, yeah." At this point, a fiery red flag rippled ominously in the breeze of my intuition. "Um.Yeah." *What the fuck is goin' on here?* Adamant, I suppressed my feelings. *A paying gig.* "See you July 30th, Buck."

I threw myself into positive visualization in a desperate bid for confidence as the date of the gig got moved further back incrementally. Each week, Buck called to announce another postponement, and railed against the poor planning of the Native American event committee. "These Indians can't seem to set a date an' stick to it!!" Now an enormous red flag waved frantically in my mind's eye—I could almost touch it! Buck's tirades conjured up images from one of those hopelessly bigoted, racist television series that polluted American collective consciousness during the '50s and '60s: A nineteenth century grizzled old wagon train master or mountain man, muttering bitterly, "Them dadburned Injuns! They've broke their treaty..." An ill omen, for sure! Still, I hungered for quality stage time and the opportunity to work with and learn from a true professional, a national headliner like Charlie Hill.

Finally, in late August, the day of the gig arrived, with showtime set for noon, in the stadium at the Mendocino County Fairgrounds in Ukiah, California. Chris drove up there with me in our funky little 1985 Renault Alliance—the Appliance, we called it. Chris'd purchased the vehicle from a friend of ours who dabbled in used auto brokerage, procuring confiscated cars dirt cheap at DEA auctions. Whatever dope slinger they cadged this baby from was hardly a cartel jefe! This piece of shit car'd been riddled with bullet holes at one point, then Bondo-ed and primered into a semblance of social acceptability—however, the spray of ammo still shone through its white paint job.

In addition to cosmetic issues with the chassis, the liner of the interior roof sagged so badly that we had to lift up the hanging fabric in order to glance in the rearview mirror. But unlike past sets of wheels we'd driven, this auto was legitimately ours—registered, insured, and paid for. We were on our way up, and the Appliance was merely a stepping-stone on the road to glory. Of course, we brought our dog Black Jack. En route to Ukiah, we purchased blocks of ice and set them on the floor in the backseat to augment the car's ailing air conditioning, so Jack could stay comfortable. The predicted high temperature that day was 100 degrees.

When we arrived at the Mendo County Fairgrounds, the sun beat down relentlessly, the thermometer registered 102 degrees, and I found out that the show would take place outdoors, in a stadium of the sort used for horse races or monster truck rallies. Buck greeted us and gave me the lineup. I would perform first, at noon, followed by Charlie Hill, then some country band—The Oakridge Boys or Rodeo Hounds or Cowchip Slingers or whatever the fuck, and then later that night, Dave Mason—of Traffic and Fleetwood Mac. *Hmmmm. Noon standup comedy. Outdoors, 102 degrees. Bleachers, country music and monster trucks. Hellllll giiiig!!!* Buck went on to say, "I'd introduce you to Charlie Hill, but he's in the limo with his manager. They're gonna keep the motor running an' the AC on." *Wow. A limo. AC. And a manager. I've got a long way to go...*

As I approached the stadium I saw people lined up at the ticket booth. But only a few. Fervently, I whispered a pep talk to myself— *The crowds are already packed in there, clamoring in the stands for live comedy. Sure, that's it. These few are latecomers, stragglers vying for standing room.*

Chris, Jack and I reached the backstage area and looked around. A man approached. "Hi, I'm Bill. Are you Marti, the opening act?"

"Yeah. Can our dog stay backstage?"

"Er, well. Not really, it's against regulations. Hey, can you, like, stretch it? Y'know, do a half hour? We need you to stall for time. The Rodeo Hounds're gonna be a little late. And, uh, we're gonna start the show around one p.m."

"Uh, okay. I'll do a half hour. Er, I'll, um, stretch it." I swallowed, realized my mouth'd gone dry. I only had ten minutes I could actually depend on for solid laughs. "Well, you gotta let my dog stay if I do that much time."

"We'll see. Anyway, I'm going to introduce you. I do kickass intros." Bill hurried away.

One peek into the stadium's bleachers spoke volumes about the hell I was poised to walk through. It was now ten minutes to showtime, yet I saw only about fifty people in the stands, and panicked. They weren't sitting together, either, they were scattered widely throughout the bleachers, as though each audience member was a psychopath, a rabid antisocial who needed to isolate. None of them were Native Americans either—they all looked to be hatchet-faced grannies or old rednecks in bib overalls. *But in Mendocino County they grow weed! Weed farmers don't look like this! Or do they? Oh, man...*

Desperately, I turned to Christopher. "Hey, honey, um...this isn't gonna be good. It's gonna suck, and I hate for you to see it. Promise me that when I go onstage you'll take Jack, get in the car, and drive all the way to the farthest reaches of the stadium parking lot and wait till my set is over. Please."

"Okay, I'll do it...if it makes you feel better. But think positive. You're gonna do great!" *Yeah...right.*

A few minutes later, someone from the sound crew told me that although the Hopland band of Pomo Indians co-sponsored the event, they didn't get to handle the scheduling. Due to a mix-up, a Tri-state Pow Wow was currently in progress, so the Native American community wouldn't be attending this event. *Perfect.* My positive visualizations curled up in a fetal position and flipped me off. Teetering on the brink of despondency, I sat down on a bench and waited for the show to start.

At one-thirty p.m., Bill, the guy who'd assured me he did kickass intros, walked out on the platform, thumped his forefinger on the microphone a couple of times and said, "Okay, everybody!

Marti's coming up here to talk to you." He whirled and stomped off the stage.

The disgruntled-looking crowd sat stonily silent. A smattering of guilt applause came from Buck Wade and a group of five Native Americans who'd just now sat down in the front row. I figured they were the event planning committee and therefore obliged to be supportive. I stepped up to the microphone and did my first joke. Silence. I continued. Silence. I would've welcomed the sound of crickets chirping. Nothing. I squinted into the sun and looked out into the angry faces scattered randomly around the stands. One of the Native American planning committee stood up and passed me a pair of sunglasses. I nodded thanks and put them on.

I knew I was bombing miserably but kept on going, glancing at my watch from time to time. *I promised them a half hour and dammit, I will deliver. No matter what this looks like, I'm a motherfucking professional.* At one point, I heard Black Jack barking in the distance. No doubt he'd heard my voice over the speakers. I wrestled with the urge to whistle and call out, "Here, boy," in hopes of summoning a friendly face in the midst of this catastrophe.

Suddenly the wind picked up, in seething, scorching gusts that scattered grit and debris around the stadium. My hair blew over my face and I fleetingly hoped it would disguise my identity. Buck Wade stood, passed me his cowboy hat. I put it on to keep my hair back and finished out my time. During the last ten minutes I found my rhythm and actually heard laughter. I walked off the stage with mouth bone dry and knees shaking.

As I slumped down the platform's steps in disgrace, taking care not to make eye contact with any other human being, someone half-whispered, "That took guts." I scuttled off, head hanging. In the seventh circle of comedy hell, people exhort you with, "That took guts." If someone had passed me a shovel, I'd have set to work then and there, digging a deep, deep hole, jumping into it and shouting for the nearest gravedigger to cover me with dirt and tamp it down.

I found Chris standing around beside the platform. He gave me a smile, and all of a sudden, everything made sense. *No matter how fucked up that set was, I'm loved, and I lead a charmed life.* We hung out to watch Charlie Hill. I laughed and learned. He worked that crowd with consummate comedic skill. Awestruck, and a little embarrassed, I resolved to make my getaway as soon as Charlie's set ended. My budding aspirations of rubbing shoulders with a true professional had wilted in the hot glare of my perceived inadequacy as a comic.

Charlie wrapped it up, did his closer and exited. I turned to Chris, "Hey, we gotta get the fuck outta here right now. I can call Buck and get him to mail me my check. Let's go before anybody from the audience recognizes me. C'mon, hurry!"

Chris put his hands on my shoulders, looked me in the eye. "Marti, you need to say something to him. Remember, the reason you did this thing was so you could hang out with a real comedian."

I thought it over. Comedy, like recovery, required me to set aside my ego in order to progress. I figured I'd better do it. With no comedy scene in my locale, I needed other comics like mountain climbers need oxygen molecules in high altitude: Infrequent chances to breathe deeply when in rarified air. Buck sauntered up to me, handed me my paycheck. "Hey Marti, Charlie's lookin' for you. He wants to talk to you."

*Uh-oh. This can't be good.* I took a deep breath, steadied myself. "Where is he?" Buck pointed. I gathered my courage, walked over to Charlie and introduced myself.

"Hey, I was looking for you! You did okay, y'know that?"

"It was a disaster!"

"No, you did all right. Because you stood your ground. That's what we do. Comedy is kinda like martial arts, you take your stance and engage the audience. They don't call it a punchline for nothing. Y'know, you remind me of me, back when I was starting out in New York. I'd be standing there, telling some story that nobody wanted to hear, and I'd keep going. I was working it out. It takes time. Lenny Bruce said that the more you are, the more it takes to develop. Richard Pryor shared that with me—Lenny helped him comin' up. Richard saw me back in my early days and kinda took me under his wing."

"Yeah? That's so cool!"

"Uh-huh, he taught me a lot. Like I said, Marti, you remind me of me when I started out. When you were climbing down off that stage, I heard somebody say, 'That took guts.' People used to say that to me, too."

"Really?" I was starting to feel a little better.

"Yeah. Y'know, kid, you've got talent. I can tell because when you stepped back from your material you were funny. You have the gift—respect it, respect yourself, and command respect from your audience. Don't get lost in the words, instead, be all that you are, up there on stage, and the words will follow. Richard Pryor told me, 'Write on your feet.' And all this comes with stage time."

We continued to converse, and I began to open up to Charlie about my past disastrous mistakes—how I'd had a Tonight Show booked, but got strung out and threw away my career.

"So you knew Jim McCauley?"

"Yeah."

"McCauley gave me my first shot too."

Some young men approached with a big bag. "Here's your pay," they told Charlie.

"Come back later," Charlie said, and waved them away. "Marti and I are talkin' shop here." He turned to me. "You came back from drug addiction. That takes a lot. You ought to let your audience know that. You'll find a way to communicate it. Y'know, Marti, there are only two kinds of standup comics—there are people who get laughs, and then there are comedians. Richard Pryor told me that. See, some comics get up there, and do jokes, and they get laughs, but when they walk away from the mike, you realize you don't know anything about them. And then there are comedians. Comedians dig down into all the pain and anguish in their souls and somehow find a way to spin it into laughter. And when they walk away from the mike, you feel certain you know them well. Richard Pryor was like that—he was a comedian. And you and me, Marti, we're comedians."

"We are?"

"Yeah, we are."

On that sweltering hot afternoon, at the Mendocino County Fairgrounds, Charlie Hill helped me to appreciate my identity as a comedian—and an individual. In that moment, I felt as if the sky had opened up and rained down all kinds of hope and promise. I learned then what I live today: Anything is possible as long as I stand my ground.

———

YEARS AGO, I DID A SHOW WITH ANOTHER COMIC AT A TRIPPY little theater in San Francisco. The theater was owned by a troupe of acrobats who used pyrotechnics—they'd dropped in to check on some of their equipment. I introduced myself to them in the lobby before going on stage. "So, what do you guys do exactly?"

"We do trapeze work—aerial stuff, y'know, while juggling fire. Flaming torches. Ralph here sometimes catches them in his teeth." One of the daredevils said this, gesturing to indicate the slender, long haired dude standing next to him was Ralph.

*Long, frizzy hair! And in his line of work. Damn!* Nervously, I acknowledged my respect. "Wow! Ralph. Hey, you guys're pretty amazing!"

They nodded, accepting my adulation. "You get used to it," one of them said nonchalantly.

Ralph spoke up. "So, how about you, lady? What do you do?"

"Oh, I do standup comedy."

The entire acrobatic troupe seemed to take a step back. Ralph, acting as spokesman, turned to look at me, eyes as big as saucers. "Standup?" He shivered. "That's the scariest thing in show business!"

"You get used to it," I said, and walked off toward the stage entrance.

I didn't make it big as a comic, but the lessons I learned and experience I gained are worth the years of effort I put into standup. I learned how to muster my enthusiasm and conquer my fear every time I stepped in front of an audience. Well, almost every time.

When a comedian friend asked me to do standup with her and a handful of other comics at a prison, I agreed without even a nanosecond of hesitation. I never even asked any details about the penitentiary in question. In the back of my mind, I was thinking it would be a women's prison.

I felt pretty stoked at the concept of making the inmates laugh. I'd only done county time, myself, and never more than ninety days at a stretch. I knew that but for chance and circumstance, I'd be doing time in prison for dope offenses. I could be in that audience. So the opportunity felt kind of karmic, in a way.

I knew that the show'd been organized through a church and a prison chaplain, so I determined to alter my act a little—for the church's sake. Normally, my act was rated R—at its mildest. But I worked on what I thought might be wholesome yet witty observational stuff. What the hell was I thinking?

On the day of the gig, all of us comics met at the church and car-pooled to the prison. That's when I found out the name of the peni-tentiary: Terminal Island. At least it sounds like a prison. Some of the names they come up with for these prisons are ludicrous. Back in the day, one of my crankster friends served a seven-year sentence in a joint called "Pleasant Valley." That sucks, doesn't it? That par-ticular prison is located on a vast, dreary, desolate, flat plain in the San Joaquin Valley, so I guess the "valley" portion of the title has tenuous credibility, although I'm sure there was absolutely noth-ing pleasant about it. Another dope fiend I knew, a heroin addict we called Skeet, did a stretch in Pelican Bay. "Pelican Bay" sounds more like a seafood restaurant. (Pelican Bay—Cell for two?)

I started getting nervous when we got to the prison. First of all, we had to go through this heavy-duty metal detector to get in-side the walls. That thing was nuclear in its intensity. Once we got through the metal detector, a guard began escorting us into the gloomy prison edifice. We would follow the guard through thick, iron- barred gates, and after each, he'd hit some kind of control switch, and the heavy metal hatchway we'd passed through would slam shut with a vengeance, clanging ominously. Every time this happened I'd jump. The whole thing gave me the creeps.

I turned to the comic who produced the show and asked, "How much time do I get?"—unlucky phrasing, perhaps, having freshly entered a prison. What I meant was, "How long do I get onstage?"

"You're doing seven minutes," she said, "And you're going first."

Lots of comics bristle at going first in a showcase line up. I'd never really minded it before, but this time I felt genuine trepida-tion. I guess it was the sound of all those cold steel gateways crashing shut behind me as I progressed toward the waiting stage. Whatever it was, my knees were knocking—something I hadn't experienced since my first few open mics. I tried breathing deeply, but only hy-perventilated, so I gave up trying to relax and simply stood, eyes closed, and listened to the emcee doing his set. Things weren't going well for him, but he trudged on, a comic warrior. After ten minutes of stony silence in response to all his jokes, he finally got a laugh. At that point, he apparently felt his work was done.

"Okay! I won't take any more of your time right now. We got some fine looking ladies to entertain you here tonight..." The emcee paused, as if considering the validity of his claim, then shrugged. "Well, some of 'em are all right—aw, fuck it, pussy's pussy. Here's your next comic." The emcee swiftly exited the stage, the only sound disturbing the mighty silence being the scuffling of his own feet.

After that questionable intro, I took a deep breath, held it too long, and walked onto the stage. I looked out over the audience and saw a couple hundred of the meanest, biggest, toughest look-ing men I have ever seen, sitting on folding chairs, staring at me. A few of them were making hand signals I couldn't decipher, but one or two in the front row leered and gestured toward their laps—not tough to decipher that message.

I started out with a comment off the top of my head. "When I signed up for this gig, I thought it was a women's prison. And if it is, you're the toughest bunch of lesbians I've ever seen." The inmates responded with a numbing silence. Several guys resumed making hand signals to each other. I pressed on, implementing a few of the squeaky clean and innocuous lines I'd imagined would be so ap-propriate and Seinfeld-esque in this particular situation, but they fell flat. I was bombing and I knew it. Minutes seemed like hours.

An inmate about nine rows back began heckling me. He was speaking at a high volume, however he somehow managed to mumble so that I couldn't distinguish any of his words. I couldn't respond to the heckler without knowing what he was saying.

Oh sure, there are a few intimidating stock phrases comics use to shut down hecklers—for some reason, only one of them came to mind in that moment, and it involves the words, "...I don't come

down to where you work and slap the dick out of your mouth..."
Clearly, this ballsy rejoinder would not land well amongst a prison
demographic.

So I stood stock still, frozen in fear, and lamely listened to the
heckler's abuses. His amazingly loud mumbles were well received
by a portion of the crowd. At least somebody was getting some
laughs. I believe that on some level I must have felt it best to be
proactive. Still terrified, I slipped into autopilot, mindlessly flail-
ing around, spewing out any old material at random, heedless of
time or place. A few days previously, when I told some of my comedian friends I was going to try standup at a prison, one of these
friends had warned me, "Whatever you do, leave out the white
supremacist joke." At that I'd laughed and said, "Of course! I'm
not that stupid!"

Unfortunately, I was that stupid—lobotomized by fear. Before I
even realized what I was saying, I delivered the lines. "I used to live
in Texas. In Texas they've got those white supremacists. Supremacists, they call themselves. Let's break that word down. The root
word is, 'supreme,' meaning, 'highest quality.' It's like these guys are
settin' themselves up to be the highest quality white people. Have
you seen these guys? Pockmarked, syphilitic cretins with close set
eyes, pointy skulls, and pencil necks. And they're always talkin'
about 'Preserving the purity of the white race.' I think these guys
belong to a special white race, don't you? Yeah, one that's kept its
purity through inbreeding and animal husbandry—literally—hey,
for these guys, safe sex would be to mark the sheep that kick." At
the moment the words exited my lips, I knew I'd possibly signed
my own death warrant. Hell, I was tempted to shank myself. Icy
silence resounded. I thought I heard an echo bouncing from walls
to ceiling—...sheep that kick - ck -ck...I began covertly scanning
the room for guards but, strangely, couldn't find a single uniform.
I braced for a shank.

Suddenly a guttural bark hacked through the disturbing silence, and I thought I heard something like, "Bitch, don' be talkin' down about white supremacy..."

Something sucked the oxygen out of my lungs but I stood my ground—for a moment. Then something—self-preservation?—took over. I put the mike back on the stand. I looked out over the audience, making eye contact with a few, straining to keep the smile plastered on my face. "Well, hey, you've been a great audience...uh, I won't take any more of your time...er, lots of good comics coming after me...thanks. Heh." And my feet started carrying me off the stage. I cast my eyes toward the floor, toward my feet as they propelled me away from ignominy and reproach.

I stumbled out into the lobby and found a folding chair, then flopped down onto its cold metal seat and buried my head in my hands. I reviewed the profundity of my failure: I'd broken the cardinal rule of standup comedy—I walked on my own act. A true comedian is a warrior, fiercely baring his or her soul, upholding the art and keeping it real, never sweating the outcome. Every authentic comedian lives by this code: Always stand your ground. No matter how bad you suck, no matter the hurt or humiliation, stand your ground. And I had fallen short of the code. I'd bailed.

I sat on that creaky metal chair and began to beat myself up for my failings. In between self-flagellations, I noticed an old Latino man approaching me, carrying a metal folding chair under one arm. "Hey," he said quietly, "I'm Hernando. Mind if I sit down?"

I waved a hand to my left, indicating there was indeed plenty of space in the zone of shame. *A comic failure never wants for elbow room...* "Sure, sit down. I'm Marti."

He cleared his throat. "I know."

*Shit! He saw.* I'd hoped he'd simply breezed in late and missed my debacle.

"Yeah," I mumbled into my closed fist.

Hernando unfolded his chair and sat down. He began speaking quietly, telling me about the truths he'd learned during his lengthy stay in the prison. He told me how he'd learned to meditate, and the freedom it afforded him. He expounded on spiritual truths and the wisdom of the ages, all of which he'd discovered and experienced in his tiny cell. His life, he told me, had grown rich through the truths he'd apprehended.

I sat in my chair, looking at him as he spoke, affecting attentiveness yet not really hearing him. I struggled to listen but all I could hear was my own ego with its self-recriminating inner monologue—self-centeredly obsessing on how bad my set went and how I'd walked on my act. Then Hernando raised his voice a fraction. "Are you listening to me? Because I'm trying to cheer you up."

And that galvanized me. *This guy Hernando is trying to share with me some truths he's learned that might cut me loose from my self-centered, egoistic torment. He's currently doing a decades-long sentence in a tiny little prison cell, while I can walk out of the penitentiary, jump in my car and go anywhere. And* he's *trying to cheer* me *up? Who's the real prisoner?* I realized how ridiculously superficial my ego is and how foolish I was to let it hold me hostage. And all of a sudden I felt good again.

There are no accidents in this universe. Everything that happens has a purpose, usually a different purpose than we think it has at first glance. I wanted to do comedy in a prison so that I could bring something inside—laughter—that might help the inmates. How phony of me. In truth, I'd been drawn to this prison in order to learn some very important lessons.

With that, I got out of myself. My spirit lightened. Who cares if I bombed? Hernando taught me that in the worst place there is human kindness—and an opportunity to grow. I knew at that moment that my visit to the joint wasn't a disaster after all. At that moment, I began to change the way I measure success.

Suddenly I heard voices in the background. It was the prisoners—chanting my name. "Marti, Marti, Marti..." The prisoners were calling me back for a second chance! Well—they probably just didn't want to go back to their cells.

The emcee spoke into the microphone—"Marti...is Marti here?"

*Well of course I'm here—I'm locked into the damn prison, aren't I?*

I took the opportunity and went back onstage. I stood up there and did my act the way I am, the way I present myself with any audience, no matter if it's a church or a prison. And you know what? I got laughs, because I wasn't uptight anymore or trying to be somebody I'm not. I wasn't worrying about what anybody thinks. I was being myself—a practice which always results in success.

After the show, I stood with the other comics in the lobby by the exit and thanked the audience members as they filed out and immediately began returning to their cells. I located Hernando and thanked him. I noticed a huge convict striding toward me from across the lobby. This guy was massive, easily as big as an NFL linebacker, very intimidating. But it was the scar on his face and his intense scowl that really unnerved me. Once again, I braced for a shank.

That badass convict shook my hand, looked me in the eye, and said, "When you go back out there, remember what you learned in here. Never let some jerk change the way you think about yourself. And never give in to fear."

I'd like to close my story on that reminder.

Never give in to fear.

Photos of a young Christopher and
Christopher and Marti present day

# EPILOGUE

LIFE IS GOOD. CHRISTOPHER AND I MARRIED, AND WE'VE STUCK together since July 1987. We bought our house—the same one where Chris ditched all those bales into the forest, and I did first aid on Firebird—on contract from our landlord. Over the years, he and I have remodeled it completely.

Our home sits on a hillside, surrounded by bay trees and redwoods. In the center of one of the redwood groves on our property stands an albino redwood tree—a rare sight, since these trees are said to be one in ten million. Its whitish needles appear translucent when the late afternoon sun shines through its branches. The Pomo Indians revere the albino redwoods, I'm told: they honor these trees as a sign of spiritual cleansing. How appropriate that we have one growing on the property where we once craved dope, sold dope, swapped and bought dope, and  made addiction the center of our lives. When we led the lives of active dope fiends the albino redwood seemed so much smaller, puny even, so we seldom paid attention to it.

In the first months after I got clean, I worked in the yard almost every afternoon. I found a lot of wreckage from our dope-obsessed years scattered over the hillside—broken glass, rusted nails and bits of copper wire, a few broken chunks of stereo components reminiscent of the stuff in the zombies' shopping carts, cigarette butts, old dope baggies, even a syringe or two. I cleared it away as part of my living amends.

One afternoon, a guy on a mountain bike pulled up in our driveway and called out to me from the top of the hill. "Hey! Did you know you've got an albino redwood tree in your yard?"

I climbed the wooden steps toward him. "We do? I mean... are you talking about the little one with the white needles? I always hoped it might be, but it's kinda scraggly, isn't it? We thought maybe it needed more sunlight..."

"Yeah—I mean, no, it's okay, that's how they look. Check it out," he said, "There's a photo of one in this book, and yours looks just like it!" He pulled the book out of his backpack and handed it to me.

I read the description, saw the photo, and learned about it being a sign of spiritual cleansing, which thrilled me. Immediately I ran downstairs to tell Christopher, who loved hearing the news. During the following weeks an arborist identified it as genuine. The albino redwood became a talisman of our recovery and healing. It's bigger now, and healthier, and each time I see that tree I say, "Thank you."

Over the years, Chris and I have seen a lot of our friends—many of the characters described in this book—get clean and create new lives for themselves. Several of them work in recovery, helping other people kick this disease. One works in forensics for a police department in a major U.S. city. Some are loving parents, grandparents, or both. Others who did not recover are dead. Some are still alive, but are out there on the streets, in their addiction. However, I'm convinced that as long as they are alive there's hope of recovery.

Hope banishes despair, peace triumphs over chaos, light illuminates darkness, serenity trumps uneasiness, forgiveness vanquishes blame, self-respect displaces shame and courage overwhelms fear. Love conquers all. As I look back over my life in recovery, that's what I see.

On August 8th, 1995, my life changed radically. Inspired and empowered by unconditional love from Chris, my daughter, and my parents, I threw off the chains of addiction and began my journey through recovery toward mental, spiritual, emotional and physical health. The process of recovery can be defined as, "building a new lifestyle, or new way of living." Through this process I've discovered and continue to discover powerful healing and life-giving forces—forces that anyone can access.

Gratitude wields a powerful life-giving force. Shame and fear fuel addiction—but gratitude takes fear and shame to the woodshed! Gratitude is the ultimate attitude adjustment. When we live in a state of gratefulness for all that we have, all that we are, and all that comes our way, we constantly receive more reasons to be grateful. Gratitude is a powerful force that instantly begins propelling us forward toward happiness, success, and health. Once established as a force within us, our gratitude naturally begins radiating out toward others.

Try it now—make a mental gratitude list in the moment. Start by thinking the words, "Thank you," and repeat as you visualize all the things you're grateful for. Take a deep breath. Acknowledge gratitude for the air you're breathing, the lung capacity you have, and the oxygen to your brain and bloodstream. Look around you, and experience gratitude for your eyesight, the view you're taking in, and your brain's power to process the image.

While acknowledging your gratitude, allow yourself to luxuriate in the feeling of joy and peace that comes from living in the moment, knowing that the future holds promise for you. As you begin to acknowledge all that you have, all that you are, and all that comes your way, you discover that everything in life, particularly that which is challenging, is a gift—a miracle. Consciously celebrate each miracle, and out of your resulting joy comes a desire to pay it forward.

It's an enriching experience when we devote ourselves to discovering how much appreciation and gratitude can be packed into the stream of life in a given moment, hour, or day. Albert Einstein said, "There are only two ways to live your life. One is as if nothing is a miracle, the other is as if everything is." When we try living as if everything, even the tiniest thing, is a miracle, gratitude bubbles over.

I BEGAN WRITING *NEVER GIVE IN TO FEAR*, IN PART BECAUSE I wanted to tell my story to recovering addicts and alcoholics, as well as those who still suffer. Reaching the families of addicts and alcoholics was also a priority, so they might take courage from the fact that even the seemingly hopeless cases—and I was one—can and do recover, as I did.

While writing this memoir, I deliberately avoided giving detailed descriptions of the physical sensations and experience of getting high—since I see that as counterproductive and encouraging drug use. Instead, I chronicled the progress of the disease in the mind of an active addict, based on my own recollections.

During the process of writing this memoir it struck me that I might be able to make a positive contribution by working as an addiction treatment professional. I obtained education in chemical dependency studies and training in addiction treatment. I now hold four professional certifications in addiction treatment, one of which is ACRPS: Advanced Certified Relapse Prevention Specialist.

In 2009, after copyrighting the first edition of *Never Give in to Fear,* I found the courage to publicly speak out against human trafficking by telling the story of what happened to me in Tokyo.

I began volunteering to speak at anti-human trafficking events at churches and universities. In June 2010, I spoke as a survivor at an MMA cagefighting event, a fundraiser for Not For Sale, a non-profit that fights modern slavery. In February 2011, I appeared as a guest speaker at the Museum of Tolerance in Los Angeles. I tell my story to raise awareness about human trafficking and hope that these small contributions will help to some day eradicate this terrible crime.

Gratitude wells up within me as I recall the period of time when I worked as a program counselor at a transitional housing facility for homeless veterans in San Francisco. This facility, founded by homeless Viet Nam veterans in 1974, accomplishes great things. I learned from combat vets that courage is not the absence of fear—it is resistance to fear. Courage is the conscious decision to move through the fear to the objective. I learned that courage is another powerful transformative force, a healing force that empowers change and reinforces hope. Courage, combined with love, is unstoppable. Take the time to embrace and celebrate courage. Never give in to fear.

---

Today, if confronted by my fears, I take courage from the memory of my father. He harnessed the transformative powers of forgiveness, love, and the courage to change.

My Dad died suddenly in March of 2010. He used his life to make the world a better place. My father grew up in the Dust Bowl during the Great Depression. He was an Eagle Scout. In the days after Dad's death, our family reviewed his military record—original documents, stored away in a metal box in Mom and Dad's closet. From reading these documents, I learned that he was still a teenager when he joined the National Guard, so when the Japanese attacked Pearl Harbor and the U.S. declared war, he was 19 years old. My father fought in the 164th Infantry at Guadalcanal and distinguished himself in battle. He received a number of medals and ribbons but never uttered a word about it to any of us.

Although my father never talked about the war, on more than one occasion when I was growing up he told me how he didn't like the hatred of the Japanese he discovered within himself after the war. He also told me how he overcame it. He entered university with his GI benefits to major in English. On his way to becoming a professor, he stepped up to teach English to Japanese immigrants in the years following the war, and he abolished the hate. He laughed with his Japanese students and helped them adjust to American society and culture. I remember my father telling me how he counted that as one of his victories in life—he overcame hatred and made a difference.

Dad taught me that, because hatred is learned, it can be unlearned; to respect all cultures and to have regard for each and every human being without prejudice. By sharing his story, my father showed me that hate blossoms from fear, but that a higher love crushes fear, and hate with it. Dad enjoyed an extensive career as an educator and helped thousands of people to enrich their lives. He carried the fire of courage and laughter and love.

My father was fond of the 13th Chapter of I Corinthians, "... Love is patient, love is kind. It does not envy, it does not boast, it is not proud. It is not rude, it is not self-seeking, it is not easily angered, it keeps no record of wrongs. Love does not delight in evil but rejoices in the truth. It always protects, always trusts, always hopes, always perseveres. Love never fails..."

Although I miss my Dad and want him back, I am consoled by the realization that he lives in me still. It's because of the things I learned from my father that I have survived—and recovered from—domestic violence, being trafficked into modern slavery, drug addiction, and homelessness. Now more than ever I am inspired to carry the Fire; to overcome fear and hate and injustice with courage, laughter, and a higher love.

I continue to speak at Anti-Human Trafficking events, and am a volunteer speaker for domestic violence shelters, to raise awareness about and funds for domestic and sexual violence survivors. Although I still do standup, it's usually for fundraisers which benefit treatment facilities and recovery homes. I will continue my career in addiction treatment, to help addicts and alcoholics who still suffer, especially those who are veterans of military service.

If you've stuck with me long enough to read this, thank you. I know you carry the fire. May we triumph in the battle to provide justice for the oppressed, and a voice for those whose voices cannot be heard.

Marti MacGibbon, CADC-II, ACRPS

If you are an addict or alcoholic, or are involved with someone who is an addict or alcoholic, here are some places to get help:

Alcoholics Anonymous http://www.alcoholics-anonymous.org

Narcotics Anonymous http://www.na.org

Alanon http://www.al-anon.org

National Institute on Drug Abuse http://www.nida.nih.gov

If you want to find out more about the crime of human trafficking, and what you can do to fight it, visit:

http://www.notforsalecampaign.org

http://www.freetheslaves.net